Teaching
Study Strategies
to Students with
Learning Disabilities

TEACHING STUDY STRATEGIES TO STUDENTS WITH LEARNING DISABILITIES

STEPHEN S. STRICHART
Florida International University

CHARLES T. MANGRUM II
University of Miami

Allyn and Bacon
Boston   London   Toronto   Sydney   Tokyo   Singapore

Copyright © 1993 by Allyn and Bacon
A Division of Simon & Schuster, Inc.
160 Gould Street
Needham Heights, Massachusetts 02194

Library of Congress Cataloging-in-Publication Data

Strichart, Stephen S.
    Teaching study strategies to students with learning disabilities /
Stephen S. Strichart, Charles T. Mangrum II.
        p.   cm.
    Includes bibliographical references and index.
    ISBN 0-205-13992-2
    1. Learning disabled teenagers—Education (Secondary)—United
States   2. Study, Method of.   I. Mangrum, Charles T.—II. Title.
LC4704.74.S77   1993
371.9—dc20   92-33136
                                                                                  CIP

Printed in the United States of America
10 9 8 7 6 5 4 3 2   96 95 94 93

To students with learning disabilities who work so hard to achieve success, we hope this book will make learning a little easier.

Contents

Preface

Although many students are able to learn to study on their own, this is not true for those with learning disabilities. Yet students with learning disabilities rarely receive instruction in how to study.

Most teachers who work with students with learning disabilities quickly realize that these students have little idea of *what to study, when to study,* or *how to study.* To be successful in school, these students must be taught how to identify what they must study, develop a plan for using their time effectively, and apply a number of study strategies.

This book is designed to help teachers teach study strategies to students with learning disabilities in the *middle and secondary grades.* Each chapter includes background information about a study strategy, a plan for teaching the study strategy, and reproducible pages for teaching the strategy. The reproducible pages ensure that students will have ample opportunity throughout the book to apply the study strategies they are taught.

We wish to express our appreciation to a number of colleagues who took the time and effort to review the manuscript and who provided many valuable suggestions. We particularly want to thank Harry L. Dangel of Georgia State University, Katherine H. Greenberg of The University of Tennessee at Knoxville, Jane D. Mangrum of Miami Dade Community College, Diane Brown of Gulliver Preparatory School in Miami, Florida, and Danny F. Reed of the Pulaski County Special School District in Little Rock, Arkansas. We also wish to thank the many middle school and high school teachers in our own university classes who critiqued the teaching activities we present in this book.

Teaching Study Strategies to Students with Learning Disabilities

Using This Book

■ HOW THIS BOOK WILL HELP STUDENTS WITH LEARNING DISABILITIES

A major goal of teachers of students with learning disabilities is to assist these students to become independent learners. To achieve this goal, teachers must provide these students with strategies they can use on their own to master a variety of learning tasks across a range of instructional settings. Teaching students with learning disabilities to use study strategies effectively is an important step in transforming dependent learners into independent learners. Once they have mastered the study strategies contained in this book, students with learning disabilities will be more successful learners.

■ WHAT IS A LEARNING DISABILITY?

Public Law 94-142, the Education for All Handicapped Children Act of 1975, provides the most widely used definition of a learning disability. Within this law, a learning disability is defined as the disorder in one or more of the basic psychological processes involved in understanding or in using spoken or written language. The disorder results in problems in such skills and abilities as listening, thinking, speaking, reading, writing, spelling, or doing mathematical calculations.

Smith and Dowdy (1989) offer a less complex definition that we find useful. They describe a learning disability as a breakdown in the sequence of taking in information (input), making sense of the information that is taken in (process), and using the information (output). Students with learning disabilities may experience a breakdown at any point in this sequence.

■ WHAT IS A STUDY STRATEGY?

We view a study strategy as a systematic plan for obtaining (input), organizing (process), and using (output) information taught in school. Study strategies are similar to what Deshler and Schumaker (1984) termed "learning strategies" or Hoover (1989b) termed "study skills." Study strategies help students master subject matter information and help them demonstrate their mastery in a variety of ways.

■ WHAT WE KNOW ABOUT STUDY STRATEGIES AND STUDENTS WITH LEARNING DISABILITIES

Many authors have described the deficient study strategies of students with learning disabilities. A common thread is disorganization. Students with learning disabilities often lack the ability to perceive and use the existing organization in their textbooks

1

and other instructional materials, fail to provide organization where it is lacking, and neglect to organize the materials they create on their own (Alley & Deshler, 1979; Derr & Peters, 1986; Hoover 1989a, 1989b; Slade, 1986).

A second common thread is inefficient and ineffective strategies for learning. Students with learning disabilities show little ability to determine what is required in a learning situation, possess a limited repertoire of strategies for responding to tasks, and demonstrate little awareness of how to evaluate the effectiveness of their responses. (Archer, 1988; Derr & Peters, 1986; Herr, 1988; McLoughlin & Lewis, 1990; Shields & Heron, 1989).

Gleason (1988) clearly showed the differences in study strategies between successful students and students with learning disabilities. She observed that when the teacher lectures, successful students listen, take notes, ask questions, answer questions, and contribute to discussions. Given an assignment, successful students make efficient use of class time, use textbooks and other resources to answer questions, and complete the assignment by the end of the class. In contrast, students with learning disabilities attend for only part of the time that the teacher lectures, write down only a word or two, and rarely contribute to the discussion. When given assignments, these students lack the self-direction and strategies needed for finding information in textbooks, looking up words in the glossary, interpreting maps, answering questions, or asking the teacher for appropriate assistance. At the end of the class, they often have not finished the assignment. Further, students with learning disabilities lack the strategies needed to complete the assignment on their own at home.

The importance of study strategies, combined with the deficiencies in study strategies common to students with learning disabilities, dictates the need for increased emphasis on assisting these students to develop effective study strategies. We believe that study strategies must be systematically introduced to students with learning disabilities in the middle school grades and must continue to be reinforced throughout the remainder of their education.

■ STUDY STRATEGIES TAUGHT IN THIS BOOK

A number of authors have identified study strategies that students with learning disabilities need to learn (Derr & Peters, 1986; Hoover, 1988, 1989b; Mandelbaum & Wilson, 1989; McLoughlin & Lewis, 1990; Shields & Heron, 1989; Smith & Dowdy, 1989). In this book, we present the important study strategies needed by students with learning disabilities to obtain information (input), organize it (process), and use it (output). The study strategies are presented in ten chapters, as follows:

Chapter 1. *Remembering Information.* The crucial test of learning information is remembering it. "Learning" something is of little value if what is learned cannot be recalled whenever necessary. In this chapter we present strategies students can use to retain the important information and ideas to which they are exposed in school.

Chapter 2. *Reading Textbooks.* Much of the information and ideas that students must learn is contained in their subject area textbooks. Students must be taught to extract information from their subject area textbooks effectively and efficiently. To do so, students must have a textbook reading strategy. In this chapter students are taught to use SQ3R, a textbook reading strategy that helps students improve their reading comprehension and their retention of information for quizzes and tests.

Chapter 3. *Solving Math Word Problems.* Students must learn how to understand and solve math word problems. They must know how to determine what the problem is, identify the steps needed to solve it, and then carry out and check the necessary calculations. In this chapter students are taught to use SQRQCQ, a math word problem-solving strategy.

Chapter 4. *Taking Notes from Class Presentations.* Students must be taught effective ways to write down the important information presented by their teachers. In this chapter students are taught a strategy for taking class notes.

Chapter 5. *Using the Library.* Students must be taught to make appropriate use of the many resources found in their school and other libraries. In this chapter we present strategies students can use to locate quickly and make effective use of the many resources available in school and other libraries.

Chapter 6. *Using Reference Books.* Students must be made aware of the many reference books they can use to achieve learning mastery. In this chapter students are taught strategies for using these reference books: dictionary, encyclopedia, thesaurus, almanac, and atlas.

Chapter 7. *Using Visual Aids.* Students must be taught how to use charts, tables, graphs, figures, and diagrams to enhance their comprehension of textual material. In this chapter strategies are presented that help students interpret these visual aids.

Chapter 8. *Writing a Research Paper.* Students must be able to organize their ideas in a written manner that communicates their ideas clearly and efficiently. In this chapter students are taught a strategy for writing a research paper.

Chapter 9. *Taking Tests.* Students must demonstrate their mastery of information and ideas by successfully completing tests given in various formats. In many cases, students have learned what is required of them but lack the necessary test-taking skills to demonstrate their mastery. In this chapter students are taught strategies for preparing for and taking tests given in these formats: multiple choice, true-false, matching, completion, and essay.

Chapter 10. *Managing Time.* Students must learn how to make effective use of their time if they are to complete their school assignments when required. In this chapter students are taught strategies for apportioning and scheduling their time.

■ HOW THIS BOOK IS ORGANIZED

Each chapter is organized according to the following structure:

1. *Purposes* of the chapter
2. *Titles of reproducibles* provided

3. *Rationale* for teaching the study strategy

4. *Background information* that explains what is taught in the chapter

5. *Teaching plan*

6. *Reproducibles* for student use

7. *"What I Have Learned"* end-of-chapter test. In all cases the end-of-chapter test uses a short essay format.

8. *Answers* for the Reproducibles.

■ HOW TO USE THIS BOOK

Read the purposes and rationale for each chapter. Then decide which chapters you want to cover and in what order. For each chapter you decide to teach, follow these steps:

1. Review the background information. This section provides all the information needed to teach the strategy.

2. Follow the teaching plan and use the reproducible activities provided to teach the strategy. You may reproduce as many copies as you need for your class.

3. Use the end-of-chapter test to determine what your students have learned and what may need to be reviewed.

■ SPECIAL NOTES

Here are some things you need to consider when using this book.

1. In any case where you decide that the instructional material provided in a reproducible is either too difficult or too easy for teaching a study strategy to your students, you may substitute your own material.

2. Go beyond the reproducibles to provide your students with additional practice in the use of the strategies. It is additional practice with materials that are directly related to classroom objectives that will enable students to achieve greater success in school.

3. Have the students use a study strategy under your supervision until they have mastered it. Mastery of a strategy means that students are able to recall it as rapidly as they can recall their own names or phone numbers. Mastery also means the ability to apply the strategy automatically to school tasks. Students have achieved mastery when they can automatically recall and apply a strategy. Until they have achieved this automaticity, there is no mastery.

4. Share the strategies with colleagues who also teach your students, and encourage your colleagues to have the students use the strategies in their classes as well. This will help to ensure that students generalize and maintain their use of the strategies.

5. Although the various study strategies are presented individually in this book, in reality students will need to use a combination of strategies to complete most assignments. For example, students studying for a test should use strategies for

remembering information, reading textbooks, and managing time, in addition to test-taking strategies. Use every opportunity to demonstrate or explain to your students how to combine the use of the various strategies presented in this book.

6. Motivate your students to want to use the study strategies taught in this book. We recommend you use the PARS motivation strategy (Forgan & Mangrum, 1989). This strategy has four components: Purpose, Attitude, Results, Success.

   Purpose. Students are more likely to want to learn a study strategy when they understand how the strategy can help them succeed in school. Be sure to explain how its use can help them acquire more information and get better grades in your class and in their other classes.

   Attitude. Your attitude is infectious. If you are enthusiastic about a study strategy, your enthusiasm will transfer to your students, who are then likely to model your positive attitude toward the use of the strategy.

   Results. It is important to give students feedback on how well they are applying a strategy. The feedback needs to be very specific so that students understand what they did correctly and what they did wrong. Students need specific feedback in order to know what to do to improve their use of each strategy.

   Success. It is important that students experience success in the application of a strategy. Nothing elicits recurrent behavior as well as success.

7. Have students work cooperatively in pairs or small groups to practice applying the strategies to class assignments. Students can take turns demonstrating how a strategy is used or providing feedback on the effectiveness of its use.

CHAPTER 1

Remembering Information

■ Purposes

The purposes of this chapter are to:

1. teach students with learning disabilities a three-step strategy for remembering information.
2. identify ways teachers can establish conditions to make it easier for their students to remember information.
3. provide reproducibles that can be used to help students learn how to remember information.

■ Titles of Reproducibles

■ RATIONALE

Learning increases students' fund of knowledge. For learning to occur, students must be able to remember newly acquired information so that they can retrieve the information and use it whenever necessary. Information that is not remembered is of no value to students for dealing with current requirements in or out of school.

Students who have difficulty remembering information typically do very poorly on tests, because all forms of tests require that students remember information in order to respond appropriately.

Students cannot retain all the information to which they are exposed. Teachers need to help students remember the important information. This is especially true for students with learning disabilities, a category of students who frequently are characterized as having difficulty remembering information (Gearheart & Gearheart, 1989; Hallahan, Kauffman, & Lloyd, 1985; Kirk & Chalfant, 1984; Mercer, 1991; Wallace & McLoughlin, 1988). Teachers of students with learning disabilities often become frustrated when they find that information their students seemed to learn on Monday is forgotten on Tuesday. Only by remembering important information over time can students with learning disabilities make appropriate progress in school.

■ BACKGROUND INFORMATION

Students with learning disabilities often approach learning tasks in a disorganized manner. They can increase their ability to remember important information by using a strategy to remember information. We propose that these students be taught a three-step remembering strategy. First, they should carefully SELECT the information that is most important to remember. Second, they should choose from a variety of techniques those they will use to REMEMBER the information. Third, they should systematically REVIEW the information.

The Remembering Strategy

SELECT

REMEMBER

REVIEW

1. The SELECT step of the remembering strategy is a crucial one. It is simply not possible for students to remember all the information to which they are exposed. Consequently, students must select the information that is important to remember. Ideally, the teacher will tell students what they need to remember. If this is not done, students should be told to ask their teacher to specificy what information is important for them to remember.

Sometimes it is necessary for students to rewrite information they need to remember. This is necessary when the information is found in many different sources. In these cases students must collect and integrate the information before applying specific techniques for remembering it.

2. In the REMEMBER step of the strategy, students must choose the technique(s) they will use to remember the information. Students should select techniques that are compatible with the nature of the information to be remembered. For

8

example, students might visualize a map to remember locations, but use a mnemonic device to recall key names.

There are several effective techniques for facilitating recall of information. Students with learning disabilities need to become familiar with each technique so that, depending on the nature of the information to be remembered, they can select the appropriate ones.

Here are the techniques that students with learning disabilities should learn to use to help them remember important information.

(a) *Visualization.* Bos and Vaughn (1988) defined *visualization* as "seeing in your mind's eye what you are trying to remember" (p. 213). Simply put, visualization means creating a picture or a series of pictures as an aid to remembering information.

Visualization is a common technique that almost everyone uses at some time or other to remember information. For example, if you want to remember the parts of an elephant, a good strategy to use is to formulate a mental picture of an elephant from which you can then recall the parts.

(b) *Association.* Bos and Vaughn (1988) noted that associating information refers to "arranging the information and associating it in such a way that is easier to remember" (p. 213). They observed that whereas non-learning-disabled students spontaneously categorize or associate items, students with learning disabilities typically do not. Consequently, it is important for teachers of students with learning disabilities to provide practice in associating and categorizing information.

For example, students asked to remember the words *milk, rose, violet, meat, bread, orchid* should organize the words into two categories: *food* and *flowers.* By doing this, they reduce the number of words in a set from six words in one set to three words in each of two sets. Students can then use association to help them remember each of the words within a set. For example, *bread* and *meat* can be associated to make a sandwich and *milk* associated as the drink to go with the sandwich. *Violet* and *rose* can be associated as two girls who each receive an *orchid* from their boyfriends.

(c) *Application.* Students use application as a way of remembering information whenever they use the information to create something. For example, when students create a diorama of a Civil War battle, they are using application to remember important information about a battle that occurred during the Civil War. Likewise, when students use a math formula to determine size and area to build a cage for a pet, they are using application to remember the math formula.

(d) *Repetition.* Repetition involves repeatedly saying, looking at, and/or writing information. When students practice spelling a list of words by writing the words several times, they are using repetition. Repeating a list of facts aloud until they are memorized is another example of repetition.

When students with learning disabilities use repetition, they should be encouraged to use all their senses simultaneously. Students should read, say aloud, and write the information they are trying to remember.

Repetition has some significant limitations when used in isolation to remember information. Frequently, students use repetition to enhance recall of information they do not understand, have not personalized, and have not applied in any way. The teacher should emphasize to students with learning disabilities that repeating

9

information is not a substitute for understanding it. Students must realize that repetition needs to be combined with efforts to understand, personalize, and apply the information to be remembered.

(e) *Mnemonic Devices.* Devine (1981) defined *mnemonic devices* as "any formal schemes designed deliberately to improve memory" (p. 285). Many mnemonic devices have been developed to help people remember. The popular books whose authors promise to improve your memory, consist largely of explanations of a variety of mnemonic devices. Teachers often resist teaching the use of mnemonic devices to their students because they erroneously believe that these are nothing more than memory tricks. Actually, mnemonic devices are very useful for helping students with learning disabilities remember information that would otherwise not be held in their memories.

Although there are many mnemonic devices, some, in our judgment, are so complex that they would be as difficult for students with learning disabilities to remember as would be the information to be remembered. We have selected the mnemonic devices we believe to be both useful and within the capabilities of students with learning disabilities. Here are the five mnemonic devices we recommend:

1. *Rhyme.* This is a simple technique often taught to young children in songs and verses. We are certain that virtually every teacher has used rhymes to help students to remember information. One good example is the use of a popular rhyme to remember the number of days in each month:

Thirty days hath September,
April, June, and November.
All the rest have thirty-one
Except February, which has twenty-eight.

Or,

In fourteen hundred ninety-two,
Columbus sailed the ocean blue.

Adler (1988) recommended that when students transform information into a rhyme, to reinforce their memory further, they should emphasize the cadence in the rhyme. In addition, students should form a mental picture of the rhyme.

2. *Acronym.* An acronym is a word made from the first letter or first syllable of other words that one wants to remember. The word CAP is an acronym for Civil Air Patrol. Similarly, Florvets is an acronym for Florida Veterans. An acronym does not have to be a real word, but it must form a word that can be pronounced. The acronym NATO stands for North Atlantic Treaty Organization. NATO is not a real word, but it is easy to pronounce and therefore easy to remember.

3. *Abbreviation.* Like acronyms, abbreviations use the first letters of words to be remembered, but the first letters do not form a pronounceable word. Common examples include CBS (Columbia Broadcasting System), FBI (Federal Bureau of Investigation), IRS (Internal Revenue Service), and SQ3R (Survey, Question, Read, Recite, Review—a textbook reading strategy presented in Chapter 2.

10

4. *Acronymic Sentence.* When using this mnemonic device, students create sentences made up of words that begin with the initial letter of the items to be remembered. Shepherd (1982) provides a good example for remembering the sequence of planets in our solar system. This sequence, starting with the planet nearest the sun and proceeding to the planet farthest from the sun, can be remembered by using this acronymic sentence: "My (Mercury) very (Venus) earthy (Earth) mother (Mars) just (Jupiter) served (Saturn) us (Uranus) nine (Neptune) pizzas (Pluto)."

Acronymic sentences are particularly useful when an acronym is difficult to formulate. By creating humorous or personalized acronymic sentences, students with learning disabilities can facilitate their memory of fairly complex sets or sequences of information.

5. *Pegwords (Rhyming Words).* This strategy is used to remember numbered or ordered information (Mastropieri & Scruggs, 1987). To use this technique, students must first memorize a set of rhyming words for the numbers *one* through *ten.* Mastropieri and Scruggs recommended the following pairings:

one	—	bun
two	—	shoe
three	—	tree
four	—	door
five	—	hive
six	—	sticks
seven	—	heaven
eight	—	gate
nine	—	vine
ten	—	hen

You can make your own pairings, but be certain that the pegword or rhyming word for a number is one for which students with learning disabilities will be able to form a visual association easily. For this reason, it is best to use nouns and verbs.

Once students have memorized the pegwords, the pegwords can be combined with numbered or ordered information to help them remember the information. Mastropieri and Scruggs (1987) provide an example of using pegwords to remember nine possible reasons that dinosaurs became extinct. We will use their first three reasons to illustrate the technique.

The first reason that dinosaurs became extinct is that the climate became too cold. Using the first pegword, *bun,* students could form an interactive mental image of a cold dinosaur holding a frozen bun.

To remember the second reason (the swamps dried up) in association with the second pegword *(shoe),* the students could form an image of a dinosaur with a shoe stuck in a dried swamp. For the third reason (exploding star), the image could be of a dinosaur watching a star on top of a Christmas tree explode. To remember reason 3, the students would then think back to the pegword *tree* and remember the exploding star.

Adler (1988) identified a number of things that must be done if mnemonic devices are to be used successfully. Teachers of students with learning disabilities must ensure that their students do the following when using mnemonic devices:

• Pay attention.
• Divide what is to be remembered into manageable chunks.

- Structure the material.
- Study the material when in a good frame of mind (i.e., do not attempt to use one of the mnemonic devices when anxious or depressed).
- Review the material.
- Use imagination.
- Have fun.

3. The REVIEW step of the remembering strategy enables students to remember information over a period of time. Techniques for remembering information are not sufficient in themselves to guarantee retention. Information that is not used is quickly lost from memory. Students must understand that they need to review information periodically to be able to recall it when needed.

There are three important things that students need to do to maintain information in memory over a period of time. First, students should periodically *reread* information to be remembered. Second, and immediately following rereading, students should *recite* information—that is, say aloud the information to be remembered. This technique is referred to as *verbal rehearsal* and has been found to be very valuable for students with learning disabilities. Third, students need to *rewrite* information in a concise form, using key words and phrases rather than complete sentences. Abbreviations should be used whenever possible.

These three review steps make up a loop through which students must periodically cycle to remember information over time. The longer the information is to be remembered, the more times students should cycle through the review loop.

■ WHAT TEACHERS CAN DO TO HELP STUDENTS REMEMBER

There are three important things teachers can do to create conditions that make it easier for students with learning disabilities to remember important information. Teachers should strive to create these conditions for remembering when they teach new information to students.

1. *Meaningfulness.* Information that is meaningful to students is easier for them to remember than is information that is not meaningful. Information is meaningful when it can be related to what is already known. This means that the teacher must present new information in a sequence such that the new information builds upon and can be related to information that students already possess.

2. *Personalization.* Remembering information can be facilitated by making the information personally relevant to students. For example, students will more likely remember a new word such as *stingy* if they can think of someone they know who is stingy. Likewise, students will more likely remember the signs of a heart attack if they have a close relative who has experienced a heart attack. Whenever possible, teachers should relate new information to their students' lives.

3. *Interest.* It is easier to remember information about interesting topics than about topics in which students have little or no interest. Teachers are constantly amazed when students who cannot remember the multiplication tables reel off the names and batting averages of all the players on a favorite baseball team. This shows how important it is for teachers to work on building student interest in the subjects they teach.

■ TEACHING PLAN

Here is a plan for teaching students with learning disabilities the strategy for remembering information.

1. Write the word *remembering* on the chalkboard. Ask students if they are good at remembering information. Ask selected students to tell how they remember information for quizzes or tests. Ask students if they would like to be better at remembering. Tell them you will show them how. Distribute copies of Reproducible 1-1, "Knowing More and Remembering It Longer." Use the information to explain the *remembering strategy*. Have the students use 1-1 to take notes as you introduce the steps in the strategy. Tell the students you are going to take them through a number of activities to show them how to remember information.

2. Use Reproducible 1-2, "Selecting What You Need to Remember," to explain how students should select the information they want to remember. Then have the students complete the four-step activity for any test you will be giving as part of your classroom program.

3. Distribute copies of Reproducible 1-3, "Using Visualization to Remember Information." Explain visualization. Have students practice visualizing events from the preceding day. Then have the students complete the activity by visualizing and drawing the home computer described in the paragraph in 1-3.

4. Once the students have finished drawing the home computer, distribute Reproducible 1-4, "Model for Visualization of Home Computer." Discuss the drawing in 1-4 and have students compare it with their own representations of the home computer.

5. In a similar way, use Reproducible 1-5, "More Practice Using Visualization," to enhance your students' visualization ability.

6. Give each student a copy of Reproducible 1-6, "Model for Visualization of Ski Race." Discuss the drawings in 1-6 and have the students compare them with their own representations of the ski race. Use 1-6 to continue to refine your students' visualization abilities.

7. Distribute Reproducible 1-7, "Using Association to Remember Information." Use 1-7 to teach students how to build associations to improve remembering. Have the students complete the activity to practice developing and using association to remember information.

8. Distribute Reproducible 1-8, "Using Application to Remember Information." Use 1-8 to discuss with students the many ways they can use application. Emphasize that using information in an active way makes it easier to remember the information. Use 1-8 to provide students with practice in selecting application activities for remembering information.

9. Use Reproducible 1-9, "Using Repetition to Remember Information," to explain the value of repetition as a technique for remembering information. Be sure the students understand the repetition procedure and follow the steps to complete the activity.

10. Distribute Reproducible 1-10, "Using Mnemonic Devices to Remember Information." Explain that mnemonic devices are not tricks but techniques used for the purpose of improving remembering. Review the five different types of mnemonic devices: *rhyme, acronym, abbreviation, acronymic sentence, pegwords.* Have students take notes as they participate in a discussion of each mnemonic device. Reproducibles 1-11 through 1-16 provide more information and practice with each mnemonic device.

11. Use Reproducible 1-11, "Rhyme as a Mnemonic Device," to explain how rhyme can be used as a mnemonic device to improve remembering. Let the students create their own rhymes for the information provided. Have students share their rhymes to further develop their understanding of rhyme as a mnemonic device for improving remembering.

12. Use Reproducible 1-12, "Acronym as a Mnemonic Device," to explain how acronyms can be used to improve remembering. Have students complete the activities to develop commonly used acronyms. Then have them prepare their own acronyms for the sets of words provided. When the students have completed the activity, have them share their acronyms.

13. Use Reproducible 1-13, "Abbreviation as a Mnemonic Device," to explain how abbreviations can be used to improve remembering. Direct the students to form abbreviations for popular organizations or groups. Then have them prepare their own abbreviations for the sets of words provided. Have them share their abbreviations.

14. Use Reproducible 1-14, "Acronymic Sentence as a Mnemonic Device," to define and provide an example of an acronymic sentence. Have the students prepare their own sentences for the eight sets of information. Later, have them share their acronymic sentences.

15. Distribute Reproducible 1-15, "Pegwords as a Mnemonic Device." Use 1-15 to teach students pegwords that go with the number words *one* through *ten*. Then have the students read and discuss how the first five pegwords were used to recall five forms of transportation. Finally, have the students use the first five pegwords to remember five vegetables. Let students share the mental images they formed to help them remember the five vegetables.

16. Distribute 1-16, "More Practice Using Pegwords." Direct students to use the ten pegwords they have memorized to remember ten rights guaranteed by the Bill of Rights. Later let the students share the mental images they formed to help them remember each of the ten rights.

17. Distribute Reproducible 1-17, "What I Have Learned." Use this reproducible to evaluate how well your students have learned the information taught in this chapter. Use any of the reproducibles as needed to review what was presented in this chapter.

Knowing More and Remembering It Longer

Here is a strategy that will help you remember information. This strategy has three steps that you must follow. By following these steps you will remember more information for a longer period of time. This will make you more knowledgeable and improve your grades.

Think about each step as your teacher tells you about the remembering strategy. Write notes too. Ask your teacher about anything you do not understand.

REMEMBERING STRATEGY

1. **Select**
   - Select what you want to remember.
     - Ask the teacher.
     - Examine your class notes.
     - Read text assignments.
     - Study the handouts.

2. **Remember**
   - Choose techniques that will help you remember.
     - Visualize.
     - Associate.
     - Apply.
     - Repeat.
     - Use mnemonic devices:
       - Rhyme
       - Acronym
       - Abbreviation
       - Acronymic sentence
       - Pegwords

3. **Review**
   - Use these techniques to keep what you want to remember in your memory:
     - Reread.
     - Recite.
     - Rewrite.

Copyright © 1993 by Allyn and Bacon

Selecting What You Need to Remember

The human brain is not like a tape recorder that records everything that goes into it. The brain does not remember everything the eyes, ears, and other senses bring to it. The brain remembers mostly what you select to remember. This is why the first step in the Remembering Strategy tells you to *select* what you need to remember.

Here is what you should do to select what you need to remember:

- Ask the teacher what is important for you to remember.

- Examine your class notes and underline or use a highlight pen to mark the information you need to remember.

- Read the text assignments and take notes on the important information and ideas you need to remember.

- Examine your handouts and underline or use a highlight pen to mark the information you need to remember.

Think about a test one of your teachers will soon be giving you. Follow these steps to *select* the information you need to remember for the test.

1. Talk with your teacher about the test. In the space below, write the important information your teacher told you to remember for the test. Use the back if necessary.

2. Look at your class notes. What information do you need to remember from your class notes for the test? Write the information here.

3. Examine the reading assignments that will be covered on the test. What information do you need to remember from your reading assignments for the test? Write the information here.

4. Review handouts that will be covered on the test. What information do you need to remember from these handouts? Write the information here.

Using Visualization to Remember Information

To **visualize** means to form a picture in your mind of something you need to remember. Be sure to include all the important parts. Also be sure you can see how one part is attached or related to another part. This helps you remember all the parts. Sometimes you will need to form more than one picture to remember the information. Visualization is a good way to remember things, places, people, and other things that are easy to picture.

Read the following paragraph that describes the parts of a home computer. As you read, form a picture of a home computer in your mind.

The Home Computer

I use my computer at home to type letters and reports. The computer looks like a typewriter but has four different parts while a typewriter has only one. The four parts are separate but attached to each other by wires. One part is a monitor that I look at as I type. The monitor looks like a 10-inch TV screen. The second part is a disk drive, and it is placed below the monitor. A third part is the keyboard on which there are letters and numbers I use to type. The keyboard is flat and is usually placed in front of the monitor. The fourth part is the printer I use to print what I have typed. The printer is larger than the keyboard and is usually placed to the left or right of the monitor. The monitor, keyboard, and printer are connected to the back of the computer by wires. The computer is connected to a power source by an electrical cord. The computer makes preparing letters and reports easier and quicker to do.

Do you have a clear picture in your mind of the home computer? If not, you should reread the selection until you do. Once you have a clear picture in your mind, use a blank sheet of paper to cover the paragraph about the home computer. On another blank sheet of paper, draw the home computer system described in the paragraph. Label all the parts. Once you start your drawing, do not reread the paragraph.

When you are through, your teacher will give you a drawing of a home computer that has all the parts and labels needed to form a good visualization of the paragraph you just read. Compare your drawing with the drawing of a home computer provided by your teacher.

1. Did you include all the parts?

2. Did you label everything?

3. Were your labels correct?

If you answered NO to any of these questions, read the paragraph again and redraw the home computer. Repeat this procedure until you have answered each question YES.

Model for Visualization of Home Computer

Power source

Printer

Monitor

Keyboard

18

More Practice Using Visualization

Read the following selection from a story. As you read, form a picture in your mind of what is happening. This time you will need to create more than one picture to remember all the information. When information is presented in a sequence, you need to form a picture for each step in the sequence.

The Ski Race

What a beautiful day it was. It was cold and there was snow on the ground but there was not a cloud in the sky. It was a great day for snow skiing and I was ready for the competition to begin. I was feeling very confident as I placed the snow skis over my shoulder and began to walk up the hill.

Joe and I had competed for top honors for fastest skier last year, too. Last year he won, but I knew this year it was my turn. During the fall and summer I worked out in the gym to improve my strength. I rode the stationary bike to build my leg muscles and lifted weights to build strength in the rest of my body. I was stronger than last year.

When I saw Joe, I couldn't believe how big he looked. He had been training too. He was prepared for this race too. Some of my confidence began to fade. But when the race was over and they placed the trophy in my hand, there was a big smile on my face. I looked at Joe who winked and whispered, "Wait 'til next year."

Use a blank sheet of paper to cover the story. On another blank sheet of paper draw the pictures you created in your mind to help you remember the story. Number your drawings to show the order in which they occurred in the story.

When you are through drawing your pictures, your teacher will provide you with a set of drawings that form a good visualization of the story you just read. Then compare your drawings with the drawings provided by your teacher and answer the following questions.

1. Did you have the same number of drawings?

2. If you had fewer drawings, what did you leave out?

3. If you had more drawings, what did you add?

4. How did visualizing the story help you remember what happened?

Model for Visualization of Ski Race

Using Association to Remember Information

To **associate** means to remember things by how they go together. For example, *bread* and *butter* go together. By using this association, if you remember *bread* you will remember *butter*. Association is a good technique to use when you are trying to remember many things that go together.

To use association, think about the things you must remember and divide them into groups that go together. For example, look at the following list of words to remember:

football, baseball, giraffe, lion, basketball, dog, elephant, hockey

You can see that some of the words refer to sports and others to animals. The first thing to do is to divide this list into two lists: *animals* and *sports*.

Animals	Sports
lion	football
giraffe	baseball
dog	basketball
elephant	hockey

Now, instead of having to remember eight separate words, you have to remember two sets of four words that go together. This makes remembering easier for two reasons:

1. It is easier to remember things that go together.

2. It is easier to remember small sets of things rather than large sets.

Examine the following list of words. Place the words into three different groups. Give each group a label or title to help you remember the words in the group.

train, hotdog, dentist, car, auto mechanic, carrots, teacher, boat, apples, airplane, lawyer, soup, waiter, musician, potatoes.

Title _____   Title _____   Title _____

_____   _____   _____

_____   _____   _____

_____   _____   _____

_____   _____   _____

_____   _____   _____

_____   _____   _____

Using Application to Remember Information

Application means to remember information by using the information in some way. Application can be used to help you remember things in all school subjects. Here are some ways you can use application to remember things in different school subjects:

a. Make a map.

b. Write a story.

c. Prepare a time line.

d. Prepare a diorama.

e. Build a model.

f. Prepare a picture album.

g. Create a rule that explains.

h. Develop a game.

i. Create a formula that can be followed.

j. Write a newspaper article.

k. Make an oral presentation.

l. Plan an itinerary for a trip.

m. Cook a meal using the ingredients.

n. Collect examples of things.

o. Collect or take photographs.

Write the letter that shows how you would remember each of the following:

1. _____ to remember the names of U.S. presidents since 1968.

2. _____ to remember the names of the states that border Canada.

3. _____ to remember how to get from one place to another.

4. _____ to remember the ingredients of a recipe.

5. _____ to remember how to formulate a chemical compound.

6. _____ to remember a series of current events.

7. _____ to remember the names of members of a team.

8. _____ to remember the things seen on a field trip.

9. _____ to recall the names of different types of dogs.

10. _____ to remember the parts of an airplane.

Using Repetition to Remember Information

You have probably used repetition many times without realizing it. Anytime you have read, said, or written something a number of times to remember it, you have used repetition.

A good way to remember information when using repetition is to **read, say,** and **write** what you want to remember. For example, if you need to remember a list of words and their definitions, here is how to use repetition to do this:

REPETITION PROCEDURE

1. **Read** aloud the word and its definition. If you need to, use a dictionary to help you pronounce a word.

2. With your eyes closed, **say** the word and its definition.

3. Without looking at the word, **write** the word and its definition.

4. Repeat the steps until you can write the word and its definition from memory three times without an error.

5. Do this for each word on the list.

Use the **repetition procedure** to learn and remember the meanings of these five words.

cordial   warm-hearted, friendly, nice, sociable

frugal   careful with money, watchful, penny-pinching

magnify   make larger, increase in size, enlarge

intricate   puzzling, complicated, difficult to follow

prohibit   stop, prevent, forbid, not allow

24

Using Mnemonic Devices to Remember Information

Mnemonic (pronounced nĭ mŏn´ ĭk) devices are used to improve remembering. They are sometimes referred to as memory tricks. But they are not tricks at all. They are ways to improve remembering. Here are five mnemonic devices you will learn more about.

1. **Rhyme.** A rhyme is a poem or verse that uses words that end with the same sound. For example, to remember the number of days in each month you can use the rhyme:

   Thirty days hath September, April, June and November. All the rest have thirty-one, except February, which has twenty-eight.

2. **Acronym.** An acronym is a word that can be pronounced that is made by using the first letter of other words. For example, the names of the five great lakes in the United States form the acronym HOMES:

   Huron, Ontario, Michigan, Erie, Superior

3. **Abbreviation.** An abbreviation is a group of letters made from the first letter of each word to be remembered. For example, FBI is an abbreviation for the Federal Bureau of Investigation.

4. **Acronymic sentence or phrase.** An acronymic sentence or phrase is formed by words beginning with the first letter of each word to be remembered. For example, the phrase *very active cat* might be used to recall the three types of blood vessels in the human body: veins, arteries, capillaries.

5. **Pegwords.** A pegword is a word that helps you remember something by forming a picture in your mind. Pegwords are used to remember lists of things. Each pegword helps you remember one thing. If you memorize 10 pegwords, then you can use them to remember 10 things. If you memorize 20 pegwords, you can remember 20 things.

Rhyme as a Mnemonic Device

Sometimes the best way to remember information is through rhyme. For example, if you want to remember that Columbus discovered America in the year 1492, you could do so using this rhyme:

In 1492, Columbus sailed the ocean blue.

You should be creative and have fun when you are trying to make a rhyme. Just let your imagination run wild. If you create a rhyme that works for you, use it. If you find that you cannot create a rhyme, try another mnemonic device.

Now try to create a rhyme that can be used to remember the following information. Write your rhyme on the line provided. If you can't think of a rhyme, write NO CAN DO on the line below the information.

1. Jefferson was president of the United States when the Louisiana Purchase was made.

   _____

2. Thomas Edison invented the electric light bulb.

   _____

3. There are 360 degrees in a circle.

   _____

4. China has the largest population in the world.

   _____

5. Lansing is the capital of Michigan and Albany is the capital of New York.

   _____

6. Shakespeare is the author of a play called *Hamlet*. The story is about a Prince of Denmark who lived a long time ago.

   _____

7. Canada, Mexico, and the United States are the three countries that make up North America.

   _____

Acronym as a Mnemonic Device

An acronym is a word made from the first letter or first syllable of each word you want to remember. It does not have to be a real word, only a word that can be pronounced. Sometimes small words like *for, the,* and *a* are not included in the acronym. They are used only when needed to make an acronym that can be pronounced.

Use the first letter of each of the following capitalized words to write an acronym.

1. National Organization for Women _____

2. Mothers against Drunk Drivers _____

3. Constable on Patrol _____

4. Civil Air Patrol _____

5. Organization of Petroleum Exporting Countries _____

6. Acquired Immune Deficiency Syndrome _____

7. North Atlantic Treaty Organization _____

Sometimes acronyms are formed by using the first syllable of each word you want to remember. Use the first syllables of the following words to write an acronym.

8. Florida Veterans _____

9. Medical Communications _____

10. Mercury, Venus _____

Make your own acronyms for the following. Use first letters or first syllables. You may need to reorder the words to form your acronym.

11. Nevada, Maryland, Arkansas _____

12. road, travel, atlas, prison _____

13. lunch, envelope, radio, eggs, table, typewriter _____

14. art, fiction, column, treaty _____

15. rope, apple, ink, lion, tank _____

16. Indian, Sioux, X-ray _____

17. Philippine Agriculture _____

18. Benson Lighting _____

Abbreviation as a Mnemonic Device

An abbreviation is formed from the first letter of each word you want to remember. For example, to remember Columbia World Airlines, you would use the abbreviation CWA. Sometimes the first letters of small words like *for, the,* and *a* are not included in the abbreviation. You do not have to be able to pronounce an abbreviation.

Write the abbreviations used to remember these famous things:

1. United States Air Force _____

2. National Football League _____

3. American Broadcasting Company _____

4. Internal Revenue Service _____

5. Better Business Bureau _____

6. Tennessee Valley Authority _____

Make your own abbreviations for the following. Sometimes you will find it helpful to reorder the words to form an abbreviation. Do not reorder the words when the abbreviation stands for a real thing.

7. Gulf Coastal Plain _____

8. University of Nevada at Las Vegas _____

9. sugar, rope, corn, chocolate, coffee _____

10. dollar, pound, yen, yuan _____

11. check, draft, bill, receipt _____

12. mint, silver, bullion, barter, bank _____

13. colonies, Jamestown, patriots, soldiers _____

14. Washington, Jefferson, Madison, Kennedy _____

Acronymic Sentence as a Mnemonic Device

Sometimes it is helpful to form a sentence to remember information. Begin by writing the first letter of each of the words you want to remember. For each letter, substitute a word beginning with that letter than can be used to form a sentence. For example, it might be difficult to remember the names of the five oceans: Atlantic, Pacific, Indian, Arctic, Antarctic. It would be easier to remember the names if you used a sentence, such as "Alan and Alice played inside." In this sentence, *Alan* helps you remember *Atlantic, and* to remember *Arctic, Alice* to remember *Antarctic, played* to remember *Pacific,* and *inside* to remember *Indian.*

Write an acronymic sentence that will help you remember each of the following:

1. Remember 5 continents: Europe, Asia, Africa, Arctic, Antarctic.

2. Remember 4 items on a grocery list: milk, sugar, bread, meat.

3. Remember 5 parts of the digestive system: liver, stomach, colon, intestine, pancreas.

4. Remember 5 musical instruments: banjo, violin, oboe, drums, piano.

5. Remember the 5 main groups of substances: elements, compounds, solutions, suspensions, mixtures.

6. Remember 6 major rivers: Snake, Mississippi, Amazon, Congo, Nile, Hudson.

7. Remember 6 things to bring to school: pencil, ruler, notebook, eraser, map, compass.

8. Remember 6 types of snakes: cobra, rattlesnake, python, garter, water, copperhead.

Pegwords as a Mnemonic Device

Pegwords are used to remember lists of things. You must memorize pegwords that rhyme with numbers and are easy to picture in your mind. Most often pegwords are used with the number words *one* through *ten*. Each thing to be remembered is pictured with one of the pegwords.

Here is a set of pegwords for the number words *one* through *ten*:

one	run
two	shoe
three	bee
four	door
five	dive
six	fix
seven	heaven
eight	plate
nine	sign
ten	men

Here is how you would use pegwords to remember five forms of transportation your teacher discussed: car, train, boat, airplane, bus. To remember *car,* start with *one* and remember the pegword *run.* Then, form a mental image of a dog running after a car, so that thinking of *one* will help you to remember *car.* To remember *train,* form a mental image of a train coming out of a shoe. To remember *boat,* form an image of a bee driving the boat. To remember *airplane,* form an image of an airplane door. To remember *bus,* form an image of a bus diving off a swimming platform. The more unusual the image, the easier it is to remember.

Using the pegwords for the number words *one* through *five,* what images would you form to remember these five important vegetables:

one/run: carrots _____

two/shoe: peas _____

three/bee: lettuce _____

four/door: corn _____

five/dive: broccoli _____

More Practice Using Pegwords

Use pegwords to memorize ten rights guaranteed under the Bill of Rights. Describe the image you form for each of the 10 rights.

one/run: Freedom of religion.

two/shoe: States can have a national guard.

three/bee: We don't have to give food or shelter to soldiers during peacetime.

four/door: Our homes can't be searched without a search warrant signed by a judge.

five/dive: A person can't be brought to trial without evidence.

six/fix: A person accused of a crime has the right to a speedy trial.

seven/heaven: You have a right to a trial by a jury of your peers.

eight/plate: Punishment for a crime must not be excessive.

nine/sign: Workers have the right to strike.

ten/men: States run the public schools.

What I Have Learned ━━━━━━━━━━━━━━━━━━

Directions. Show what you have learned about remembering information by writing an answer for each of the following:

1. Name the three steps in the remembering strategy.

2. What do you do when you use each of the following to remember information:

   Visualization

   Association

   Application

   Repetition

3. What is a mnemonic device?

4. Explain what you do when you use each of the following mnemonic devices to remember information:

   Rhyme

   Acronym

   Abbreviation

   Acronymic sentence

   Pegwords

Answers for Chapter 1 Reproducibles

1-1 Notes will vary.

1-2 Answers will vary.

1-3 Students draw picture of computer on separate paper. Answers will vary.

1-4 No writing required.

1-5 Students draw pictures to represent ski race on separate paper. Answers will vary.

1-6 No writing required.

1-7 *Food:* hotdog, carrots, apples, soup, potatoes. *Occupations:* dentist, auto mechanic, teacher, lawyer, waiter, musician. *Transportation:* train, car, boat, airplane.

1-8 1. c. 2. a. 3. l. 4. m. 5. i. 6. j. 7. o. 8. f. 9. n. 10. e.
1-9 Students write the definition for each word as part of the repetition procedure.

1-10 Notes will vary.

1-11 Responses will vary.

1-12 1. NOW. 2. MADD. 3. COP. 4. CAP. 5. OPEC. 6. AIDS. 7. NATO. 8. Florvets. 9. Medcom. 10. Merven. 11. Man. 12. Trap or Part. 13. Letter. 14. Fact. 15. Trail. 16. Six. 17. Philag. 18. Benlight.

1-13 1. USAF. 2. NFL. 3. ABC. 4. IRS. 5. BBB. 6. TVA. 7. GCP. 8. UNLV. 9–14. Answers will vary.

1-14 Answers will vary.

1-15 Answers will vary.

1-16 Answers will vary.

1-17 1. Select, Remember, Review. 2. *Visualization:* Form a picture in your mind. *Association:* Remember things by how they go together. *Application:* Use the information in some way. *Repetition:* Read, Say, and Write something a number of times. 3. A way to improve remembering. 4. *Rhyme:* Write a poem or verse that uses words that end with the same sound. *Acronym:* Form a word that can be pronounced using the first letter of words to be remembered. *Abbreviation:* Form a group of letters made from the first letter of each word to be remembered; *Acronymic sentence or phrase:* Create a sentence or phrase in which the first letter of each word begins with the first letter of the words to be remembered; *Pegwords:* Use memorized pegwords to remember things.

CHAPTER 2

Reading and Taking Notes from Textbooks

■ Purposes

The purposes of this chapter are to:

1. teach students with learning disabilities how to use the SQ3R textbook reading and notetaking strategy.
2. provide reproducibles that can be used to teach students with learning disabilities how to use the SQ3R strategy.

■ Titles of Reproducibles

2-1 Components of SQ3R
2-2 A Visit to Ancient Rome
2-3 Textbook Notes for "A Visit to Ancient Rome"
2-4 Practicing with SQ3R
2-5 Textbook Notes for "Political Parties"
2-6 "What Europeans Found: The American Surprise" (Part 1)
2-7 Textbook Notes for "What Europeans Found: The American Surprise" (Part 1)
2-8 "What Europeans Found: The American Surprise" (Part 2)
2-9 Textbook Notes for "What Europeans Found: The American Surprise" (Part 2)
2-10 Lobbying on Gun Control
2-11 Textbook Notes for "Lobbying on Gun Control"
2-12 What I Have Learned

■ RATIONALE

Many students with learning disabilities have difficulty comprehending the information they read in their textbooks. They also have difficulty retaining the information. Teachers must teach students with learning disabilities a textbook reading and notetaking strategy that will improve their comprehension of textual information as well as help them retain the information for later discussions, quizzes, or tests.

Robinson (1978) developed a textbook reading strategy known as SQ3R that improves reading comprehension and prolongs the period of time information can be retained. SQ3R is an effective strategy for improving the textbook comprehension and retention of information for students with learning disabilities. It is also an effective strategy for taking notes from textual materials.

We believe the systematic nature of SQ3R makes it an excellent strategy for students with learning disabilities to use.

■ BACKGROUND INFORMATION

The SQ3R Textbook Reading Strategy

The formula SQ3R stands for the five steps of this textbook reading strategy: **survey, question, read, recite,** and **review.** The first three steps, **survey, question,** and **read,** are used by the reader to comprehend the textual information. The last two steps, **recite** and **review,** are used to help the reader retain the information. SQ3R can be used with textbooks that contain side headings as well as those that do not contain side headings.

In this section we describe the use of SQ3R for reading textbook assignments that contain side headings. We also describe the use of SQ3R for reading assignments that contain no side headings.

Here is the information you need to teach each step in SQ3R to students with learning disabilities. Students should apply the steps to any textbook reading assignments that contain side headings.

To Improve Comprehension

Survey. The purpose of this step is to activate the prior knowledge of the reader and to familiarize the reader with the content of the reading selection. Here is what the student must do:

- Read the **title** and think about what it means.
- Read the **introduction,** which is usually found in the first paragraph or two.
- Read the **side headings** to learn what the selection is about.
- Examine all the **visuals** and read their captions.
- Read the **conclusion,** which is usually found in the last paragraph or two.

Question. The purpose of this step is to provide the reader with questions to think about and answer while reading. These questions force the reader to interact with the author to locate information that will answer the questions. While reading to answer questions, the reader remains active in the reading process. Students who read without a clear purpose in mind frequently become inactive readers. Their eyes move across lines and from page to page while their minds record nothing.

38

Questions are formed by placing the words *who, what, where, when, why,* or *how* in front of the title to form one or more questions about the title. Each side heading is changed into one or more questions by following the same procedure. More than one question should be written for a title or side heading if a single question would be too complex.

In many cases teachers will assign parts of chapters to be read. In these cases there may be no title. When this occurs, the students should be instructed to proceed by writing questions for side headings only.

Students should write their questions in their notebooks. We recommend the use of the format shown in Figure 2.1, "Textbook Notes," for doing this. Instruct students to leave the title section blank if the reading assignment contains no title.

Read. The purpose of this step is for the reader to get the information needed to answer the questions formed in the previous step. Students should be encouraged to skim, skip, read, and/or reread material as appropriate to answer each question. They should write the answers to each question on the form shown in Figure 2.1. It is not necessary for students to write answers in complete sentences. Students should be encouraged to use abbreviations and to write answers with as few words as possible. The written answers to the questions then become textbook notes, which students can use to review the chapter information and prepare for tests.

Students should be told that sometimes while reading they will discover that a question they formed does not match the information presented by the author. When this is the case, students should be directed to change their question to match the information presented.

Recite. The purpose of this step is for students to fix the information in their short-term memory. Immediately after textbook notes have been completed, for each question students should:

• Read the question and its answer **aloud.**
• Read the question **aloud,** then look away and say the answer **aloud.**
• Read the question **aloud,** then with eyes closed say the answer **aloud.**
• **Repeat** this procedure three times.

Review. The purpose of this step is for the reader to fix the information in long-term memory. The same procedure used in the Recite step is followed. The difference is that the recitation is done over a number of days to fix the questions and answers in long-term memory. Students will vary in the number of times and days needed for review. Students with memory difficulties will have to review more often. We recommend that students review for at least three days.

Some textbooks used by students will not contain side headings. In this case, only the Question step of SQ3R must be modified. Since there are no side headings to change into questions, students must read the text to create questions. To do this, students should start by reading the first paragraph of their assignment and continue reading until the author changes the topic. Then the students should reread the information to create a question for the topic the author discussed in that section. Students should write the question on the form shown in Figure 2.2. This procedure is repeated for the remainder of the assignment.

FIGURE 2.1 Textbook notes

Name of Textbook _____

Pages _____

Title: _____

Question

Answer

(Add more questions and answers as necessary)

Side heading:

Q

A

(Add more questions and answers as necessary)

Side heading:

Q

A

(Add more questions and answers as necessary)

Side heading:

Q

A

(Add more questions and answers as necessary)

FIGURE 2.2 Textbook notes when there are no side headings

Name of Textbook _____

Pages _____

Title: _____

Question

Answer

Topic:

Q

A

Topic:

Q

A

Topic:

Q

A

■ TEACHING PLAN

Here is a plan for teaching students with learning disabilities how to use the SQ3R textbook reading strategy.

1. Tell your students you are going to show them a magical formula that will increase their reading comprehension and prolong their memory of what they have read. Tell them the magical formula is called SQ3R. Write the formula on the chalkboard where all the students can see it. Prepare and distribute copies of Reproducible 2-1, "Components of SQ3R." Use 2-1 as you explain what each letter stands for in the

SQ3R formula. Point out to students that, depending on the reading assignment, there may or may not be a title, introduction, visuals, and/or conclusions. However, students should be instructed to use whatever part of the strategy applies to a specific assignment.

2. Distribute copies of Reproducible 2-2, "A Visit to Ancient Rome" and Reproducible 2-3, "Textbook Notes for 'A Visit to Ancient Rome,' " to your students. Use 2-2 and 2-3 to demonstrate the survey, question, and read steps and guide the students through their use. Encourage students to ask questions to ensure that they understand how to apply the first three steps to a reading assignment. Then tell the students that if this were an actual reading assignment, they would also need to do the recite and review steps.

   When using Reproducible 2-3, it may be necessary for students to write additional questions and answers for the title or side headings on the back of the reproducible page. This will not be the case when students write questions and answers in their notebooks. Because we could not predict the number of questions each student would create for a title or side heading, we included space for only one question and one answer. Students should be told to label each question and answer on the back as pertaining to the title or to a specific side heading. Writing and labeling questions and answers on the back of the reproducible may also be necessary for Reproducibles 2-5, 2-7, and 2-9.

3. Distribute copies of Reproducible 2-4, "Practicing with SQ3R," and the corresponding Reproducible 2-5, "Textbook Notes for 'Political Parties.' " Again, use these reproducibles to take your students through the first three steps of SQ3R.

4. Distribute copies of Reproducible 2-6, "What Europeans Found: The American Surprise (Part 1)," and the corresponding Reproducible 2-7, "Textbook Notes for 'What Europeans Found: The American Surprise' (Part 1)." Organize students into learning partner pairs or cooperative learning groups. Have them apply the first three steps of SQ3R to the selection in 2-6. Circulate to be sure students are completing each step in the manner you discussed. When the students have finished applying SQ3R to the selection, have them share with the entire class the questions they formed and the answers they obtained.

5. In the same manner, provide additional practice by extending the assignment using Reproducible 2-8, "What Europeans Found: The American Surprise (Part 2)," and Reproducible 2-9, "Textbook Notes for 'What Europeans Found: The American Surprise' (Part 2)."

6. If your students must read textbook assignments without side headings, you can use Reproducible 2-10, Lobbying on Gun Control, and Reproducible 2-11, "Textbook Notes for 'Lobbying on Gun Control,' " to teach them how to modify the use of SQ3R for this purpose. Emphasize that the only step changed is the Question step. If students need more space when using 2-11, have them use the back of the reproducible page to continue writing additional questions and answers.

7. Have your students use SQ3R with textbooks used in your classes. Insist that they use SQ3R for all textbook reading assigments. For the SQ3R strategy to be of maximum use to students, they must be able to apply the strategy automatically—as automatically as they can recall their own names.

8. Distribute Reproducible 2-12, "What I Have Learned." Use this reproducible to evaluate how well your students have learned the information taught in this chapter. Use any of the reproducibles as needed to review what was presented in this chapter.

Components of SQ3R

1. Survey

- Read the **title** and think about what it means.
- Read the **introduction,** which is usually found in the first paragraph or two.
- Read the **side headings** to learn what the selection is about.
- Examine all the **visuals** and read their **captions.**
- Read the **conclusion,** which is usually found in the last paragraph or two.

2. Question

- Change the **title** into one or more questions. Use these key words to form your questions: *who, what, where, when, why, how.*
- Change each **side heading** into one or more questions. Use these key words to form your questions: *who, what, where, when, why, how.*
- **Write** the questions.

3. Read

- **Read** to **answer** the **questions.**
- **Change questions,** as necessary, to answer the questions the author is addressing.
- **Write answers** to questions to form textbook notes.

4. Recite

Immediately following the reading assignment, do the following for each question:

- Read the question and its answer **aloud.**
- Read the question **aloud,** then look away and say the answer **aloud.**
- Read the question **aloud,** then with eyes closed say the answer **aloud.**
- Repeat these steps three times.

5. Review

Review by doing the same things you did for the **recite** step. Do this once each day for the next three days. Review for more than three days if you need to.

A Visit to Ancient Rome

What do you think living in Rome was like a thousand or more years ago? It was quite exciting for the times because Rome was the cultural center of the known world. By taking a visit to ancient Rome, you will obtain a feeling for this marvelous city.

ROMAN DRESS

The first thing a traveler to ancient Rome would see would be some male citizens going about their daily business dressed in long, woolen shirts called tunics. Those men who were involved in more formal routines would be wearing undyed wool togas over their tunics. In most weather all Romans wore strap sandals. The ladies of the city dressed in long stolas, tunics belted at the waist, worn over an inner tunic. They might wear a rectangular cloak if the weather was cold. Roman women often carried parasols and fans in hot weather. All the citizens dressed as comfortably as they could.

FORMS OF ENTERTAINMENT

As he toured the city, the newcomer might wonder what forms of entertainment amused the citizens. He would probably hear shouts and cheers coming from an area where spectators were enjoying a circus, a play, or gladiatorial combat. These events took place often and lasted from sunrise to sundown. Admission was free so anyone who chose to could attend.

Another popular leisure time activity in ancient Rome was public bathing. Bathing establishments were quite elaborate. One would find games, lectures, and muscial performances presented there. There were areas where people could lounge and gossip if they were not enjoying the baths. At the center of everything were the baths themselves, a cold bath, a warm bath, and a steam bath which bathers passed through in order. The baths were actually a large complex of business and entertainment areas.

LIMITATIONS OF THE CITY

The tourist would be impressed with the Roman's love of grandeur as evidence by the beauty of baths, but if he walked around the city long enough, he would become aware of the limitations it had. It would soon be obvious that as a visitor he would have to ask directions in order to get around. Most of the residential streets did not have names and the houses

LIVING LONG AGO   101 did not have numbers. There were few sidewalks and the streets were narrow and crowded. The tourist would have to be alert when he strolled down a residential street because at that time people disposed of their trash the easiest way, by throwing it out the window! Thus, walking around Rome was not only confusing, it was also dangerous.

ROME AT NIGHT

Anyone visiting Rome would be well advised to do his sightseeing during the day because a walk through Rome at night was a dangerous adventure. There were no street lights to illuminate the heavy traffic that clogged the streets. During the day law prohibited chariots and tradesmen's carts from filling the streets of the city, so there was a great deal of traffic at night. There was also a lot of crime in the dark, crowded streets. Smart Romans stayed at home after sunset.

HAZARDS OF TRAVEL

When the visitor to Rome decided to leave, he would have to choose his route home carefully. Travel outside the city was dangerous and difficult. Wealthy people traveled by carriage, usually accompanied by their household slaves and servants. Travelers would not stop at the inns and hotels along the way because they were apt to be dirty. They also tended to be the hangouts of robbers. Instead the Roman traveler would sleep in his carriage or in a tent put up by the side of the road. If the traveler was fortunate and had a friend who lived along the route, he could stay with him. There was an elaborate social system of *hospitium* or "guest friendship" that was similar to membership in a lodge. People were obligated to give those who were their friends protection and hospitality while they were on the road. Romans had to plan their journey well if they were to arrive at their destination safely.

You can see that living in the ancient city of Rome was both adventurous and dangerous. Life was very different from what we experience in the twentieth century. Dress, entertainment, travel, and conditions of living are much better today.

102   LIVING LONG AGO

Textbook Notes for "A Visit to Ancient Rome"

1. **Title:** A Visit to Ancient Rome

   <u>Q</u>uestion

   <u>A</u>nswer

2. **Side heading:** Roman Dress

   Q

   A

3. **Side heading:** Forms of Entertainment

   Q

   A

4. **Side heading:** Limitations of the City

   Q

   A

5. **Side heading:** Rome at Night

   Q

   A

6. **Side heading:** Hazards of Travel

   Q

   A

Practicing with SQ3R

Directions: Use SQ3R to read this assignment. Write your questions and answers in the handout titled "Textbook Notes for 'Political Parties.' " If you need to write more than one question for the title or a side heading, do so on the back of the handout.

Political Parties

Political parties propose programs that concern voters. Voters hold public officials accountable. Unless a party makes its program work, voters may vote for the other party in the next election. Thus, the parties provide a way for people to express their support for, or opposition to, the government.

POLITICAL PARTIES AND CANDIDATES

One of the most important goals of either the Democratic Party or the Republican Party is to win elections. Each party nominates candidates for public office. The party needs workers and money to get its candidates elected. Therefore, the party must constantly look for workers to help candidates, and raise money to support candidates.

1

Reprinted with permission from *Civics, Government and Citizenship* by J. R. Fraenkel, F. T. Kane, & A. Wolf, copyright © 1990 by Prentice Hall, Englewood Cliffs, NJ, pages 338–340.

Political parties buy advertising time on television, and advertising space in newspapers. They organize public meetings where candidates can speak. They send workers to homes, shopping centers, factories, and other places to get people to register and to vote. Parties pass out campaign pamphlets and urge people to vote for their candidates. On election day, party workers telephone people registered with their party to remind them to vote. They drive voters to the polls. They offer baby sitting services. It would be very difficult, if not impossible, for a candidate to win an election without party support.

POLITICAL PARTIES IN CONGRESS

The Constitution states that each house of Congress may set up its own rules of operation and select its own leaders. In practice, it is the majority party in each house that selects the leaders and decides what the rules will be. Usually the same party has a majority in both houses. Sometimes, however, one party has a majority in the Senate and another has a majority in the House of Representatives.

At the beginning of a new Congress, the members of each party in each house hold a party caucus. At a caucus, each party elects its leader and assigns its members to various committees. The majority and minority leaders are their party's floor leaders and key planners. They try to influence party members to vote on the important bills as the party recommends. When 75 percent of the party's legislators vote the same way, it is considered a party vote.

The majority party in Congress usually has enough support from its members to pass bills. When it does not have this support, the leaders of the majority party may work with leaders of the minority party to get help to pass bills.

One of the advantages of a two-party system is that the two parties will debate issues and work out compromises. Most compromises are made when the majority party needs the minority party's help to pass a bill. At such times, the minority party can have influence over what the bill will contain.

POLITICAL PARTIES AND STATE LEGISLATURES

The Democratic and Republican parties are represented in state legislatures too. The power and influence of the parties in the state legislatures are similar to their power and influence in Congress. Party caucuses elect leaders and assign members to various committees. The majority party

2

elects the leaders in each house. The leaders of each party try to persuade their members to support the bills their party proposes.

THE PRESIDENT AS A PARTY MEMBER

You learned in an earlier chapter that Presidents are legislators as well as leaders of their parties. The President, the President's advisers, and the leaders of the President's party in Congress often work together to develop bills.

There are times when the President's views on issues are different from the views of party members in Congress. When this happens they try to compromise, but at times they fail to reach agreement. Members of Congress, for example, may want a large tax cut. The President may feel that taxes should not be reduced. As a result, the President may veto a tax bill that some of his own party members helped to pass.

The President uses the position as party leader and the power to make appointments to reward party members who support presidential programs in Congress. The President may ask these members to suggest people to be appointed as judges, cabinet members, and ambassadors. The President also rewards loyal party members by campaigning for them—making personal appearances and issuing statements of support for them.

As you can see, political parties are an important part of our government system. They provide a way for people with common beliefs to work together to do the important business of government. They also help insure that important issues are debated. Each political party polices the actions of the other party to ensure fairness in government.

3

Textbook Notes for "Political Parties"

1. **Title:** Political Parties

   Question

   Answer

2. **Side heading:** Political Parties and Candidates

   Q

   A

3. **Side heading:** Political Parties in Congress

   Q

   A

4. **Side heading:** Political Parties and State Legislatures

   Q

   A

5. **Side heading:** The President as a Party Member

   Q

   A

What Europeans Found: The American Surprise (Part 1)

Directions: Use SQ3R to read and study the information in this assignment. Write your questions and answers in the handout "Textbook Notes for 'What Europeans Found: The American Surprise' (Part 1)." If you need to write more than one question for the title or a side heading, do so on the back of the handout.

What Europeans found: the American surprise

The discovery of America was the world's greatest surprise. When the first Europeans came, their maps of the world left no place for America. They knew only three continents—Europe, Asia, and Africa. These seemed to be merged together into one huge "Island of the Earth." That big island was indented by lakes, and a few seas like the Mediterranean and the Western Ocean. The planet seemed covered mostly by land, and there was no room for another continent.

Columbus was not looking for a new continent. He thought he was on his way to China and India. Europeans were disappointed to find unexpected lands in their way. Still they insisted on calling the natives here the "Indians." So America was discovered by accident.

As more Europeans came and explored the unknown lands, their disappointment became surprise. They had found a world for new beginnings.

1. CHRISTOPHER COLUMBUS

The adventure that Columbus had in mind was exciting enough. He aimed to sail westward from the shores of Europe until he reached the shores of Asia. Asia was then Europe's treasure-house. It supplied peppers and spices and tea for the table, silks and gold brocade for the dresses of noble ladies and for draperies in palaces, diamonds and rubies for rings and bracelets and necklaces. Until then the main way to the Orient had been the slow, long trek overland. From Venice it might take a year to reach Peking. You would not arrive at all unless you survived the attacks of bandits, the high-mountain snows, and torrid desert heats. Even after you arrived in

5

Asia, it was hard to bring your treasure back overland. For there were no wagon highways and you had to pack your treasure in caravans on the backs of donkeys, horses, and camels.

A direct westward voyage by sea would make all the difference. You could avoid bandits and mountains and deserts. The spacious hold of your ship would safely carry back your treasure. This was a simple and appealing idea. The wonder is why more people before Columbus did not try it.

Earlier in the 1400s a few sailors had tried. But they were not prepared for so long a voyage, and they did not know the winds. Some reached out into the Atlantic Ocean as far as the Azores and beyond. But the winds were against them and the seas rough. They all soon turned back for home.

As a determined young man Christopher Columbus decided that he would sail into the Western Ocean—to Asia and back. He had no doubt he could do it. He knew the sea, the winds, and the currents.

Early experiences. Columbus was born in 1451 in bustling Genoa, Italy, "that noble and powerful city by the sea." He was the son of a prosperous wool-weaver. For the first 22 years of his life he lived there. He saw ships bringing rich cargo from the eastern Mediterranean where the treasures of the Orient had been taken overland. When he went to sea, he sailed in all directions where ships went at the time. Once his cargo was wool and dried fish and wine carried from Iceland and northern Ireland to Lisbon and the islands of the Azores. Then he lived for a while in the Madeira Islands off the coast of Africa. He even sailed down the steaming African coast to distant Portuguese trading posts on the Gulf of Guinea.

When he left Genoa to settle in Lisbon, Portugal, that city was "the street corner of Europe." Its deep, sheltered harbor was the point of arrival and departure, a place of exchange, for the seaborne commerce of the whole western end of the continent. From there shipments went northward to the British Isles or the North Sea, southward for trade into Africa. And, why not westward—to Asia?

There in Lisbon the single-minded young Columbus laid his plans for his grand "Enterprise of the Indies." He called it an "enterprise" because he expected it to be not just a voyage of discovery but a money-making project. "The Indies" was the name for India and the other Asian lands of the Far East. Convinced that they had a great project to sell, Christopher and his brother Bartholomew made Lisbon their headquarters.

The "Enterprise of the Indies" would not be inexpensive. Ships would have to be bought or hired, crews found and paid. Food and other supplies had to be collected for the long voyage there and back. No ordinary merchant would have the wealth and the power needed. It would take a rich monarch. There was hope of great profit, but there was also great risk. Was there a ruler bold enough to take the big gamble?

6

No one knew exactly what the risks might be—or even how far it was from the coast of western Europe to the coasts of Asia. No one had ever made that trip before. The questions could not be answered from experience.

The learned men disagreed in their guesses. Some said it was about 2000 miles. Others said it was two or three times that long. The leading authority was the ancient Greek geographer Ptolemy. Columbus read the best geography books he could find. We still have some of them with his own marks. He underlined the passage that said, "this sea is navigable in a very few days if the wind be fair." He believed the writers who said the distance was short, and accordingly he made his plans.

Seeking support. Christopher and his brother traveled to the capitals of Europe trying to sell their project. The monarchs shunned Columbus's grand Enterprise of the Indies. When in 1484 King John II of Portugal asked his committee of experts if Columbus could succeed, they said it was too far to Asia and told him not to take the risk. Instead King John sent daring sailors on the long way round Africa eastward to India. In 1488 Bartholomeu Dias succeeded in rounding the Cape of Good Hope, at the southern tip of Africa. Now the eastern route to India was open. Why risk the uncertain way west when there was a sea-path to the east?

Columbus then went next door to Spain, where Queen Isabella had a mind of her own. The bold mariner awakened her interest. To finance the trip she needed money from the royal treasury, but her committee of experts refused to approve the project. She kept the impatient Columbus waiting for six years. Finally, he gave up and prepared to take ship for France. At the last moment, the court treasurer convinced Isabella the gamble was worth the risk. She now became so enthusiastic she was even prepared to pawn her jewels to help Columbus. But that was not necessary. She was told the royal treasury could pay the cost. So Queen Isabella sent Columbus a promise of royal support. She also granted all his demands for noble titles and a 10 percent share of whatever wealth came from land he might discover.

Columbus formed his enterprise in the small port of Palos, which had done something illegal. As a penalty the Queen fined it two caravels—light, swift sailboats—to go with Columbus. The caravels were the *Niña* and the *Pinta*. The third vessel of the expedition was the biggest, the *Santa Maria*, which Columbus chartered. The crew was mostly from Palos and nearby, and they were courageous and expert sailors.

The great voyage. With his three ships Columbus set sail from the coast of Spain on August 3, 1492. In the next weeks he proved that he was the greatest mariner of the age.

Still, it is hard to be at sea for weeks when you are not sure what—if

7

anything—is ahead. So Columbus's men grew rebellious and reached the verge of mutiny. But Columbus was a true leader. A man taller than most, blue eyed and red haired, he was respected by his followers. He altered the records of distances they had covered so the crew would not think they had gone too far from home. He convinced them to go on. Still, on October 9, Columbus agreed that if they did not find land in three days, he would turn back. But by then there were more and more signs of land—birds in the air, leaves and flowers floating in the water.

It was not enough to know the sea. The winds were the engine that took you there and back. Others had failed because they did not know how to use the winds. They had tried going straight west from Spain. That was their mistake. Instead Columbus first had sailed south to the Canary Islands off the coast of Africa, then sailed west from there. That was where the winds blowing from the east would carry his ships straight on to his destination. Also the Canaries were on the same latitude as Japan, so if he went due west he thought he would arrive where he wanted to be.

The winds blew just as Columbus expected. This, the most important sea voyage in history, had good weather and clear sailing. At 2 o'clock in the morning on October 12, 1492, after thirty-three days at sea, a lookout sighted the white cliffs of an island in the Bahamas. The natives called it Guanahani, and Columbus named it San Salvador—Holy Savior. Columbus had discovered America—though he did not know it.

Columbus cruised about in the Caribbean Sea for several months. He landed on Cuba, which he thought and hoped might be Japan. After the *Santa Maria* was wrecked on the reef off Haiti, he built a fort on the island. They named the island Hispaniola (after Spain). He left about 40 men when he headed for home January 4, 1493. Columbus had found no great cities in his travels—but he had seen gold ornaments and found a little gold in a stream on Hispaniola. So he thought he had reached the outposts of the rich empire of Cathay (China).

By great luck Columbus did not try to sail back the way he had come. It would have been a mistake, for at that latitude the winds came from the east. Instead Columbus sailed north to about 35° north latitude. There the prevailing winds from the west blew him back to Spain.

When he arrived on March 15, 1493, he had accomplished much more then he knew. He had discovered a new world. The king and queen loaded him with honors and made his two sons pages at the court. Meanwhile he had shown sailors how to sail and where to sail so the winds would carry them to America *and back!* This made it possible for countless other ships to follow.

Columbus's other voyages. Three times on later voyages Columbus returned to the islands that he called the "Indies," or lands of the East. On

8

these trips he established the first permanent settlement of Europeans in the Western Hemisphere, he skirted the shore of South America, and he explored the coast of Central America. He was always trying to prove that he had found the treasure lands of the East. But he finally reaped only misfortune and disgrace. When he returned to Spain in 1504 after his last voyage, he found Queen Isabella dying and his friends, his influence, and his reputation gone. Two years later Columbus died still believing that he had sailed to the coast of Asia.

9

Textbook Notes for "What Europeans Found: The American Surprise" (Part 1)

1. **Title:** What Europeans Found: The American Surprise

   Question

   Answer

2. **Side heading:** 1. Christopher Columbus: Who he was and why he came

   Q

   A

3. **Side heading:** Early experiences

   Q

   A

4. **Side heading:** Seeking support

   Q

   A

5. **Side heading:** The great voyage

   Q

   A

6. **Side heading:** Columbus' other voyages

   Q

   A

What Europeans Found: The American Surprise (Part 2)

Directions: Use SQ3R to read this assignment. Write your questions and answers in the handout "Textbook Notes for 'What Europeans Found: The American Surprise' (Part 2)." If you need to write more than one question, use the back of the handout.

---

2. BEFORE DISCOVERY

If it hadn't been for Columbus, years might have passed before the people of Europe "discovered" America. But it was only for the people of Europe that America had to be "discovered." Millions of Native Americans were already here! For them, Columbus, and all the sailors, explorers, and settlers who came later, provided their "discovery" of Europe!

For Europeans the "discovery" of America offered vast lands, treasures of gold and silver and timber, places to build cities and places of refuge. For them this was a happy discovery. In the long run it would be a great discovery for the world. But for the millions of Native Americans already here their "discovery" of Europeans was not quite so happy. For some it meant the end of their Native American civilization. For some it meant slavery. For nearly all of them Europeans brought shock, disease, and change.

The first people to come to America were the ancestors of those who Columbus by mistake called Indians. No one knows when they came. A widely held theory is that sometime between 35,000 and 11,500 years ago during the last great ice age the first small groups arrived. They were people on the move. They had come from Northern China and Siberia.

So much of the sea had frozen into ice that it lowered the water in the Bering Strait. Then as they tracked wild game they could walk across the 56 miles from Siberia to Alaska. Without knowing it, they had discovered two large continents that were completely empty of people but were full of wild game—huge mastodons and mammoths, giant ground sloths, camels, antelopes, and great long-horned bison, In the thousands of years afterwards many other groups followed. These small bands spread all across North and South America.

The high mountains and broad rivers separated the communities. There were hundreds of languages and many different styles of life. Some small bands of people had no fixed homes. They followed their quarry and lived

10

the wandering life of hunters. Others settled down and after centuries built vast kingdoms with flourishing cities, temples and palaces, and lively commerce.

Mayas, Incas, and Aztecs. The grandest of these Native American cultures astonished the Europeans. South of the present United States—from central Mexico to Peru—they found the Aztecs, the Mayas, and the Incas.

In the mountains, deserts, and rain forests of Guatemala, Belize, Honduras, and Mexico the Mayas had built temples and pyramids clustered about broad plazas. We can still climb them. The Mayas invented their own writing. Although they had no telescope, they built their own kind of observatory and made accurate calendars. Their "Indian corn" (maize) had never been seen in Europe. It was originally a wild grass, but would become a staple food for the world.

In Peru the Incas had constructed palaces surrounded by high walls, and had connected their mountain-towns with a network of roads. To farm their steep land they had built terraces. Where water was scarce, they had cut canals and erected stone aqueducts to irrigate their crops. The Incas gave us the potato and the tomato.

When European explorers came to Peru, they were amazed by the Incan government. They never expected to find such powerful rulers so well organized in the mountain wilderness. The Incas had succeeded even without a system of writing. No Americans were richer. In Cuzco, the mountain capital of the Incan empire, even the buildings were covered with gold!

The Aztecs were a warlike people who lived in central Mexico. They were clever architects. Like the Mayas, they too built grand temples and high pyramids. Their capital, where Mexico City is today, was a bustling metropolis. And they fashioned their gold into jewelry so ornate as to make European kings jealous.

These peoples had found their own ways of progress—different from the ways of Europe. They had never invented the wheel. They had no iron tools. Their beasts of burden were the dog and, in Peru, the llama. Unlike the peoples of Europe, they had not built ships to cross the oceans. They had not reached out to the world. In their isolation they found it hard to learn new ways. When the Spanish came, it seemed that the Incas, the Mayas, and the Aztecs had ceased to progress. They were ripe for conquest.

North American Indians. Of course there was no census of early America. But in 1500 the people in Mexico probably numbered about 12 million. Farther north in what is now the United States and Canada there

11

were only some 4 million. The great empires of old America—of the Mayas, the Incas, and the Aztecs—were all in Mexico or south.

North of Mexico most of the people lived in wandering tribes and led a simple life. North American Indians were mainly hunters and gatherers of wild food. An exceptional few—in Arizona and New Mexico—settled in one place and became farmers.

The most advanced Indians of North America lived in the Southwest. The Anasazi came to be known as Pueblo Indians, after their style of building. A "pueblo" was a kind of apartment several stories tall, built of stone or adobe. The Anasazi also built cliff dwellings where they could defend themselves against enemy tribes. They and their descendants—the Hopi, Zuñi, and Acoma—made pottery, textiles, and baskets which we still admire.

When the Europeans came, the largest population of Indians north of Mexico was in California. They were a tenth of all the Indians in what is now the United States. They and the Indians of the Northwest lived by hunting and fishing and by gathering the plentiful nuts and berries.

Before Columbus and the Spanish came to America, they were not many Indians on the Great Plains. They walked for miles in pursuit of the herds of buffalo. The buffalo supplied them with skins to wear, meat to eat—and even (in dried buffalo chips) with fuel for their fires. Their only beast of burden was the dog. There were no horses in America until the Spanish brought them.

In the Eastern Woodlands the many tribes were mainly hunter–food gatherers, but they also did some farming. some of them had joined in their own small version of a United Nations. Five tribes of Huron-Iroquois-speaking people—the Mohawk, Seneca, Oneida, Onondaga, and Cayuga—in upper New York State formed the Iroquois League. The council of chiefs who governed the league was chosen by certain women of high station. The council had no power to make war but planned defense. The powerful Chief Powhatan formed his own league (in Virginia), and there were others.

Down south in Mississippi the Natchez Indians seemed more like the Mexican Indians. Mainly farmers, they were divided into nobles and commoners, and were ruled by a man they called the Great Sun.

The Indians of North America were as varied as the peoples of Europe. There were countless tribes and hundreds of languages. Some tribes made elegant gold jewelry, but others were still in the Stone Age. Some wove handsome rugs and wore textiles of beautiful design. Others knew only skins and furs. Their meat depended on the place. Deer were nearly everywhere, and on the plains were herds of buffalo. The seashores and streams abounded in fish and shell food. The Indians planted corn, which made their bread, and beans, squashes, and many other crops. They knew where

12

to find, and how to enjoy, the nuts and berries and mushrooms and other delights of the woods. They raised and smoked tobacco.

Because the Indians lived so close to nature, most of them had religions in which natural things played a major role. The Indians saw and worshiped Nature. They had learned to know the stones, the animals, and the plants. They were adept at using what they found for food, shelter, and clothing.

3. WHY EUROPEANS WENT EXPLORING

For centuries all these people and their cultures lay hidden from Europe: What happened to stir Europeans to reach out to this vast unknown?

The Renaissance, 1300–1600. Near the end of the Middle Ages, the Christians of western Europe launched crusades to take Jerusalem back from the Muslims. When thousands of Europeans traveled across the Mediterranean and reached the Holy Land, they discovered that they had much to learn from the East. Commerce grew and minds were opened. Scholars translated books of poetry, adventure, and science from Greek, Arabic, Hebrew, Persian, and other eastern languages. They revived the questioning spirit of the ancient Greeks. Ambitious princes led new city-states in Italy. They built palaces and churches in the style of Greece and Rome. For the first time artists discovered the science of perspective. Leonardo da Vinci and Michelangelo painted their masterpieces and kept notebooks of all the wonders of the world.

Of course there were books before there was printing. But those early books were all copied by hand. It would take six months to make one copy of a long book. Books were costly and few people could read. Then Johann Gutenberg at Mainz in Germany invented movable type. Here was a way to make many copies of a book—and at much less cost. In 1456 he printed his first Bible and opened a new world for books. Within only fifty years 10 million copies of printed books appeared in Europe.

Modern astronomy was born. Copernicus showed that the earth revolved around the sun, and the word went everywhere in books.

The rise of nation states. At the same time, the modern nation state took shape. Strong kings conquered weak feudal lords. The nation's laws, taxes, armies, and courts replaced those of the local nobles. People began to glory in the power of their king. They were proud to be French, English, Spanish, or Portuguese. For "king and country" they sought glory in war, riches in commerce, honor in the arts. And the more adventurous went out

13

to plant their country's flag abroad. The wealth of the nation commanded by the new monarchs would outfit the ships to explore the world.

The lure of the East. The fabled Orient had a wonderful charm for the people of Europe. In 1271 the Venetian merchants Maffeo and Nicolo Polo, and Nicolo's young son Marco, traveled to China. They spent seventeen years there in the service of the Khan. Upon the Polos' return, the people of Venice were astonished by the gold and silks and jewels they had brought back. Marco Polo's book about his adventures was printed two centuries later on the new presses. When Columbus read Marco Polo's book, it whetted his appetite for the East.

Meanwhile the rich people of Europe wanted more and more of the goods from the Orient. These had come partly overland by risky trails through mountain and desert and partly by sea. Much was lost to bandits or to shipwrecks. The rising monarchs began to think of finding a direct way to the East entirely by sea.

The techniques of discovery. In Columbus's time all educated people and most sailors believed that the earth was a sphere. They disagreed about the size of the globe, and about how much was land and how much water. The coast of Africa was only beginning to be explored.

Prince Henry "the Navigator" (1394–1460) had set up a school for explorers at Cape St. Vincent on the southwestern tip of Portugal. He began to push voyages of discovery along the coast of Africa. He trained the sailors and their captains, improved the design of ships, and gathered maps and charts. Within fifty years, his sailors made more progress exploring the west coast of Africa than Europeans had made in the thousand years before.

Since about 1200, sailors had had the compass to help them find their way. To figure latitude and see where they were on the map, they used other simple instruments—the astrolabe, the quadrant, and the cross-staff. They had no way to discover longitude. This meant that they could not figure exactly where they were east or west, or how wide was the Western Ocean.

During their African voyages of discovery the Portuguese designed a new kind of sailing ship—the "caravel." It was a lithe, but sturdy, three-masted or four-masted vessel that was excellent for exploration. Caravels had sails that could be set to catch the wind so if they sailed somewhere with the wind they could still sail back, even with the wind against them.

14

Textbook Notes for "What Europeans Found: The American Surprise" (Part 2)

1. **Side heading:** 2. Before discovery

   Q

   A

2. **Side heading:** Mayas, Incas, and Aztecs

   Q

   A

3. **Side heading:** North American Indians

   Q

   A

4. **Side heading:** 3. Why Europeans went exploring

   Q

   A

5. **Side heading:** The Renaissance, 1300–1600

   Q

   A

6. **Side heading:** The rise of nation states

    Q

    A

7. **Side heading:** The lure of the East

    Q

    A

8. **Side heading:** The techniques of discovery

    Q

    A

Lobbying on Gun Control

Directions: Use SQ3R to read this assignment that has no side headings. Write your questions and answers in the handout "Textbook Notes for 'Lobbying on Gun Control.'" If you run out of space, continue writing questions and answers on the back of the handout.

Think of the television shows and movies you have seen in the past month. Did you watch westerns, science fiction, crime thrillers? How many programs showed scenes with guns? How many scenes involving guns do you suppose you have watched in your entire lifetime?

Guns are so familiar on television and in the movies that we take them for granted. But in real life guns are the focus of much debate. Do all American citizens have the right to bear arms? Or should the right to bear arms be regulated? Powerful interest groups have spoken out on both sides of this question. The National Rifle Association (N.R.A.) is the best-known group lobbying in favor of the right of every citizen to bear arms. Groups such as Handgun Control, Inc., and the Center to Prevent Handgun Violence lead the fight to limit the sale and possession of firearms.

No one denies that guns play a significant role in violent crimes. But interest groups disagree whether or not gun control is an effective way to stop crime. Opponents of gun control argue that private citizens often need guns to protect themselves. A homeowner, for example, might own a gun to stop an intruder from breaking in and stealing property. Some foes of gun control further contend that crime would increase if citizens could not own guns, because criminals then would be able to get away with more crimes.

Gun control advocates see things differently. They believe that owning a gun does not significantly improve one's chances of defending oneself against a criminal. They also point out the great number of accidents that were caused by guns. In 1987, gun accidents were the fourth leading cause of accidental death for children under the age of 15 in the United States.

Supporters of gun control believe that violent crime would be reduced if criminals found it harder to get guns. The 1968 Gun Control Act forbids the purchase of guns by convicted felons, minors, drug addictrs, and mentally ill persons. Some states have laws against carrying concealed weapons. Others require pistol owners to register their guns. Supporters of gun control want more; they would like to see a two-week waiting period in all states before anyone can purchase a gun. This would allow time to check the buyer's background.

Groups like the N.R.A. oppose such regulations. They argue that gun control laws affect only law-abiding people who want to own guns. Criminals, they say, will get guns no matter what the laws are. The N.R.A. puts its faith in better law enforcement and stiffer penalties for criminals.

34

Much of the debate on gun control focuses on the second Amendment to the Constitution. The Amendment reads:

A well-regulated militia being necessary to the security of a free state, the right of the people to keep and bear arms shall not be infringed.

Interest groups that support gun control point out that when the Amendment was written, the War for Independence was fresh in the minds of Americans. People remembered that British soldiers had taken charge of the colonial militia, and they wanted an amendment that would prevent the new federal government from ever disarming a state's militia. Gun control supporters insist that the Second Amendment gives the military, not individual citizens, the right to carry guns.

Interest groups opposing gun control could not disagree more. The Second Amendment, they argue, says in black and white that all American citizens have the "right to bear arms." This includes owning guns for self-defense, target shooting, and hunting.

The Supreme Court has not ruled directly on whether individuals can own guns. But citizens of Morton Grove, Illinois, presented the question to lower courts in 1973. Morton Grove was the first town in the United States to ban the possession of handguns. The two federal courts that heard the case both ruled that the town's ban did not violate the Second Amendment.

Crackling gunfire continues to keep the gun control issue alive. In 1981, John Hinkley, Jr., wounded President Reagan and Press Secretary William Brady with a handgun. More recently, the use of semiautomatic, or "assault," rifles has stirred public controversy. These military-type guns are often linked to drug-related violence. In February, 1989, five schoolchildren in Stockton, California, were killed in their school playground by a man with a semiautomatic rifle. Gun control groups have called for a ban on these weapons. Opponents of gun control reply that semiautomatic weapons should be allowed for lawful purposes such as hunting.

The debate over guns is not likely to be resolved soon. Interest groups for both sides will continue to lobby for their positions. The final verdict, when it arrives, will determine whether citizens have the right to buy any weapon they choose—or whether they can own a gun only under strict regulation.

35

Textbook Notes for "Lobbying on Gun Control"

1. **Title:**

   Q

   A

2. **Topic:**

   Q

   A

3. **Topic:**

   Q

   A

4. **Topic**

   Q

   A

5. **Topic:**

   Q

   A

6. **Topic:**

   Q

   A

What I Have Learned

Directions: For each of the following letters in the SQ3R formula:

    1. Identify the step the letter stands for.

    2. Tell the important things you are to do when applying that step.

S

Q

R

R

R

    Explain what you must do in the Q step when the assignment you are reading does not have side headings.

Answers for Chapter 2 Reproducibles

2-1   No writing required.

2-2   No writing required.

2-3   1. (Q) What would you see if you visited ancient Rome? (A) Types of dress, forms of entertainment, and what city life was like. 2. (Q) How did Roman men dress? (A) Tunics, togas, sandals. (Q) How did Roman women dress? (A) Astolas, cloaks, sandals. 3. (Q) What kinds of entertainment would you see? (A) Circuses, plays, gladiators, public baths. 4. (Q) What were the limitations of ancient Rome? (A) Hard to find places, crowded, dirty. 5. (Q) What was Rome like at night? (A) Dangerous, very dark, lots of crime, many travelers. 6. (Q) What were the hazards of travel? (A) Robbers. (Q) How did Romans plan their travel? (A) Stayed out of inns and hotels. Wealthy Romans traveled with slaves and servants for protection.

2-4   No writing required.

2-5   1. (Q) Why do we have political parties? (A) To give people a way to support or oppose government. 2. (Q) What are the names of the political parties? (A) Democratic, Republican. (Q) What do political parties do to get candidates elected? (A) Advertise, hold meetings where candidates speak, get people to vote for their candidate. 3. (Q) What do political parties do in Congress? (A) Try to get their bills passed. 4. (Q) What do political parties do in the state legislature? (A) Try to get their bills passed. 5. (Q) What does the president do as a party member? (A) Works with the party to develop bills and appoints party members to important jobs. (Q) What happens when the president does not agree with the party members on an issue? (A) They try to reach a compromise.

2-6   No writing required.

2-7   1. (Q) What did the Europeans find in America? (A) They found a world for new beginnings. 2. (Q) Who was Christopher Columbus? (A) A determined young man who liked adventure. (Q) Why did he come to America? (A) He discovered America by accident while trying to reach Asia. 3. (Q) What were his early experiences like? (A) He was the son of wealthy parents who was fascinated by the sea. He did a lot of sailing and wanted to find a route to Asia by water. He hoped to make a lot of money by doing this. 4. (Q) How did he get support for his adventure? (A) He tried to get many European monarchs to support him with money. (Q) Who gave him support? (A) Queen Isabella of Spain. (Q) What three ships did Columbus take on his adventure? (A) Niña, Pinta, Santa Maria. 5. What was his great voyage like? (A) He was a great leader. He convinced the crew to continue on. He had good weather and clear sailing. He discovered America in 1492 and returned to Spain in 1493. 6. (Q) What were Columbus' other voyages? (A) He sailed to America three more times. He started a settlement and explored the coastlines of South and Central America. At his death, he still believed that he had found Asia.

2-8   No writing required.

2-9   1. (Q) What was America like before Columbus discovered it? (A) It was inhabited by people Columbus called Indians, who had many languages and different ways of living. 2. (Q) Who were the Mayas, Incas, and Aztecs? (A) Indians who built civilizations that were advanced in many ways. They were very different from the Europeans. 3. (Q) What were the North American Indians like? (A) About 12 million lived in what is now known as Mexico and 4 million in what is now known as the United States and Canada. They were mostly hunters and gatherers of food. They had no horses. Some tribes joined together for protection. The tribes were as varied as the people of Europe. 4. (Q) Why did the Europeans go exploring? (A) The Renaissance, the rise of nation states, and the lure of the East. 5. (Q) What was the Renaissance? (A) A period of time in which there were many changes and advances in Europe as a result of what was learned by travelers to the East. 6. (Q) Why did nation states come about? (A) People began to take pride in being a citizen of a certain country. They wanted their country to become wealthy and important. 7. (Q) What was the lure of the East? (A) Gold, silk, and jewels. 8. (Q) What techniques were used to make discoveries? (A) Compass and other instruments of navigation, good maps and charts, trained sailors, improved design of ships.

2-10 No writing required.

2-11 1. (Q) Why is there lobbying on control of guns? (A) People disagree on whether there should be control of guns. Each side lobbies for its position. 2. (Q) Who lobbies for gun control? (A) Groups like Handgun Control, Inc. 3. (Q) Who lobbies against gun control? (A) Groups like the National Rifle Association. 4. (Q) What are the arguments from people who want gun control? (A) Having guns does not make people safer and there would be fewer violent crimes if criminals could not get guns. 5. (Q) What are the arguments from people who want the right to own guns? (A) Criminals would still get guns, the Second Amendment to the constitution gives people the right to have guns. 6. (Q) Has there been a solution to this controversy? (A) Not yet.

2-12 S = Survey: Read title, introduction, side headings, visuals, and conclusions. Q = Question: Use the words *Who, What, Where, When, Why,* or *How* to form questions from the title and side headings. R = Read: Read to answer the questions. R = Recite: Say the questions and answers aloud until they can be recalled. R = Review: Do the same things as in the Recite step from time to time to make sure the information is remembered. When the assignment does not have side headings, look for topics and change them into questions.

CHAPTER 3

Solving Math Word Problems

■ Purposes

The purposes of this chapter are to:

1. teach students with learning disabilities how to use the SQRQCQ strategy for solving math word problems.
2. provide reproducibles that can be used to teach students with learning disabilities how to use the SQRQCQ strategy.

■ Titles of Reproducibles

■ RATIONALE

Many students with learning disabilities have difficulty solving math word problems even though they may have little difficulty with the basic operations of addition, subtraction, multiplication, and division. They have difficulty because they frequently lack a strategy for solving math word problems.

Teachers must instruct students with learning disabilities in the use of a strategy that helps them to solve word problems. SQRQCQ is a strategy particularly well suited for these students because it is logical and simple to use. Furthermore, SQRQCQ is a natural extension of the SQ3R textbook reading strategy presented in Chapter 2. Together these strategies provide students with learning disabilities with an effective way to approach two of the most important requirements they face in school: reading textbooks and solving math word problems.

■ BACKGROUND INFORMATION

Learning about SQRQCQ

SQRQCQ is a mnemonic that stands for the six steps in a math word problem-solving strategy developed by Leo Fay (Forgan & Mangrum, 1989). The six steps are: Survey, Question, Read, Question, Compute, and Question.

What Students Need to Know about SQRQCQ. Here is a summary of the ideas students with learning disabilities must learn to associate with each step in the SQRQCQ strategy:

Survey	Students must carefully read the entire word problem to learn what it is about. If there are terms or ideas they do not understand, they must get them clarified before they go to the next step. Students should ask the teacher and/or other students for clarification.
Question	Students must state the problem in the form of a question. This will help them understand what must be done to solve the problem. Sometimes reading the problem out loud, visualizing it, or even drawing a picture helps students to state the problem as a question.
Read	Students must identify the information that is needed to answer the question. To do this, they must differentiate between the information needed and any extraneous information contained in the word problem. The information needed should be written down as specific facts that will be used to answer the question.
Question	In this step, students must ask: "What computation(s) must I do to get the answer to the question?"
Compute	Students must set up the problem on paper and do the computation(s). Then they must check their computation(s) to make sure there are no errors.
Question	In this step, students must ask: "Does my answer make sense?"

To do this, students must look at their answer to see if it is possible given the facts in the problem. A check of the relationship between the question and the answer will allow students to do this.

How Is SQRQCQ Applied to Word Problems? Here is how SQRQCQ is applied to word problems.

Sample Problem

This year 1,300 students attend Morrison School. Last year there were only 950 students. The school newspaper reported that next year there will be a 7% increase in the number of students attending Morrison School. The principal wants to know how many students will be attending Morrison School next year if the newspaper report is correct.

Survey	By reading the problem carefully, the student learns that the principal wants to know how many students may attend Morrison School next year.
Question	Here the student decides that the question is: "How many students are likely to attend Morrison School next year?"
Read	Here the student reads the problem slowly and carefully to find the information needed to solve the question. The information needed is:

- Last year's enrollment was 1,300 students.
- A 7% increase is expected.

The extraneous information that should be ignored is:

- 950 students attended the school last year.

Question	Here the student must ask: "What computation(s) must I do to solve the problem question?" Two computations must be done. First, the student must calculate how much 7% of 1,300 is. Second, the student must add the result to 1,300 to obtain the answer to the problem question.
Compute	In this step, the student does the necessary computation(s) to answer the question.

$$
\begin{array}{ll}
1,300 & 1,300 \\
\times\ .07 & +\ \ 91 \\
\hline
91.00 & 1,391 \\
\end{array}
$$
likely to attend Morrison School next year

The student then checks the computation(s) to make sure they were done correctly.

Question	Finally, the student asks: "Does my answer to the question make sense?" By looking at the problem question and the answer, the student can determine if the answer makes sense. The student knows that the number

of students attending Morrison will be greater next year. Since the answer shows a reasonable increase in size, the answer makes sense.

■ TEACHING PLAN

Here is a plan for teaching students with learning disabilities how to use the SQRQCQ math word problem-solving strategy.

1. Prepare and distribute copies of Reproducible 3-1, "Learning about SQRQCQ." Use 3-1 as you explain what each letter stands for in this strategy for solving math word problems.

2. Distribute copies of Reproducible 3-2, "Guided Use of SQRQCQ." Use 3-2 to review what each letter in the mnemonic SQRQCQ stands for and to provide a demonstration of how the strategy is used to solve math word problems.

3. Use Reproducible 3-3, "More Guided Use of SQRQCQ," to provide a second demonstration of how SQRQCQ is used to solve math word problems.

4. Use Reproducible 3-4, "Identifying Important Information," to teach students how to write questions and differentiate between important and extraneous information in math word problems.

5. Arrange students into learning pairs. Each learning pair should be composed of one high- and one low-achieving student. Distribute a copy of Reproducible 3-5, "Applying SQRQCQ," to each student. Have the students work together in pairs to apply SQRQCQ and solve the math word problem. When all the pairs have finished their work, review the steps in the SQRQCQ strategy as applied to this problem.

6. Regroup students into new learning pairs and use Reproducible 3-6, "More Practice Applying SQRQCQ," to give students another opportunity to work together to solve a math word problem. When all pairs are finished, review the steps.

7. Select from Reproducibles 3-7 through 3-10 those appropriate for use with your students. The four reproducibles apply to different types of problems. Have the students work independently. The reproducibles are:

    Reproducible 3-7, "Using SQRQCQ to Solve a Percent Problem"

    Reproducible 3-8, "Using SQRQCQ to Solve a Fraction Problem"

    Reproducible 3-9, "Using SQRQCQ to Solve a Money Problem"

    Reproducible 3-10, "Using SQRQCQ to Solve a Measurement Problem"

8. Use Reproducible 3-11, "Using SQRQCQ to Solve a Math Word Problem Provided by Your Teacher," to present your own word problem. Write your problem in the box on Reproducible 3-11 before you duplicate this reproducible.

9. Distribute Reproducible 3-12, "What I Have Learned." Use this reproducible to evaluate how well your students learned what was taught in this chapter. Use any of the reproducibles for review purposes as needed.

For SQRQCQ to be of maximum usefulness to students, they must be able to apply the strategy automatically. You can help your students achieve automaticity by providing practice sessions with the strategy and insisting that your students use the strategy to solve word problems assigned in class and for homework.

Learning about SQRQCQ

SQRQCQ is a strategy you can use for solving math word problems. Each of the letters stands for one of the six steps in the strategy. Read about each step as your teacher discusses it with you.

Survey   Read the entire word problem to learn what it is about. Ask your teacher and/or other students to explain any terms or ideas you do not understand. Be sure you understand everything in the word problem before you go to the next step.

Question   Change the problem into a question. Sometimes it is helpful to read the problem out loud or to form a picture of the problem in your mind or to draw a picture of the problem. Doing these things will help you change the problem into a question. When you have changed the problem into a question, you are ready to go on to the next step.

Read   Read to find all the information you need to answer the question. Write the information down where you can see it. Check to be sure you have all the necessary information. Ignore information in the problem that is not needed to answer the question.

Question   Ask, "What computations must I do to answer the question?" Decide if you need to add, subtract, multiply, divide, or do these in some combination.

Compute   Set up the problem on paper and do the computations. Check your computations for accuracy.

Question   Look at your answer, and ask: "Does my answer make sense?" You can tell if it does by going back and looking at the question you tried to answer. Sometimes you will find that your answer simply could not be right because it does not fit with the facts in the problem. When this happens, go back through the steps of SQRQCQ until you arrive at an answer that does make sense.

Write the words for which each of these letters stands:

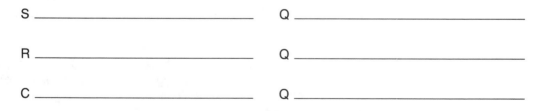

S _____   Q _____

R _____   Q _____

C _____   Q _____

Guided Use of SQRQCQ

Read this problem, which is like many of the word problems you see in your math books.

> This year 1,300 students attend Morrison School. Last year there were only 950 students. The school newspaper reported that next year there will be a 7% increase in the number of students attending Morrison School. The principal wants to know how many students will be attending Morrison School next year if the newspaper report is correct.

Here is how SQRQCQ is used to solve this math word problem.

Survey   **Read the problem to find out what it is about.**
Ask your teacher and/or other students to define or explain anything you do not understand. For example, you may need to ask what a "7% increase" means. From a survey of this problem, you learn that the principal wants to know how many students will attend Morrison School next year.

Question   **Restate the problem as a question.**
By restating the problem as a question, you will have a better idea of how to solve the problem. Sometimes reading the problem out loud, visualizing it, or drawing a picture will help you restate the problem as a question. The problem here is:

> "How many students will attend Morrison School next year if there is a 7% increase?"

Read   **Read the problem and write down the information you need to answer the question.**
Here is the information you need to write:

- The number of students attending Morrison School this year (1,300)

- The percentage by which this number is expected to increase next year (7%)

Cross out or ignore information you do not need. In this problem, you do not need to know the number of students who attended Morrison School last year. If you cross out this unnecessary information, it will not get in the way as you answer the question.

Question   **Ask, "What computations must I do to answer the question?"**
In this problem you will need to multiply 1,300 by 7%. Then you must add this result to 1,300 to answer the question.

Compute   **Do the computations on paper. Circle your answer.**

$$
\begin{array}{cc}
1{,}300 & 1{,}300 \\
\times\ .07 & +\ 91 \\
\hline
91.00 & 1{,}391 \\
\end{array}
$$

Be sure to check that you have done your computations correctly.

Question   **Ask, "Does the answer make sense?"**
Look at the question and decide if your answer makes sense. The answer 1,391 make sense for this problem because you knew there would be more students at Morrison School next year. Your answer, 1,391, is more than the 1,300 students now attending Morrison School. If your answer was less than 1,300, you would know you had done something wrong. You would then have to go back through the steps in SQRQCQ to get the correct answer.

Answer these questions:

1. Why is it important to change a problem into a question?

    _____

    _____

    _____

2. Why is it a good idea to cross out information not needed to answer the question?

    _____

    _____

    _____

3. What should you do if you decide your answer does not make sense?

    _____

    _____

    _____

More Guided Use of SQRQCQ

Here is another word problem like many you find in your math books.

> Luis earns $27 a week working at the supermarket. He works 9 hours a week. He has been working at the supermarket for 6 months. He works 3 days a week. How much money does Luis earn an hour?

Here is how SQRQCQ is used to solve this math word problem.

Survey   After reading this problem, you know that you must find out how much money Luis earns each hour he works.

Question   You restate the problem as a question:

"How much money does Luis earn an hour?"

Read   You decide the following information is needed to answer the problem question:

- Earns $27 a week.
- Works 9 hours a week.

You decide the following information is not needed to answer the problem question:

- Has been working for 6 months.
- Works 3 days a week.

Question   You decide that you will need to divide $27 by 9 hours to know how much money Luis earns an hour.

Compute   You do the computation.

$$\overset{\displaystyle \$3 \text{ an hour}}{9\overline{)27}}$$

Question   You decide your answer makes sense. You know that your answer must be more than $1 an hour and less than $27 an hour.

Answer these questions:

1. Was there anything in the problem you did not understand?

   _____

   _____

2. If yes, what did you not understand?

   _____

   _____

3. Did you read the problem aloud, try to visualize it, or draw a picture to help you restate the problem as a question?

   _____

   _____

4. What information was not needed to answer the question?

   _____

   _____

5. Write the six key words that help you remember the strategy for solving math word problems.

   _____

   _____

Identifying Important Information

Here are some word problems. For each problem, write a question. Cross out any information you do not need to answer the question.

The city of Louisville is about 300 miles from Sam's home town of Ashley. Sam has lived in Ashley for 13 years. Sam drives to Louisville at a speed of 50 miles an hour. Sam's dad wants to know the number of hours it will take Sam to get to Louisville.

1. Question _____

_____

Sal has hit 150 home runs during his baseball career. He has played baseball for 10 years and has been on 3 different teams. He expects to play baseball for 5 more years. Determine the average number of home runs Sal has hit each year.

2. Question _____

_____

Jax is 14 years old today. In his home state he will be able to vote at 18 years of age. Jax wants to know how long it will be before he is able to vote.

3. Question _____

_____

Oxford has a population of 370,890. It has two airports, 6 hospitals, and 22 schools. Its sister city of Bowtown has a population of 78,987. Bowtown has fewer hospitals and schools and does not have an airport. Bowtown is only 13 miles from Oxford. Figure out the population difference between the two cities.

4. Question _____

_____

Applying SQRQCQ

Work with your partner to solve the following problem by using the SQRQCQ strategy. Show what you did for each step. Be prepared to explain how you solved the problem.

In Swanyee there is an average of 32 inches of rain each year. A tree planted in Swanyee grew 3 inches the first year it was planted. It grew 7 inches the second year and 14 inches the third year. This tree will take almost 100 years to reach its full height. Find the average yearly growth rate for this tree.

S What is the problem?

Q Write the question.

R Write the information needed to answer the question. (Cross out any information not needed.)

Q Tell what computations you will use.

C Show your computations. Circle your answer. (Remember to check your computations.)

Q Did your answer make sense? How do you know?

More Practice Applying SQRQCQ ━━━

Work with your new partner to solve the following problem by using the SQRQCQ strategy. Show what you did for each step. Be prepared to explain how you solved the problem.

> There are 32 students in Ms. Henry's math class. Unfortunately, she only has 23 math textbooks and 16 math workbooks. She also found 19 social textbooks. Two more students will be added to the class beginning tomorrow. The principal wants to know the number of additional math textbooks Ms. Henry needs for her class.

S What is the problem?

Q Write the question.

R Write the information needed to answer the question. (Cross out any information not needed.)

Q Tell what computations you will use.

C Show your computations. Circle your answer. (Remember to check your computations.)

Q Did your answer make sense? How do you know?

Using SQRQCQ to Solve a Percent Problem

Working on your own, solve the following math word problem by using SQRQCQ. Be prepared to explain how you used SQRQCQ to solve the math word problem.

There are 780 students and 46 teachers at John Martin School. The school secretary reported that 56% of the students are boys. The principal, Ms. Adams, wants to know the number of boys attending the school. She has been asked for this information by the president of the PTA.

S What is the problem?

Q Write the question.

R Write the information needed to answer the question. (Cross out any information not needed.)

Q Tell what computations you will use.

C Show your computations. Circle your answer. (Remember to check your computations.)

Q Did your answer make sense? How do you know?

Using SQRQCQ to Solve a Fraction Problem

Working on your own, solve the following math word problem by using SQRQCQ. Be prepared to explain how you used SQRQCQ to solve the math word problem.

> Juan and Susan ordered a large pizza with extra cheese and pepperoni for an after school snack. A large pizza has 12 slizes and costs $9.60. Juan said he had a big appetite and would eat ⅔ of the pizza. Susan said that was fine but that Juan would then have to pay ⅔ of the cost of the pizza. Juan wants to know what his cost will be.

S   What is the problem?

Q   Write the question.

R   Write the information needed to answer the question. (Cross out any information not needed.)

Q   Tell what computations you will use.

C   Show your computations. Circle your answer. (Remember to check your computations.)

Q   Did your answer make sense? How do you know?

Using SQRQCQ to Solve a Money Problem

Working on your own, solve the following math word problem by using SQRQCQ. Be prepared to explain how you used SQRQCQ to solve the math word problem.

Paula has been offered a job working after school each day at the Town Pharmacy. She would be paid $4 per hour for stacking shelves and waiting on customers. Paula's mother wants to know how much money Paula would be earning each week. Here is the schedule Paula would have to work:

Monday and Wednesday: 3:00–5:00

Tuesday and Thursday: 3:30–6:15

Friday: 5:15–7:45

S What is the problem?

Q Write the question.

R Write the information needed to answer the question. (Cross out any information not needed.)

Q Tell what computations you will use.

C Show your computations. Circle your answer. (Remember to check your computations.)

Q Did your answer make sense? How do you know?

Copyright © 1993 by Allyn and Bacon

Using SQRQCQ to Solve a Measurement Problem

Working on your own, solve the following math problem by using SQRQCQ. Be prepared to explain how you used SQRQCQ to solve the math word problem.

> Marvin wants to build a cage for his pet rabbit. He wants to build the top and bottom out of wood and the rest of the cage from wire. The top and bottom each need to be 4 feet long and 3 feet wide. His sister needs to know the number of square feet of wood to buy at the lumber yard.

S   What is the problem?

Q   Write the question.

R   Write the information needed to answer the question. (Cross out any information not needed.)

Q   Tell what computations you will use.

C   Show your computations. Circle your answer. (Remember to check your computations.)

Q   Did your answer make sense? How do you know?

Using SQRQCQ to Solve a Math Word Problem Provided by Your Teacher

Solve the following math word problem by using SQRQCQ. Be prepared to explain how you used SQRQCQ to solve the math word problem.

S What is the problem?

Q Write the question.

R Write the information needed to answer the question. (Cross out any information not needed.)

Q Tell what computations you will use.

C Show your computations. Circle your answer. (Remember to check your computations.)

Q Tell how you decided that your answer made sense.

What I Have Learned

Directions: Show what you have learned about using SQRQCQ to solve math word problems by writing an answer to each of the following:

1. The first step in SQRQCQ is **survey.** What do you do in this step?

2. The second step in SQRQCQ is **question.** What must you do to complete this step?

3. The third step in SQRQCQ is **read.** What information must you identify when using this step?

4. The fourth step in SQRQCQ is **question.** What question must you ask to complete this step?

5. The fifth step in SQRQCQ is **compute.** What three things should you do in this step?

6. The sixth step in SQRQCQ is **question.** What question must you ask to complete this step?

7. What should you do if your answer to the question in step 6 is NO?

Answers for Chapter 3 Reproducibles

3-1   S = Survey. Q = Question. R = Read. Q = Question. C = Computer. Q = Question.

3-2   1. To understand what must be done to solve the problem. 2. So information not needed will not get in the way of answering the question. 3. Repeat the steps.

3-3   1–3. Answers will vary. 4. Luis has been working at a supermarket. He works three days a week. 5. Survey, Question, Read, Question, Compute, Question.

3-4   1. How many hours will it take to get from Ashley to Louisville? (Students should cross out "Sam has lived in Ashley for 13 years.") 2. What is the average number of home runs Sal hit per year? (Cross out ". . . and has been on 3 different terms. He expects to play baseball for 5 more years.") 3. In how many years will Jax be able to vote? (Nothing needs to be crossed out). 4. How many more people live in Oxford than Bowtown? (Cross out "It has two airports, 6 hospitals, and 22 schools. Bowtown has fewer hospitals and schools and does not have an airport. Bowtown is only 13 miles from Oxford.").

3-5   S = Find the average yearly growth rate for the tree. Q = What is the average yearly growth rate for the tree? R = Grew 3 inches the first year, 7 the second year, 14 the third year. Q = Add 3 + 7 + 14. Divide sum by 3. C = 8 inches average yearly growth. Q = Yes. It is more than the first year's growth but less than the third year's growth. (Students should cross out "In Swanyee there is an average of 32 inches of rain each year. This tree will take almost 100 years to reach its full height.").

3-6   S = To find how many more math textbooks Mrs. Henry will need for her class. Q = How many more math textbooks will Mrs. Henry need for her class? R = 32 students; 23 textbooks; 2 more students tomorrow. Q = Add to get total number of students. Subtract to get number of books needed. C = 11 textbooks needed. Q = Yes. The number of textbooks needed was less than the number of students in the class. (Students should cross out ". . . and 16 math textbooks. She also found 19 social studies textbooks.").

3-7   S = To find the number of boys who attend John Martin School. Q = How many boys attend John Martin School? R = 780 students; 56% boys. Q = Multiply 780 × 56%. Round to nearest whole number. C = 437 boys. Q = Yes. The number of boys is fewer than the number of students. (Students should cross out "The school secretary reported that . . . and 46 teachers. She has been asked for this information by the president of the PTA.").

3-8   S = To find the amount Juan must pay for the pizza. Q = How much will the pizza cost Juan? R = Pizza cost $9.60. Juan will pay ⅔ of cost. Q = Divide $9.60 by ⅔. C = Juan's cost is $6.40. Q = Yes. Juan's cost was less than the cost of the whole pizza. (Students should cross out "Juan and Susan ordered a large pizza with extra cheese and pepperoni for an after school snack. Juan said he had a big appetite and would eat ⅔ of the pizza. Susan said that was fine but that . . . then").

3-9   S = Find out how much money Paula will earn each week. Q = How much money will Paula earn each week? R = Is paid $4 an hour. Works Monday and Wednesday 3:00–5:00, Tuesday and Thursday 3:30–6:15, Friday 5:15–7:45. Q = Subtract ending from starting time for each day. Sum differences. Convert minutes to hours and minutes. C = $48 per week. Q = Yes. Paula works 2 to 3 hours per day for 5 days each week and is paid $4 an hour. This means the answer must be between $40 and $60 per week. (Students should cross out "Paula has been offered a job working after school each day at the Town Pharmacy and ". . . for stacking shelves and waiting on customers.").

3-10 S = Find the number of square feet needed to build a wood top and bottom for a cage. Q = How many square feet of wood will Marvin's sister need to buy? R = Needs to build a wood top and bottom that are each 4 feet long and 3 feet wide. Q = Multiply length × width × 2. C = 20 square feet of wood. Q = Yes. 4 × 3 × 2 = 24. (Students should cross out ". . . for his pet rabbit . . . and the rest of the cage from wire.").

3-11 Answers will depend on the problem provided by the teacher.

3-12 1. Read the problem to learn what it is about.   2. State the problem in the form of a question.   3. The information needed to answer the question.   4. What computation(s) must I do?   5. (a) Set up the problem on paper. (b) Do the computation(s). (c) Check for errors.   6. Does my answer make sense?   7. Repeat the steps to locate and correct any errors.

CHAPTER 4

Taking Notes from Class Presentations

■ Purposes

The purpose of this chapter are to:
1. teach students with learning disabilities a three-stage strategy for taking notes from class presentations.
2. identify ways teachers can organize their lectures to facilitate notetaking.
3. provide reproducibles that can be used to teach students with learning disabilities how to use the three-stage strategy for taking notes.

■ Titles of Reproducibles

4-1   Get Ready Stage
4-2   Take Notes Stage
4-3   Two-Column Notetaking Format
4-4   Pete's Rough Notes
4-5   After Notes Stage
4-6   Pete's Revised Rough Notes
4-7   Pete's Final Notes
4-8   The Notetaking Strategy
4-9   Writing Shorter Sentences or Phrases
4-10 Using Cue Words
4-11 More Cues to Important Information
4-12 Using Abbreviations
4-13 More Abbreviations
4-14 The Middle East Today
4-15 Lecture for "The Middle East Today"
4-16 The American Revolution
4-17 Lecture for "The American Revolution"
4-18 What I Have Learned

■ RATIONALE

Research shows that students at both the elementary and secondary school levels spend the majority of their time listening to oral presentations by teachers (Bos & Vaughn, 1988; Mastropieri & Scruggs, 1987). Teachers of students with learning disabilities frequently report that when they examine notes taken by their students, the notes are incomplete, disorganized, and illegible; do not contain the essential information; and cannot be used for recreating what was presented. Students with learning disabilities approach notetaking in a passive, nonsystematic manner. Alley and Deshler (1979) emphasized the importance of getting these students to take notes in an active manner, thereby contributing to long-term learning. As Bos and Vaughn observed, given the deficits in attention, listening, and writing that typify students with learning disabilities, it is vital that teachers provide these students with direct instruction in notetaking.

The task of taking notes from class presentations is relatively complex. Vogel (1987) pointed out that notetaking requires simultaneously listening to, understanding, and recognizing and synthesizing important ideas, while retaining the ideas long enough to write them down quickly and accurately. It is not surprising, then, that so many students with learning disabilities are poor notetakers. Vogel observed that these students have deficits that significantly interfere with their ability to take effective notes. Auditory deficits at the phonemic level make discrimination of unfamiliar vocabulary difficult, while poor listening comprehension diminishes the likelihood of comprehending what is being said. A slow rate of comprehension makes it difficult for students with learning disabilities to keep up with the flow of language that occurs during a lecture. Most debilitating is the frequently found deficit in auditory short-term memory, which results in students forgetting what is said almost as quickly as it is said.

Further problems for students with learning disabilities were noted by Wood, White, and Miederhoff (1988). Students with visual processing deficits may not be able to move their eyes from the teacher (far point) to their paper (near point) smoothly enough to take notes quickly. A deficit in fine motor control may result in poor handwriting that is difficult to read later. Given these various problems, the need for direct instruction in notetaking for students with learning disabilities is apparent.

■ BACKGROUND INFORMATION

Students with learning disabilities should be taught a three-stage notetaking strategy that will enable them to record the important information given to them by their teachers. The three stages of the notetaking strategy are: (1) how to **GET READY** to take notes, (2) how to **TAKE NOTES,** and (3) what to do **AFTER NOTES** have been recorded.

Get Ready Stage

During the **Get Ready** stage students develop the necessary mental set required for taking good notes. The Get Ready stage requires the students to do the following:

1. Have available all the materials necessary to take notes. Each student should have an 8½″ by 11″ notebook with sufficient blank pages for notes. Preferably, there

should be a separate tabbed section in the notebook for each school subject the student is taking. Students should also have several sharpened pencils with erasers. Teachers know the frustration of having students say that they do not have paper or a pencil.

2. Review notes from the previous class session to determine the connection between what was taught before and what will be taught today. Students should be encouraged to ask questions about anything not understood after reviewing notes from the previous session.

3. Complete assigned readings in order to have the necessary background information to be able to follow and understand the day's presentation. Again, students should ask for clarification of anything they do not understand in the reading assignment.

4. Ask the teacher to specify the purpose(s) of the presentation when this is not clear. Frequently the teacher will provide an outline, a listening guide , or some type of handout to guide students as they are listening and taking notes. When this is not done, however, it is important that students ask for specification. Knowing the purpose(s) of the presentation gives students a basis for knowing what to listen for and what is important to write in their notes.

Take Notes Stage

Once students are prepared to take notes, they must do so using a consistent format. We recommend the use of a two-column format for taking notes, as shown in Figure 4.1. The first column is labeled "Rough Notes" and is used to write down what students think is important. The second column is labeled "Don't Understand" and is used to write questions about whatever is not understood, for which later clarification is needed. At the bottom of the page is a "Vocabulary" section for recording any words the teacher uses whose meaning students do know know. Students will subsequently need to look up these words in the dictionary and write their definitions. We refer to the initial notes taken using the two-column format as "rough notes."

In using this format, it is important that students with learning disabilities efficiently and accurately record what the teacher presents during class lectures. A number of authors have recommended procedures that students may use to accomplish this (Alley & Deshler, 1979; Anderman & Williams, 1986; Beirne-Smith, 1989; Bos & Vaughn, 1988; Mann, Suiter, & McClung, 1987; Mastropieri & Scruggs, 1987; Shepherd, 1982). Their recommendations should be incorporated into the use of our notetaking strategy. According to these authors, students with learning disabilities should be taught the following:

1. Take notes on one side of the paper only. This makes it possible to lay notes side by side to study for a test. It also eliminates the possibility that notes written on one side of a page will interfere with the reading of notes taken on the other side of the page.

2. Skip lines to show changes in ideas. This requires students to process actively the points made by the teacher. When students review their notes, the spaces highlight the flow of the lecture and allow each major idea to be focused on as necessary.

FIGURE 4.1 Two-column notetaking format

Class _____ Period _____ Date _____ Page _____

Rough Notes   Don't Understand

Vocabulary

3. Write ideas or phrases—not complete sentences. Attempting to write complete sentences makes it difficult for students to keep up with a fast-paced lecture. Also, there is the danger that students may attend more to the grammatic formulation of a sentence than to what the teacher is communicating. Ideas and phrases may be put into complete sentence form at a later time. If students are unable to rewrite a sentence as an idea or phrase, they should rewrite it as a shorter sentence.

4. Underline or place an asterisk before information that the teacher emphasizes as important. If they do this, students are more likely to review essential information at a later time.

5. Write down the information that the teacher writes on the chalkboard or displays using a transparency or other overhead. This includes tables, charts, diagrams, and formulas. Information that is displayed by a teacher is apt to be that which the teacher regards as particularly important. If it is not available in the textbook, it is important for students to record it as accurately as possible. This is especially true for any material that the teacher underlines or highlights in some other manner (e.g., circles, writes in boldface print, writes larger).

6. Leave blanks for information that is missed. This allows students to fill in the information at a later time by asking the teacher, asking another student, or locating the information in the textbook. A question mark may be placed in the blank space to signify that something was missed.

7. Do not worry about spelling. Notes are for student use. What is important is that students write words in a form that will be easily recognized at a later time. Worrying about correct spelling is analogous to worrying about sentence construction; it slows down the notetaking process and increases the possibility that students will miss important ideas or information presented by the teacher.

8. Listen to the lecture in an active manner. Rather than attempt to copy down everything the teacher says, students should engage in a continual process of deciding what is and what is not important to record.

9. Make certain that notes are reasonably clear and legible. It is essential that students be able to read their notes easily at a later time. Notes that are written illegibly will lose their value almost immediately after they are recorded.

10. Notes should be written in the students' own words. Aside from technical terms, students should paraphrase what the teacher says. In this way, students will ensure understanding of their notes when they are reread.

11. Be alert for cues that a particular idea or some specific information is important. Students should listen for cues such as "This is important," or for pauses and changes in the volume and tone of the teacher's voice, as well as for statements that are repeated.

12. Include examples in the notes. In this way, difficult or abstract concepts will be more easily understood when received.

13. Do things that maximize the ability to concentrate. Where possible, students should select a seat that is in the center and front of the room, with an

uninterrupted view of the teacher and the chalkboard. Students should be neither too warm nor too cold, not hungry, and not in need of the restroom.

14. Utilize structure provided by the teacher. For example, if the teacher states, "There are three forms that water can take," students should make certain their notes contain a list numbered 1, 2, 3.

15. Increase notetaking speed. Although legibility is important, notes should be taken using a simplified handwriting that minimizes the number of lines, curves, and flourishes. Speed can also be increased by using common abbreviations as well as invented ones for frequently occurring words. However, caution should be taken here, as too many abbreviations may present a puzzle rather than a clear model for review and study.

16. Do not write down what is already known. Notes should be as concise as possible. If students do not recording what they already know, their review of notes will focus on what they need to know.

After Notes Stage

As soon as possible after the presentation, students should revise their rough notes by doing the following:

1. Add any important information they remember the teacher saying but they did not write down.

2. Locate the information needed to answer any questions listed in the "Don't Understand" column. The information can be obtained from the teacher, from other students, or by looking in the textbook or a reference book.

3. In the same manner, locate the information needed to complete any blanks.

4. Look up and write the definition for each unknown word written in the "Vocabulary" section at the bottom of the page.

5. Use these revised rough notes to prepare the "final notes." The final notes should be written without the use of columns and should incorporate information from the "Rough Notes" and "Don't Understand" columns of the revised rough notes. At the bottom of each page some space should be reserved for students to rewrite the vocabulary words and definitions from their rough notes. This section should be labeled "Vocabulary." The final notes should be written in a separate notebook reserved only for final notes. Students use the final notes to study for quizzes and tests. Figure 4.2 shows a final notes page format.

When writing the final notes, students should include additional information they obtain from the teacher, other students, their textbook, or reference books. This allows students to expand their rough notes. Also, students should rewrite phrases and short sentences into complete sentences. Both spelling and grammar should be corrected, although more attention should be given to the information value of the notes than to these written English aspects.

Either a looseleaf notebook or a bound notebook may be used for writing the

FIGURE 4.2 Final notes page format

Class _____ Period _____ Date _____ Page _____

_____

Vocabulary

final notes. Some teachers of students with learning disabilities prefer that students use a looseleaf notebook so that they can remove those pages they need to study from for a test. Other teachers prefer the use of a bound notebook to prevent the possibility of pages being lost.

Example of the Notetaking Strategy

Here is a transcription of a portion of an oral presentation made by a teacher on the topic "Mining Gold." This transcription mimics reality in that it contains pauses, omissions, repetitions, interruptions, and other characteristics associated with oral presentations such as lectures. Following the transcription are notes taken by Pete, a student in the class.

Teacher: Hi, folks. Today we are going to talk about how gold is mined. That means, how it is taken out of the ground. I'm sure you all know that, uh, that gold is very valuable. Anything made from gold costs a lot of money. It is beautiful to look at and soft to touch. Anything made from gold lasts forever. And there isn't very much of it.

Can anyone here think of uses of gold? Let's make a list of uses of gold. Who has an idea to get us started? Be sure to write these things down.

Sam: Some watches are made from gold.

Teacher: Good, that gets us started.

Marta: You can have gold fillings in your teeth.

Paul: Sure would be expensive teeth.

Teacher: Sure would. Anything else?

Pearl: Coins. Many years ago they used gold to make money. My dad has some old coins that are worth a lot of money.

Steve: Yeh. I saw some gold coins at the flea market last week. This guy was selling the coins too. Boy, were they expensive.

Teacher: Good ideas. How about some uses?

Tom: All kinds of jewelry such as bracelets, necklaces, and rings.

Teacher: Good list. I hope you all got those in your notes. Gold is also used in the space industry and in medicine. I would say that the most common use of gold is for making expensive jewelry.

Gold is found in many places throughout the world. While it is rare, it is still found in many places all over the world. Some of the places where gold is found might surprise you. You may have some gold right next door to you. Wouldn't that be great? Your own gold mine in your back yard.

Paul: Yeah, my yard, my yard!

Teacher: Well, maybe not in your yard, but there are many places in the United States where gold can be found.

Ben: I heard there is gold in Russia, too.

Teacher: That's right! And there is also a lot of gold in Australia, too. Australia is a country as large or maybe even larger than the United States. Anyone know where Australia is?

Pete, show us where Australia is on our big wall map. That's right! Good!

CHAPTER 4 ■ TAKING NOTES FROM CLASS PRESENTATIONS

By the way, that won't be on the test. But you will have to know the different ways to mine gold. Let me talk about that now.

Now, this is important for you to know. Mining gold means getting it out of the ground. That is not an easy task. Many people have tried. Some have become very wealthy. Others have died trying to get gold from the earth.

There are three ways to mine gold. First is placer mining. That means techniques that are used to separate gold from sand and gravel. This is what the Forty-Niners did in the famous California Gold Rush of 1849. They used a method called panning. They used a pan that looked like a pan your mother might cook breakfast with. They would go to a stream where the water was moving fast and scoop up some sand and gravel from the bottom of the stream. They would shake the pan real fast so that the lighter sand and gravel would spill out, leaving the heavier little bits of gold in the pan. A lot of men rushed to California in 1849 because some men had found some gold in a stream next to a mill owned by a man named Sutter—it was called Sutter's Mill.

Sue: It must have taken a long time to get an ounce of gold that way.

Teacher: Sure did. Many miners worked for weeks to get an ounce or two of gold. They would use some of the money they got for the gold to buy grub. *Grub* is another word for grub—I mean it's another word for food. They would call that money a grub-stake because it staked them to some food. But they were always hoping to find that big nugget or the mother lode."

Oscar: What's the mother lode?

Teacher: Good question, Oscar! The mother lode is the, uh, it's, I guess, I guess the place in the ground or in a mountain where the biggest amount of gold is. Don't worry about just what it means. I'm going to do a little research and give you its exact meaning tomorrow.

Vein mining is another way to get gold from the earth. More than half of the gold in the world is gotten this way. The miners looked for veins of gold in the mountains. Does anyone know what a vein is? Here, look at the word on the board.

Sam: It's like a vein in your hand or leg. It runs from one place to another. It's small.

Teacher: That's the idea of it, except gold veins are yellow and your veins are blue. You might want to look up the word *vein* in your dictionary. In vein mining, the miners would break off a piece of rock and look for a vein of gold. If they found the vein, they would follow the vein through the rock to get more gold.

Pete: It sounds like you can make more money from vein mining than pan mining.

Teacher: Yes, you can. A third way gold can be obtained is in the, uh, the processing of other metals. For example, when copper is refined, some gold is obtained as a by-product. More gold is gotten this way than from placer mining, but not as much as from vein mining.

Well, we have to stop now. We'll talk more about mining gold tomorrow.

Figure 4.3 shows the rough notes Pete took during class. An examination of the notes shows that in the first column there is a gap in the notes. The gap is shown by the space Pete left after the number 2 for vein mining. In the second column Pete wrote three questions he had concerning the information presented by the teacher.

FIGURE 4.3 Pete's rough notes

Class ____U.S. History____ Period _____3_____ Date ____10/14/91____ Page ___1___

Rough Notes   Don't Understand

Mining gold means taking it out of ground. Gold is valuable—costs lot. Soft. Lasts forever. Not much of it.	

Uses of gold—watches
            coins
            jewelry   *expensive jewelry
	How is gold used in teeth?

Gold is found all over world—
  US
  Russia
  Ostraila	

3 ways to mine gold 1. placer mining—panning. 49ers used pan to scoop gold from a stream using sand.	
49ers went to California & found gold at Sutter's Mill in 1849. Bought grub—food. Got a grubsteak. Looked for mother lode? Teacher will tell us about this.	Is there gold in California now? Are there miners there?
2. Vein mining. ½ the gold gotten this way.	
3. Processing other metals. Get gold as a by-product. Get more than placer mining—but not as much as vein mining.	

Vocabulary:
by-product
grubsteak   sp
vein

At the bottom of the page, Pete wrote three words for which he did not know the meaning. He wrote "sp" after one of the words to indicate that he was uncertain about how it was spelled.

Figure 4.4 shows Pete's revised rough notes. The boldface type shows Pete's revisions to his rough notes:

1. Pete added two more uses of gold that he recalled his teacher talking about.

2. Pete obtained information from his textbook to fill in the gap in his rough notes concerning the second of three ways to mine gold.

3. Pete answered his three questions.

FIGURE 4.4 Pete's revised rough notes

Class ___U.S. History___ Period _____3_____ Date ___10/14/91___ Page ___1___

Rough Notes   Don't Understand

Rough Notes	Don't Understand
Mining gold means taking it out of ground. Gold is valuable—costs lot. Soft. Lasts forever. Not much of it. Uses of gold—watches **industry** coins **medicine** jewelry *expensive jewelry Gold is found all over the world— US Russia Ostraila	 How is gold used in teeth? **Gold is used to fill cavities in teeth and sometimes to make new teeth.**

3 ways to mine gold
1. placer mining—panning. 49ers used pan to schoop gold from a stream using sand.
 	
   49ers went to California & found gold at Sutter's Mill in 1849.
   bought grub—food. Got a grubsteak.
   Looked for mother lode? teacher will tell us about this.
	
	Is there gold in California now? Are there miners there?
	There are some commercial gold mines. Also, some independent miners are still prospecting for gold.

2. Vein mining. ½ the gold gotten this way. **Miners find veins of gold in the mountains. Break off pieces of rock and follow vein to find all the gold.** 3. Processing other metals. Get gold as a by-product. Get more than placer mining— but not as much as vein mining.	

Vocabulary
  by-product
  grubsteak   sp
  vein

by-product   **Something produced in the making of something else.**

grubstake   **Money or supplies advanced to a prospector against future profits.**

vein   **Like a vein in the body but its ore and its found in rock.**

4. Pete wrote definitions for the three unknown words.

5. Pete corrected the spelling of one of the unknown words.

Figure 4.5 shows Pete's final notes. Pete used his revised rough notes to prepare his final notes. In writing the final notes, Pete corrected errors in language structure and spelling. He also rearranged some of the notes and expanded some sections. Pete also added more details to the definitions of words in the Vocabulary section. Overall, his final notes are better organized, more complete, and more legible. The final notes provide Pete with an excellent study tool.

FIGURE 4.5 Pete's final notes

Class ____U.S. History____ Period _____3_____ Date ____10/14/91____ Page ___1___

Gold is a very valuable mineral found in the ground. Because it is found in the ground it has to be mined. Gold is usually found in veins. Miners follow the veins as they mine the gold. Because the veins are small, it's hard work getting at the gold.

Gold is very valuable because it can be used for many things and there is not much of it. It is found in different parts of the world such as USA, Russia, and Australia. Some of the common uses of gold are:

1. make jewelry

2. make coins

3. filling teeth or making new teeth

4. medicine

5. space industry

Three ways to mine gold:

1. Placer mining. The miners would scoop out sand from the bottom of a stream and then sift out the sand to see if any pieces of gold remained in the pan. The small lumps of gold were called nuggets. Smaller pieces were called flecks.

2. Vein mining. Miners would break pieces of rock off the side of a mountain to see if there was a yellow vein. If there was a vein, they would dig into that part of the mountain to follow the vein to see if it led to the mother lode. The mother lode was the big deposit of gold.

3. Processing other metals. Sometimes we get gold as a by-product of making or doing something else. Sometimes when miners are mining for ore or other metals, they find small amounts of gold. The gold would be a by-product of the mining.

Gold was discovered at Sutter's mill in California in 1848. The next year many people went there to find gold and they were called 49ers. It cost a lot of money to get started—the miners needed a place to live, food, and tools. They would get a grubstake from a bank or some person. They would use this money to get started and would pay back the loan from their profits. There is still gold in California and there are prospectors still mining gold. Some of the prospectors work for big companies and others work for themselves.

Vocabulary and Definitions

by-product: Something produced in making or doing something else. e.g., finding gold while mining for copper or iron ore.

grubstake: Money or supplies advanced to a prospector in return for a share of any profit he would make.

vein: Like a vein in the body. A thin piece of metal that runs through a rock or mountain. It sometimes leads to a big deposit of that metal, and it is the color of that metal.

Listener-Friendly Lectures

Bos and Vaughn (1988) stated that one of the most important aspects of teaching notetaking is to ensure that lectures are listener-friendly. That is, lectures given by teachers should be carefully organized to help students see relationships among concepts, to distinguish important from less important information, and to relate new information to old. A number of authors suggested that teachers do the following (Alley & Deshler, 1979; Beirne-Smith, 1989; Bos & Vaughn, 1988; Hoover, 1988; Mann et al., 1987; Wood et al., 1988):

1. Use key words and phrases such as "first" and "the most important point." These statements help students focus on main ideas and organize information.

2. Repeat important statements. Repetition cues students to the importance of the statement.

3. Summarize ideas. This helps students to recognize what is most important.

4. Pause occasionally for 5 to 10 seconds. This allows students to fill in gaps and to catch up to the last statement.

5. Provide advance organizers. Providing students with a topic outline or even a partially completed set of notes helps them record notes in an organized way. Advance organizers may take the form of guided notes in which the teacher provides a structured outline of a class lecture. In this case students follow along with the outline by filling in missing words or documenting important points. Other variations include a slot outline wherein students take notes by filling in the blanks, and a graphic organizer in which the relationship among concepts is presented visually.

6. Write important points on the chalkboard. This not only allows students to recognize important information, but also gives them time to record the information accurately and, if necessary, completely.

7. Cue students as to when to leave space between different ideas. Without such cues, students might run important but discrete points together.

8. Observe students during the lecture and adjust the pace of the lecture accordingly. Slow down and occasionally pause for several seconds to allow students to write down all the important information.

9. Vary voice tone and quality to emphasize important ideas. When lectures are delivered in a monotone, students have difficulty separating important ideas from less important ones. Further, there is the possibility that students' attention will wane. By using voice variation, the teacher gives students discriminative cues to what is most important, as well as sustaining their interest and attention.

10. Use cues such as "first," "next," "last," and "then." These cues help students take and organize their notes.

11. Write technical words and difficult-to-spell words on the chalkboard so that students' attention is not diverted from what is being said as they attempt to spell words correctly.

12. Use pictures and diagrams to show the relationships among ideas. Many students with learning disabilities require visual reinforcement of abstract concepts.

13. Ask questions during the lecture. This requires students to listen in an active manner to integrate what has been said with their prior knowledge so they can answer a question.

14. Encourage students to ask questions during the lecture. Again, this procedure produces active listening and notetaking.

15. Provide examples of the concepts that are presented. This facilitates understanding on the part of the students.

16. Provide time at the end of the lecture for students to review their notes and ask for clarification. This minimizes the possibility that students will have difficulty understanding their notes when reviewing them later.

■ TEACHING PLAN

Here is a plan for teaching students with learning disabilities how to use the three-stage strategy for taking notes from class presentations.

1. Write the names of the three stages on the chalkboard.

Notetaking Strategy

Get Ready
Take Notes
After Notes

Use relevant facts from the "Background Information" section of this chapter to introduce the notetaking strategy. Tell the students that the strategy will help them take good notes that will better enable them to prepare for quizzes and tests.

2. Distribute copies of Reproducible 4-1, "Get Ready Stage." Discuss the four things to do in 4-1. In the space provided after each step, have the students write information that is important for its understanding.

3. Distribute copies of Reproducible 4-2, "Take Notes Stage." Discuss the six things to do in 4-2. In the space provided after each step, have the students write information that is important for its understanding. Have the students write any additional things you see as necessary from the presentation included in the "Background Information" section.

4. Distribute copies of Reproducible 4-3, "Two-Column Notetaking Format." Point out the identifying information to be included at the top of each notetaking page. Explain the use of each column and the "Vocabulary" section.

104

5. Distribute copies of Reproducible 4-4, "Pete's Rough Notes." Explain how Pete used the two-column format to take notes.

6. Distribute copies of Reproducible 4-5, "After Notes Stage." Discuss the five things to do in 4-5. In the space provided after each step, have the students write information that is important for its understanding.

7. Distribute copies of Reproducible 4-6, "Pete's Revised Rough Notes." Explain how Pete revised his rough notes. Call attention to the boldface type to show Pete's revisions.

8. Distribute copies of Reproducible 4-7, "Pete's Final Notes." Explain how Pete rewrote his revised rough notes into a set of final notes.

9. Distribute copies of Reproducible 4-8, "The Notetaking Strategy." Use 4-8 to summarize the stages and things to do of the notetaking strategy.

10. Distribute copies of Reproducible 4-9, "Writing Shorter Sentences or Phrases." Tell the students that when they take notes they should write short sentences. Use the introductory material and the first four items in 4-9 to demonstrate how to write short sentences or phrases. Then have the students complete the remaining items on their own. Review the students' responses as a group activity.

11. Distribute copies of Reproducible 4-10, "Using Cue Words." Tell the students that when they take notes they should be alert for cue words their teachers use to signal that they are about to say something that is important to write down. Read the introductory statement in 4-10 with the students and go over the cue words. Have the students locate these cue words in the reading selection "Losing Your Hair." Review the students' responses as a group activity. Have the students identify other cue words they have heard teachers use.

12. Distribute copies of Reproducible 4-11, "More Cues to Important Information." Tell the students that sometimes teachers use statements as cues that important information will follow. Go over the examples of cue statements with the students and then have them write some others. Have the students locate cue statements in the reading selection "The Roman Army." Review the students' responses as a group activity.

13. Distribute copies of Reproducible 4-12, "Using Abbreviations." Tell the students that when they take notes they have to write quickly in order to record all of the important information their teacher gives them. Tell them that a good way to increase their notetaking speed is to use abbreviations whenever possible. Use the first section in 4-12 to show how words can be abbreviated. Have the students complete the second section on their own. Review the students' responses as a group activity.

14. Distribute copies of Reproducible 4-13, "More Abbreviations." Tell the students they can write entire statements using abbreviations, as well as use abbreviations to write the names of organizations or titles. Use the examples of grade point average, home computer, the Federal Bureau of Investigation, and chief executive officer to show how this is done. Have the students write the complete meaning of each of the abbreviations in the first section. Review the students' responses as a group activity. Next, have the students write an abbreviation for each of the items in the second section. Point out that they can create their own abbreviations to help remember things. Again, review the students' responses as a group activity. Finally, ask the students to share other abbreviations they have used.

15. Tell the students you are going to give them a brief lecture on the topic "The Middle East Today." Have the students use the two-column format provided in Reproducible 4-14, "The Middle East Today," to take rough notes as you read the lecture. Then have the students revise their rough notes and use a separate piece of paper to prepare their final notes. Distribute Reproducible 4-15, "Lecture for 'The Middle East Today.' " As a group activity, have the students compare their final notes to the transcription of the lecture. Make suggestions for how they could have improved their notes.

Here is the lecture that you should give to the students. Allow students to ask questions and make comments as you would normally do when you give a class lecture.

The Middle East Today

The Middle East is an area defined as much by language and culture as by geography. Fifteen countries make up the Middle East. It is important to know that Islam is the chief religion of the Middle East. Most of the people in the Middle East speak Arabic. But Hebrew is the main language used in Israel.

A large part of the Middle East is desert. Be certain that you remember this when you try to understand the history and politics of this region. Although food can be grown mainly in the river valleys or coastal areas, the people of the Middle East cannot raise enough food to feed themselves.

There is not much fertile land in the Middle East. You should know, however, that there is a lot of oil there. There is a great need for oil all over the world. Three things that oil is needed for are automobiles, airplanes, and industry. This makes the land where the oil is found very valuable.

In 1960, the countries that produced oil formed the Organization of Petroleum Exporting Countries, which is known as OPEC. This is an important organization to remember. The purpose of OPEC is to control the supply of oil to try to keep world prices high.

The Suez Canal is very important to the countries in the Middle East. This canal connects the Mediterranean Sea and the Red Sea. It was opened in 1869. Today it is controlled by Egypt. Huge quantities of food, oil, and other essential goods pass through the canal. In 1967 President Nasser of Egypt stopped Israel from using the canal. This led to a war between Israel and Egypt. These two countries fought another war in 1973. In 1978 President Carter of the United States got Egypt and Israel to sign a peace treaty at Camp David, Maryland.

16. Use Reproducible 4-16, "The American Revolution," and Reproducible 4-17, "Lecture for 'The American Revolution,' " to provide additional practice in using the notetaking strategy. Follow the same procedure as you used for "The Middle East Today."

The American Revolution

The American nation began its life under the control of England. In 1607 English colonists settled in Jamestown, Virginia, and in 1620 the Pilgrims settled in the Massachusetts Bay Area. Before leaving their ship, the *Mayflower,* the Pilgrims adopted the Mayflower Compact. In the Mayflower

Compact they agreed to enact laws for the welfare of the colony. By 1682, 13 colonies extended along the eastern coast of North America.

In 1755 England and France went to war over who should own the colonies. England won this war, which ended in 1763. Because the French got Indians to fight on their side, this war was known as the French and Indian war. The important thing to know here is that the war cost England a lot of money. To help get some of the money back, King George III of England made the colonists pay taxes. In 1773 a tax was levied on tea. Now, be sure you pay attention to this. Some of the colonists in Boston got angry and dumped tea into Boston Harbor. This became known as the Boston Tea Party. From that time on the colonists began to fight back against England and began to dream of having their own country.

In 1775 the colonists fought the British in Massachusetts. This is a very important date because it was the beginning of the American Revolution. In 1776 Thomas Jefferson wrote the Declaration of Independence. This said that all people were created equal and were born with certain rights. In 1781 England gave up fighting and the colonists had won their independence. In 1789 George Washington was elected as the first president of the United States of America. Remember his name—he was the father of our country.

17. Go back to Reproducible 4-8, "The Notetaking Strategy," to review and reinforce the three stages of the strategy.

18. Provide additional practice as necessary, using your own lecture material.

19. Distribute Reproducible 4-18, "What I Have Learned." Use this reproducible to evaluate how well your students have learned what was taught in this chapter. As needed, use any of the reproducibles for review purposes.

Get Ready Stage

1. Have notetaking materials ready.

2. Review your notes.

3. Do all assigned reading.

4. Identify your purpose for listening.

Take Notes Stage

1. Listen for your purpose.

2. Use short sentences, phrases, and abbreviations.

3. Skip lines between new ideas.

4. Copy information from the chalkboard.

5. Note things you do not understand.

6. Note words whose meaning you do not know.

Two-Column Notetaking Format

Class _____ Period _____ Date _____ Page _____

Rough Notes

Don't Understand

Vocabulary

Pete's Rough Notes

Class ___U.S. History___ Period ___3___ Date ___10/14/91___ Page ___1___

Rough Notes   Don't Understand

Rough Notes	Don't Understand
Mining gold means taking it out of ground.	
Gold is valuable—costs lot. Soft. Lasts forever. Not much of it.	

Uses of gold—watches
        coins
        jewelry   *expensive jewelry
	How is gold used in teeth?

Gold is found all over world—
  US
  Russia
  Ostraila	

3 ways to mine gold	
1. placer mining—panning. 49ers used pan to scoop gold from a stream using sand.	Is there gold in California now? Are there miners now?

49ers went to California & found gold at Sutter's Mill in 1849.
   Bought grub—food. Got a grubsteak.
   Looked for mother lode? Teacher will tell us about this.	

2. Vein mining. ½ the gold gotten this way.	
3. Processing other metals. Get gold as by-product. Get more than placer mining—but not as much as vein mining.	

New Vocabulary:
 by-product
 grubsteak   sp
 vein

After Notes Stage

1. Add important information left out of rough notes.

2. Answer any questions in the "Don't Understand" column.

3. Complete any blanks in the rough notes.

4. Write definitions for each unknown word.

5. Prepare final notes.

Pete's Revised Rough Notes

Class ___U.S. History___ Period _____3_____ Date _____10/14/91_____ Page ___1___

Rough Notes   Don't Understand

Mining gold means taking it out of ground. Gold is valuable—costs lot. Soft. Last forever. Not much of it.	How is gold used in teeth? **Gold is used to fill cavities in teeth and sometimes to make new teeth.**

Uses of gold—watches   **industry**
            coins   **medicine**
            jewelry   *expensive jewelry

Gold is found all over the world—
  US
  Russia
  Ostraila

3 ways to mine gold
  1. placer mining—panning. 49ers used pan to scoop gold from a stream using sand.

(49ers went to California & found gold at Sutter's Mill in 1849. bought grub—food. Got a grubsteak. Looked for mother lode? teacher will tell us about this.	Is there gold in California now? Are there miners there? **There are some commercial gold mines. Also, some independent miners are still prospecting for gold.**

  2. Vein mining. ½ the gold gotten this way. **Miners find veins of gold in the mountains. Break off pieces of rock and follow vein to find all the gold.**

  3. Processing other metals. Get gold as a by-product. Get more than placer mining—but not as much as vein mining.

Vocabulary
  by-product
  grubsteak   sp
  vein

by-product	**Something produced in the making of something else.**
grubstake	**Money or supplies advanced to a prospector against future profits.**
vein	**Like a vein in the body but its ore and its found in rock.**

Pete's Final Notes

Class __U.S. History__ Period _____3_____ Date ____10/14/91____ Page __1__

Gold is a very valuable mineral found in the ground. Because it is found in the ground it has to be mined. Gold is usually found in veins. Gold miners follow the veins as they mine the gold. Because the veins are small, it's hard work getting at the gold.

Gold is very valuable because it can be used for many things and there is not much of it. It is found in different parts of the world such as USA, USSR, and Australia. Some of the common uses of gold are:

1. make jewelry

2. make coins

3. filling teeth or making new teeth

4. medicine

5. space industry

Three ways to mine gold:

1. Placer mining. The miners would scoop out sand from the botton of a stream and then sift out the sand to see if any pieces of gold remained in the pan. The small lumps of gold were called nuggets. Smaller pieces are called flecks.

2. Vein mining. Miners would break pieces of rock off the side of a mountain to see if there was a yellow vein. If there was a vein, they would dig into that part of the mountain to follow the vein to see if it led to the mother lode. The mother lode was the big deposit of gold.

3. Processing other metals. Sometimes we get gold as a by-product of making or doing something else. Sometimes when miners are mining for ore or other metals, they find small amounts of gold. The gold would be a by-product of the mining.

Gold was discovered at Sutter's Mill in California in 1848. The next year many people went there to find gold and they were called 49ers. It cost a lot of money to get started—the miners needed a place to live, food, and tools. They would get a grubstake from a bank or some person. They would use this money to get started and would pay back the loan from their profits. There is still gold in California and there are prospectors still mining gold. Some of the prospectors work for big companies and others work for themselves.

Vocabulary and Definitions

by-product: Something produced in making or doing something else. e.g., finding gold while mining for copper or iron ore.

grubstake: Money or supplies advanced to a prospector in return for a share of any profit he would make.

vein: Like a vein in the body. A thin piece of metal that runs through a rock or mountain. It sometimes leads to a big deposit of that metal, and it is the color of that metal.

The Notetaking Strategy

GET READY

1. Have notetaking materials ready.

2. Review notes.

3. Do all assigned reading.

4. Identify your purpose for listening.

TAKE NOTES

1. Listen for your purpose.

2. Use short sentences, phrases, and abbreviations.

3. Skip lines between new ideas.

4. Copy information from the chalkboard.

5. Note things you do not understand.

6. Note words whose meaning you do not know.

AFTER NOTES

1. Add important information left out of rough notes.

2. Answer any questions in the "Don't Understand" column.

3. Complete any blanks in the rough notes.

4. Write definitions for each unknown word.

5. Prepare final notes.

Writing Shorter Sentences or Phrases

When you take notes, you should use phrases or short sentences as much as possible. For example, instead of writing the long sentence, "Scientists would like to be able to predict with great accuracy where or when earthquakes will appear," you could simply write, "Scientists want to predict where and when earthquakes will happen." Or, instead of writing, "As air cools it loses its ability to hold water vapor," you could write, "Cool air can't hold water vapor."

For each sentence below, rewrite the sentence in a shorter form or as a phrase.

1. No machine has ever been designed that will put out more work than that put in.

2. As we have noted, the Constitution gives to each branch of the government its own distinctive field of governmental authority: legislative, executive, and judicial.

3. The weight at which you look and feel most comfortable is your "ideal" weight or the healthiest weight for your body.

4. Although India developed great oral literature, the development of writing itself was slow.

5. Any water used for drinking purposes not only must be free of salt but also should be free of foreign matter.

6. Our system of government depends on the ability of the people to make sound, reasoned judgments on matters of public concern.

7. The common cold is really a group of symptoms and signs caused by a variety of viruses.

8. The most prominent person in the village was the headman, who was appointed by the prince or lord on whose land the village stood.

9. Each of the colonies was born out of a particular set of circumstances, and so each had its own character.

10. A good time manager is someone who completes daily tasks, works toward long-term goals, and still finds time to relax, all in a day's work.

Using Cue Words

During a lecture your teacher will often use words that tell you that something is very important to write down. These words are called *cue words.* If you listen for cue words, you will be more likely to write down important information.

Here are some cue words used by teachers that tell you that what they are about to say is important to write down. Get to know these cue words.

first   second   next
then   finally   several

Read the following selection to see how these cue words call your attention to important information. Underline each of these cue words as you read the selection.

Losing Your Hair

As people get older they typically lose some of their hair. Men usually lose their hair at an earlier age than women. However, there are many bald women just as there are bald men. People don't like to lose their hair because they think it makes them look older. There are several things that can be done to stop the loss of hair. The first thing most people try is to take better care of their hair by regular shampooing. There are many different types of shampoos available, many of which promise to stop the loss of hair. The second remedy is to massage the scalp regularly with a stiff brush or with one's fingers. When this doesn't work, the next thing people usually try is a vitamin therapy. There are many different vitamins that are thought to encourage hair growth.

Finally, when all else fails, people go out and buy a wig or toupee. Both are used to cover part or all of the scalp. As you can see, then, it is natural to lose hair, but there are things you can do to keep that "young look."

Write the cue words in the order they appeared in this selection.

More Cues to Important Information

Sometimes teachers use statements instead of single words to cue you to important information. Teachers may use statements such as:

"Here is something you should know."

"I wouldn't forget this point if I were you."

"Remember this."

"This is particularly important."

"There are five things you have to know."

1. Think of other statements teachers use to cue you to important information. Write them here.

_____

_____

_____

Read the following selection and underline any statements that cue you to important information.

The Roman Army

The expansion of Rome was made possible in part by the courage and skill of its soldiers. Be sure to remember that the Roman army became a match for any army in the Western world. The Roman army was made up mostly of foot soldiers. In early times, the soldiers were organized into groups of 8,000 called phalanxes. Make sure that you know that a phalanx was a group of soldiers massed together with shields joined and spears overlapping. Later the army replaced phalanxes with legions. A legion was made up of 3,600 men. Write in your notes that the legion was much more effective in battle than a phalanx. Roman soldiers were tough, loyal, practical men. The major thing to know is that they could handle just about any task from repairing weapons to sewing their own clothes. They had to obey rules or face a very severe punishment. The most important point is that because of its great army, Rome took over all of Italy. I am going to expect you to know that when the Roman army began to weaken, Rome began to lose its control of Italy.

2. Write the cue statements you found in this selection.

Using Abbreviations

When you are taking notes, it is important for you to write quickly. A good way to increase your notetaking speed is to use abbreviations. An abbreviation is a short way of writing something. Here are some common words and abbreviations that can be used to write these words in a short way:

Word	Abbreviation	Word	Abbreviation
psychology	psy	medicine	med
English	Eng	diameter	dia
month	mo	year	yr
vocabulary	vocab	Florida	Fl

Here are some more common words. For each word, write an abbreviation. You can make up any abbreviation as long as you are able to recognize the word from your abbreviation.

September _____

tropical _____

chemistry _____

national _____

secretary _____

anatomy _____

agency _____

general _____

manager _____

auditorium _____

science _____

mathematics _____

More Abbreviations

Sometimes you can write entire statements with abbreviations. For example, you can abbreviate "grade point average" as "gpa" or "home computer" as "ho comp." You can also abbreviate the names of organizations or titles. For example, the Federal Bureau of Investigation is commonly known as the FBI. Likewise, the chief executive officer of a company is commonly known as the CEO.

Here are some other common abbreviations. Write what each one means:

1. USA _____

2. IRS _____

3. NASA _____

4. CIA _____

Create an abbreviation that will help you recall each of the following:

5. North Atlantic Treaty Organization ____

6. United States Air Force _____

7. school principal _____

8. biology textbook _____

9. home work _____

10. longitude and latitude _____

11. Strategic Arms Limitations Talks _____

The Middle East Today

Class _____ Period _____ Date _____ Page _____

Rough Notes   Don't Understand

Vocabulary

Lecture for "The Middle East Today"

The Middle East is an area defined as much by language and culture as by geography. Fifteen countries make up the Middle East. It is important to know that Islam is the chief religion of the Middle East. Most of the people in the Middle East speak Arabic. But Hebrew is the main language used in Israel.

A large part of the Middle East is desert. Be certain that you remember this when you try to understand the history and politics of this religion. Although food can be grown mainly in the river valleys or coastal areas, the people in the Middle East cannot raise enough food to feed themselves.

There is not much fertile land in the Middle East. You should know, however, that there is a lot of oil there. There is a great need for oil all over the world. Three things that oil is needed for are automobiles, airplanes, and industry. This makes the land where the oil is found very valuable.

In 1960 the countries that produced oil formed the Organization of Petroleum Exporting Countries, which is known as OPEC. This is an important organization to remember. The purpose of OPEC is to control the supply of oil to try to keep world prices high.

The Suez Canal is very important to the countries in the Middle East. This canal connects the Mediterranean Sea and the Red Sea. It was opened in 1869. Today it is controlled by Egypt. Huge quantities of food, oil, and other essential goods pass through the canal. In 1967 President Nasser of Egypt stopped Israel from using the canal. This led to a war between Israel and Egypt. These two countries fought another war in 1973. In 1978 President Carter of the United States got Egypt and Israel to sign a peace treaty at Camp David, Maryland.

The American Revolution

Class _____ Period _____ Date _____ Page _____

Rough Notes   Don't Understand

Vocabulary

Lecture for "The American Revolution"

The American nation began its life under the control of England. In 1607 English colonists settled in Jamestown, Virginia, and in 1620 the Pilgrims settled in the Massachusetts Bay area. Before leaving their ship, the Mayflower, the Pilgrims agreed to enact laws for the welfare of the colony. By 1682, 13 colonies extended along the eastern coast of North America.

In 1755 England and France went to war over who should own the colonies. England won this war, which ended in 1763. Because the French got Indians to fight on their side, this war was known as the French and Indian war. The important thing to know here is that the war cost England a lot of money. To help get some of the money back, King George III of England made the colonists pay taxes. In 1773 a tax was levied on tea. Now be sure you pay attention to this. Some of the colonists in Boston got angry and dumped tea into Boston Harbor. This became known as the Boston Tea Party. From that time on the colonists began to fight back against England and began to dream of having their own country.

In 1775 the colonists fought the British in Massachusetts. This is a very important date because it was the beginning of the American Revolution. In 1776 Thomas Jefferson wrote the Declaration of Independence. This said that all people were created equal and were born with certain rights. In 1781 England gave up fighting and gave the colonists their independence. In 1789 George Washington was elected as the first president of the United States of America. Remember his name—he was the father of our country.

What I Have Learned

Directions: Show what you have learned about taking notes from class presentations by completing the following chart. First, write the name of each stage in the notetaking strategy. Next, list the things to do for each stage.

Stage 1 _____

    1. _____

    2. _____

    3. _____

    4. _____

Stage 2 _____

    1. _____

    2. _____

    3. _____

    4. _____

    5. _____

    6. _____

Stage 3 _____

    1. _____

    2. _____

    3. _____

    4. _____

    5. _____

Answers for Chapter 4 Reproducibles

4-1 Notes will vary.

4-2 Notes will vary.

4-3 No writing required.

4-4 No writing required.

4-5 Notes will vary.

4-6 No writing required.

4-7 No writing required.

4-8 No writing required.

4-9 The teacher provides model answers for items 1–4. Responses will vary for items 5–10.

4-10 Several, first, second, next, finally, then.

4-11 Answers will vary. 2. Be sure to remember; Make sure that you know; Write in your notes; The major thing to know; The most important point; I am going to expect you to know.

4-12 Answers will vary.

4-13 1. United States of America. 2. Internal Revenue Service. 3. National Aeronautics and Space Administration. 4. Central Intelligence Agency. 5–11. Answers will vary.

4-14 Answers will vary.

4-15 No writing required.

4-16 Answers will vary.

4-17 No writing required.

4-18 *Get Ready:* 1. Have notetaking materials ready. 2. Review your notes. 3. Do all assigned reading. 4. Identify your purpose for listening. *Take Notes:* 1. Listen for your purpose. 2. Use short sentences, phrases, and abbreviations. 3. Skip lines between new ideas. 4. Copy information from the chalkboard. 5. Note things you do not understand. 6. Note words whose meaning you do not know. *After Notes:* 1. Add important information left out of rough notes. 2. Answer any questions in the "Don't Understand" column. 3. Complete any blanks in the rough notes. 4. Write definitions for each unknown word. 5. Prepare final notes.

CHAPTER 5

Using the Library

■ Purposes

The purposes of this chapter are to:
1. teach students with learning disabilities a three-step strategy for using the library.
2. provide reproducibles that can be used to help students learn to use the library.

■ Titles of Reproducibles

■ RATIONALE

Students with learning disabilities often view the library as a boring place containing endless stacks of books. They may fail to realize that the modern library, or media center as many libraries are now called, is an exciting place containing a wide array of valuable learning aids and recreational materials. Because they are unaware of the many ways they can use the library, these students rarely visit the library. By failing to become familiar with the use of the library, they diminish their opportunities for learning (Smith, 1983).

Smith (1983) observed that, for students with learning disabilities, the library can be a source of information or, alternatively, a source of confusion. She urged teachers to help students become comfortable with the organization of the library and with the reference aids it contains. As she put it, students must view the library as an ally rather than an enemy. It is important, therefore, for teachers to promote use of the library. Devine (1981) suggests that teachers take students to the library, invite the librarian to give a talk in class, encourage library research projects, and teach basic library skills.

Teachers must convince students with learning disabilities that the library is an extension of the classroom. Students should recognize that the library provides additional resources for mastering important information about any school subject. Further, students should recognize that the library is a good place to go whenever they want to learn more about a subject or need to clarify something they did not understand in class or in their textbook. By teaching students with learning disabilities how to use the library, teachers help these students move from being dependent on teachers to becoming independent learners.

■ BACKGROUND INFORMATION

It is important to teach students with learning disabilities a strategy for using the library. We recommend a three-step strategy, as follows:

1. Determine how the library is organized. Students need to be familiar with the two major systems used for organizing libraries: Dewey Decimal and Library of Congress.

2. Use three primary references to locate information. Students need to be familiar with the use of the card catalog, the *Readers' Guide to Periodical Literature,* and the *New York Times Index* as the primary references to consult when trying to locate information.

3. Identify secondary references for locating information. These include dictionaries, almanacs, encyclopedias, biographies, government publications, and databases. These references should be used to supplement the information that is located through use of the primary references.

■ SYSTEMS FOR ORGANIZING LIBRARIES

Most libraries in the United States are organized according to either the Dewey Decimal System or the Library of Congress System. Most school libraries use the less complex Dewey Decimal System, whereas university libraries and the main libraries in major cities, along with the congressional library in Washington, D.C., use the Library of Congress System. The Library of Congress System is used when there is a need to classify a broader range of topics and wider range of materials.

Dewey Decimal System

Melvil Dewey developed a system for organizing nonfiction books on the shelves in libraries. His system, which is used in many school and public libraries to help library users quickly find the book they want, is called the Dewey Decimal System.

The Dewey Decimal System consists of ten primary classes. Each primary class is organized using a set of numbers. Figure 5.1 shows the ten primary classes. Novels and biographies are classified separately.

Novels: These are usually found in a separate section of the library and are arranged alphabetically by the first author's last name.

Biographies: These are arranged on the library shelves in alphabetical order by the name of the person who is being written about.

The ten primary classes are intentionally very broad so each can be divided into subclasses. Each primary class is divided into subclasses as seen in Figure 5.2.

By using a decimal point and a number, each subclass can be broken down still further into subdivisions. Figure 5.3 presents an example for the "Library Science 020" subclass, which is further broken down into subdivisions to allow for greater detailing.

Notice that some numbers are not used. This shows the flexibility of the system, which allows for more subdivisions as needed. The use of the decimal point means that the Dewey Decimal System has endless possibilities for the development of subdivisions. By using the subdivisions with the decimal point and numbers, the Dewey Decimal System can be expanded to classify books on any topic.

Using the Dewey Decimal System, students locate books in the library by their call numbers. The call number obtained from the card catalog is used to locate the book a student wants. The call number appears on the spine of the book, as seen in Figure 5.4, where the call number 028.7 identifies the specific location of the book on the library shelves.

To locate this book, a student should scan the bookshelves for the section between 000 and 099. Once this section is located, the student then reads the call numbers on the spines of the books until the 020 section is located. Then the student needs to locate the specific number 028.7. Sometimes more than one book has the same call number. When this is the case, the second number, B513.f, must be used to locate the specific book of interest. Figure 5.4 shows how the information looks on the spine of a book.

The numbers on the spine of a book are a code that will tell you things about the

FIGURE 5.1 Dewey Decimal System ten primary classes

000–099	Generalities	500–599	Pure Science
100–199	Philosophy and Related	600–699	Technology (Applied Sciences)
200–299	Religion	700–799	The Arts
300–399	The Social Sciences	800–899	Literature and Rhetoric
400–499	Language	900–99	General Geography and History, etc.

FIGURE 5.2 Dewey Decimal System primary classes and subclasses

000 Generalities
010 Bibliographies and catalogs
020 Library science
030 General encyclopedic works
040 Collected essays
050 General periodicals
060 General organizations
070 Newspapers and journalism
080 General collections
090 Manuscripts and book rarities

100 Philosophy and Related
110 Ontology and methodology
120 Knowledge, cause, purpose, man
130 Pseudo- and parapsychology
140 Specific philosophic viewpoints
150 Psychology
160 Logic
170 Ethics (moral philosophy)
180 Ancient, medieval, Oriental philosophy
190 Modern Western philosophy

200 Religion
210 Natural religion
220 Bible
230 Christian doctrinal theology
240 Christian moral & devotional theology
250 Christian pastoral, parochial, etc.
260 Christian social and ecclesiastical theology
270 History & geography of Christian church
280 Christian denominations and sects
290 Other religions and comparative religions

300 The Social Sciences
310 Statistical method & statistics
320 Political science
330 Economics
340 Law
350 Public administration
360 Welfare & association
370 Education
380 Commerce
390 Customs & folklore

400 Language
410 Linguistics & nonverbal language
420 English & Anglo-Saxon
430 Germanic languages
440 French, Provençal, Catalan
450 Italian, Romanian, etc.
460 Spanish & Portuguese
470 Italic languages
480 Classical & Greek
490 Other languages

130

500 Pure Science
510 Mathematics
520 Astronomy & allied sciences
530 Physics
540 Chemistry & allied sciences
550 Earth sciences
560 Paleontology
570 Anthropology & biological sciences
580 Botanical sciences
590 Zoological sciences

600 Technology (Applied Sciences)
610 Medical sciences
620 Engineering & allied operations
630 Agriculture & agricultural industries
640 Domestic arts & sciences
650 Business & related enterprises
660 Chemical technology, etc.
670 Manufactures processible
680 Assembled & final products
690 Buildings

700 The Arts
710 Civic & landscape art
720 Architecture
730 Sculpture & the plastic arts
740 Drawing & decorative arts
750 Painting & paintings
760 Graphic arts
770 Photography & photographs
780 Music
790 Recreation (Recreational arts)

800 Literature and Rhetoric
810 American literature in English
820 English & Anglo-Saxon literature
830 Germanic languages literature
840 French, Provençal, Catalan literature
850 Italian, Romanian, etc., literature
860 Spanish & Portuguese literature
870 Italic languages literature
880 Classical & Greek literature
890 Literatures of other languages

900 General Geography and History, etc.
910 General geography
920 General biography, genealogy, etc.
930 General history of ancient world
940 General history of modern Europe
950 General history of modern Asia
960 General history of modern Africa
970 General history of North America
980 General history of South America
990 General history of rest of world

FIGURE 5.3 Breaking down a subclass into subdivisions

028.074	Exhibits and Displays
028.1	Book Reviews
028.5	Reading of Children and Young Adults
028.52	Bibliography and Catalogs
028.7	Use of Books in the Library as a Source of Information
028.8	Use of Books as a Source of Recreation and Self-Development
028.9	Reading Interests and Habits

FIGURE 5.4 Information found on the spine of a book

Berkman
Find It Fast
028.7
B513.f

book as well as help you locate it. The book we are looking for is 028.7, B513.f. The number 028.7 tells you the book belongs to the 000–099 primary class, "Generalities." The number 028.7 tells you that within the Generalities primary class, the book belongs to the subclass "Library Science." The subdivision 028.7 further shows that this is a book that deals with the use of books in the library as a source of information.

The second number is B513.f. The B stands for the first letter in the author's last name (Berkman), the number 513 is assigned to all books written by this author, and the f stands for the first letter in the title of the book *(Find It Fast)*.

Once students with learning disabilities understand how to use the card catalog along with the Dewey Decimal System, they will be able to locate books in the library very rapidly. The card catalog is discussed later in this chapter.

Library of Congress System

One of the world's largest libraries, the Library of Congress, is located in Washington, D.C. The special system that was developed to organize this library is known as the Library of Congress System.

Many college and university libraries as well as other large libraries are organized using the Library of Congress System. Students with learning disabilities who

FIGURE 5.5 Library of Congress System twenty primary classes

Primary Classes	Call Numbers Start with Letter
General Works	A
Philosophy, Psychology, Religion	B
Auxiliary Sciences of History	C
History: General and Old World	D
History: America	E–F
Geography. Anthropology. Recreation	G
Social Sciences	H
Political Sciences	J
Law	K
Education	L
Music	M
Fine Arts	N
Language and Literature	P
Sciences	Q
Medicine	R
Agriculture	S
Technology	T
Military Science	U
Naval Science	V
Bibliography. Library Science	Z

will be using libraries organized using the Library of Congress System should become familiar with this system.

The Library of Congress System uses single letters to identify twenty primary classes. Figure 5.5 presents the twenty primary classes for the Library of Congress System.

These letters are combined with numbers and decimals to generate call numbers for books. Figure 5.6 shows a call number as it would appear on a card in the card catalog as well as on the spine of a book. An explanation of each part of the call number is also provided.

FIGURE 5.6 Library of Congress call number

```
DA  ⎫
754 ⎬ 1
.A1 ⎭
K4    2
1933  3
C2    4
```

1. Refers to primary class and subdivisions.

2. K4 The letter K refers to the first letter of the author's last name; for example, Kane, Paul. The number 4 tells you that he is the fourth authors whose last name begins with the letter K to have written a book in this primary class and subdivision.

3. Refers to year of publication.

4. Refers to the number of copies of this particular book in the library.

Students with learning disabilities frequently have difficulty locating books using the Library of Congress call numbers. The numbers following the decimal points are used to show the order in which books are placed on library shelves. Students need to be taught that any part of the call number following a decimal point is a decimal. In the following example, the second book (H2479.K39) follows the first (H2479.K3) because the decimal .39 follows .3 in numerical order. Similarly, the third book (H2479.54) follows the second book (H2479.K39) because the decimal .54 follows .39 in number order.

H	H	H
2479	2479	2479
.K3	.K39	.54

Once students with learning disabilities understand decimal order, they can locate books in libraries using the Library of Congress System.

■ THREE BASIC REFERENCES

Students need to know how to find nonfiction books in a library; the best reference tool for this purpose is the *card catalog*. Students also need to know how to find information in magazines; the best reference tool for this purpose is the *Readers' Guide to Periodical Literature*. Students also need to know how to locate information found in newspapers; the best reference tool for this purpose is the *New York Times Index*. These are the three basic reference tools every student should know how to use in the library.

Card Catalog

For each book in the library, there are three types of cards found in the card catalog. The *author card* is used to locate a book when you know the name of the author. The *title card* is used to locate a book when you know the title of the book but not the author. The *subject card* is used to locate a book when you know the subject but do not know the author or the title.

All three types of cards are filed in alphabetical order in the card catalog. Author cards are filed alphabetically by the author's last name. Title cards are filed alphabetically by title. However, words like *the, a,* and *an* are not used to alphabetize titles. Subject cards are filed alphabetically by the name of the subject. Figures 5.7 through 5.9 present examples of the three types of cards with the information contained in each card identified.

In the upper left-hand corner of each type of card there is a call number. If the library is organized using the Dewey system, every card will have a Dewey Decimal System call number. If the library is organized using the Library of Congress System, a Library of Congress call number will appear. Figure 5.10 shows the Dewey call number as it would appear on the author, title, and subject cards and on the binding of the corresponding book. Figure 5.11 shows the Library of Congress call number as it would appear on the author, title, and subject cards and on the binding of the corresponding book.

FIGURE 5.7 Author card

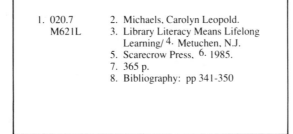

1. Call number. Always found in upper left-hand corner.
2. Author. Last name first.
3. Title. Sometimes the subtitle is also given.
4. Where published. City and state usually included.
5. Publisher.
6. Year of publication.
7. Number of pages in the book.
8. This area is used to provide any special information. In this case it tells that there is a bibliography included in the book.

FIGURE 5.8 Title card

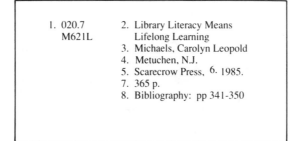

1. Call number.
2. Title of book.
3. Author.
4. Where published.
5. Publisher.
6. Year of publication.
7. Number of pages in the book.
8. This area reserved for special information.

135

FIGURE 5.9 Subject card

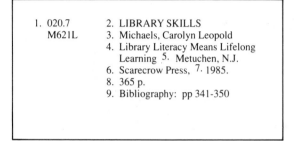

1. Call number.
2. Subject
3. Author.
4. Title
5. Where published.
6. Publisher.
7. When published.
8. Number of pages in the book.
9. This area reserved special information.

FIGURE 5.10 Dewey Decimal call number

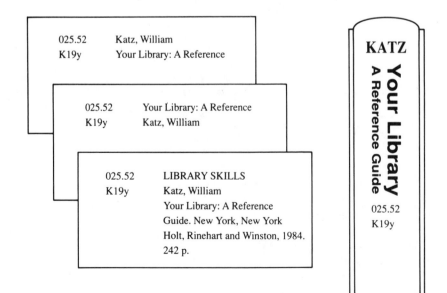

FIGURE 5.11 Library of Congress call number

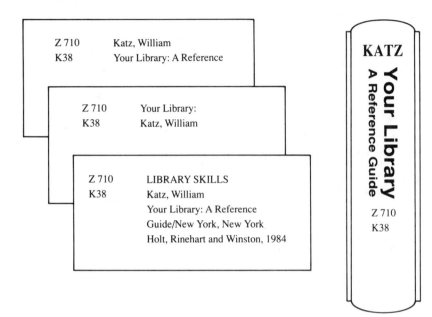

Readers' Guide to Periodical Literature

Students with learning disabilities often need to use periodicals to find information they need. The *Readers' Guide to Periodical Literature* is the best reference to use for this purpose. It is an index to 175 of the most popular magazines published on a variety of topics. The *Readers' Guide to Periodical Literature* is often referred to by its shortened title, *Readers' Guide*.

Because magazines are published on a frequent basis, *Readers' Guide* is updated every two weeks. At the end of every three months, a separate volume of *Readers' Guide* is published. An annual bound edition is published for each year. Because *Readers' Guide* is published so frequently, it enables students to obtain current information on a topic.

Articles in *Readers' Guide* are arranged alphabetically by subject and author. Figure 5.12 presents a list of entries as found in *Readers' Guide*. As you can see, the entries are for articles found in a variety of magazines.

Figure 5.13 explains the information found in two typical entries in *Readers' Guide*. Part of the information found in entries is in the form of abbreviations. Students will need to become familiar with the basic abbreviations used in the entries.

Entries sometimes contain a "See" or "See also" reference to help students locate more information on a topic. "See" identifies other headings the student should use to locate the desired information. "See also" identifies related headings that may also be useful for locating desired information.

Figure 5.14 shows examples of "See" and "See also" notations.

FIGURE 5.12 Entries found in *Readers' Guide*

MOTION PICTURE FILMS
Conservation and restoration
See Motion Pictures—Conservation and restoration
MOTION PICTURE INDUSTRY
See also
Brooksfilms Inc.
Columbia Pictures Entertainment Inc.
Fox Inc.
MGM/UA Communications Co.
Motion picture production and direction
Orion Pictures Corporation
Paramount Pictures Corp.
Pathe Communications Corp.
Acquisitions and mergers
International aspects
Does Steve Ross know who he's dealing with? [G. Parretti] S. Duffy and others. il pors *Business Week* p32–3 Ap 23 '90
The mysterious Italian who took Hollywood by storm [G. Parretti] J. Hammer. il pors *Newsweek* 115:46–7 Ap 30 '90
What makes Giancarlo run? [G. Parretti deals for MGM/UA Communications] J. Greenwald. por *Time* 135:63 Ap 23 '90
Communist activities
Hollywood goes Havana [support of G. Garcia Márquez's Foundation for New Latin American Cinema] M. L. Wohn. *The New Republic* 202:17–20 Ap 16 '90
History
Academy Awards collector's edition! [cover story; special issue] il *Architectural Digest* 47:20+ Ap '90
Cuba
See also
Foundation for New Latin American Cinema
United States
See Motion picture industry
MOTION PICTURE PRODUCERS
See also
Guber, Peter
Mayer, Louis B. (Louis Burt), 1885–1957
Roach, Hal, 1892–
Selznick, David O., 1902–1965
Thalberg, Irving Grant, 1899–1936
MOTION PICTURE PRODUCT PLACEMENT
Hollywood: the ad [cover story] M. C. Miller. il *The Atlantic* 265:41–5+ Ap '90
MOTION PICTURE PRODUCTION AND DIRECTION
See also
Motion pictures—Setting and scenery
Alfred Hitchcock goes Psycho [excerpt from Alfred Hitchcock and the making of Psycho] S. Rebello. il *American Film* 15:38–43+ Ap '90
MOTION PICTURE REVIEWS
Single works
The bear
Field & Stream il 94:172 Mr '90. C. Errig
Casualties of war
American Film il 15:52 Ap '90. P. Rainer
Chattahoochee
Newsweek 115:73 Ap 23 '90. J. Kroll
The cook, the thief, his wife & her lover
The Nation 250:644–6 My 7 '90. S. Klawans
The New Republic 202:26 Ap 23 '90. S. Kauffmann
New York il 23:66+ My 7 '90. D. Denby
The New Yorker 66:88–90 My 7 '90. T. Rafferty
Newsweek il 115:73 Ap 23 '90. J. Kroll
Rolling Stone il p38 Ap 19 '90. P. Travers
Crazy people
Maclean's il 103:61 Ap 23 '90. B. D. Johnson
The Nation 250:646–7 My 7 '90. S. Klawans
People Weekly il 33:19 Ap 30 '90. R. Novak
Cry-baby
American Film il 15:32–7 Ap '90. P. Aufderheide
Newsweek il 115:86 Ap 16 '90. J. Kroll
People Weekly il 33:17 Ap 16 '90. R. Novak
Rolling Stone p37 Ap 19 '90. P. Travers
Time il 135:90+ Ap 23 '90. R. Corliss
Distant voices, still lives
Video il 13:62+ Mr '90. J. Silberg
Do the right thing
Jet il 78:27+ Ap 16 '90
Driving Miss Daisy
New York il 23:68+ Ap 16 '90. D. Denby

Ernest goes to jail
People Weekly 33:15 Ap 23 '90. R. Novak
For all mankind
People Weekly il 33:19–20 Ap 30 '90. R. Novak
The gods must be crazy II
Maclean's 103:62 Ap 23 '90. B. D. Johnson
People Weekly il 33:19 Ap 30 '90. R. Novak
H-2 worker
The Nation 250:611 Ap 30 '90. S. Klawans
The handmaid's tale
Christianity Today il 34:56 Ap 9 '90
Commonweal 117:257–8 Ap 20 '90. P. D. Baumann
Henry: portrait of a serial killer
The New Yorker 66:91 Ap 23 '90. T. Rafferty
Henry V
Mademoiselle il por 96:139–40+ Ap '90. R. Rosenbaum
House party
American Film il 15:51 Ap '90. R. Seidenberg
People Weekly il 33:18+ Ap 16 '90. R. Novak
The hunt for Red October
America 162:431 Ap 28 '90. R. A. Blake
Commonweal 117:258 Ap 20 '90. P. D. Baumann
I love you to death
Maclean's il 103:61 Ap 16 '90. B. D. Johnson
Newsweek 115:86 Ap 16 '90. J. Kroll
People Weekly il 33:17–18 Ap 16 '90. R. Novak
Rolling Stone il p35 My 3 '90. P. Travers
Time il 135:92+ Ap 23 '90. R. Corliss
Impulse
People Weekly 33:20 Ap 16 '90. R. Novak
In the blood
Field & Stream 94:172–3 Mr '90. D. E. Petzal
Outdoor Life il 185:106 Ap '90. N. Seifert
In the spirit
The New Republic 202:28 Ap 30 '90. S. Kauffmann
People Weekly il 33:14–15 Ap 23 '90. R. Novak
Joe versus the volcano
American Film il 15:20–5+ Ap '90. C. Troy
Rolling Stone p38 Ap 19 '90. P. Travers
Lethal weapon 2
Video il 13:61 Mr '90. J. Young
The Mahabharata
The New Republic 202:28–9 My 7 '90. S. Kauffmann
Mama, there's a man in your bed
Maclean's il 103:61–2 Ap 23 '90. B. D. Johnson
Time 135:94 Ap 23 '90. R. Corliss
Miami blues
Maclean's il 103:63 Ap 30 '90. B. D. Johnson
New York 23:70 Ap 16 '90. D. Denby
The New Yorker 66:90–1 Ap 23 '90. T. Rafferty
Newsweek il 115:67 Ap 23 '90. D. Ansen
Rolling Stone il p36 My 3 '90. P. Travers
Time il 135:90 Ap 23 '90. R. Corliss
Monsieur Hire
The New Republic 202:26–7 Ap 23 '90. S. Kauffmann
Newsweek 115:73 Ap 23 '90. D. Ansen
Rolling Stone p36 My 3 '90. P. Travers
Opportunity knocks
Newsweek il 115:86 Ap 16 '90. J. Kroll
The package
Video il 13:62 Mr '90. J. Silberg
Paperhouse
Video il 13:63 Mr '90. D. Schweiger
Parenthood
Video il 13:16 Mr '90. K. Korman
Pretty woman
Commonweal 117:296–7 My 4 '90. P. D. Baumann
The New Republic 202:26–7 Ap 16 '90. S. Kauffmann
Rolling Stone il p37 My 3 '90. P. Travers
Psycho
American Film il 15:38–43+ Ap '90. S. Rebello
Q & A
Maclean's 103:63 Ap 30 '90. B. D. Johnson
New York il 23:92+ Ap 23 '90. D. Denby
Newsweek il 115:65+ My 7 '90. D. Ansen
Red desert
Video il 13:66 Mr '90. S. L. Siegel
Roger Corman's Frankenstein unbound
American Film il 15:50–1 Ap '90. R. Seidenberg

From *Readers' Guide to Periodical Literature*, page 179, 1990, Volume 69, Number 6. Copyright 1990 by The H. W. Wilson Company. Material reproduced with permission of the publisher.

FIGURE 5.13 Information found in typical entries in *Readers' Guide*

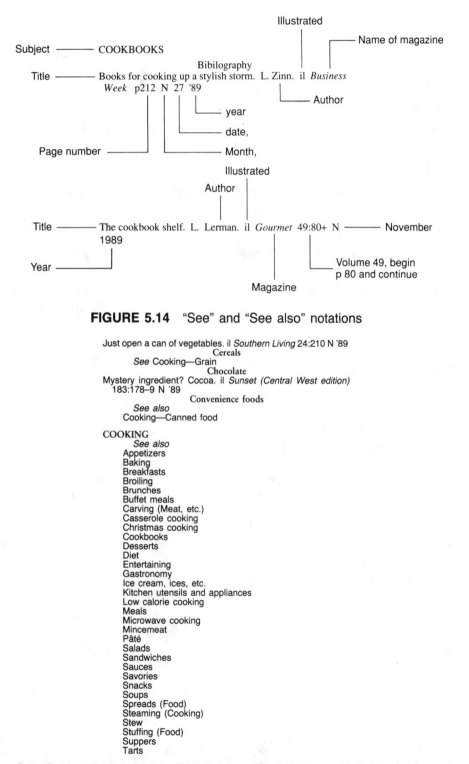

FIGURE 5.14 "See" and "See also" notations

Just open a can of vegetables. il *Southern Living* 24:210 N '89
                       Cereals
      See Cooking—Grain
                    Chocolate
Mystery ingredient? Cocoa. il *Sunset (Central West edition)*
   183:178–9 N '89
                  Convenience foods
      See also
      Cooking—Canned food

COOKING
      See also
      Appetizers
      Baking
      Breakfasts
      Broiling
      Brunches
      Buffet meals
      Carving (Meat, etc.)
      Casserole cooking
      Christmas cooking
      Cookbooks
      Desserts
      Diet
      Entertaining
      Gastronomy
      Ice cream, ices, etc.
      Kitchen utensils and appliances
      Low calorie cooking
      Meals
      Microwave cooking
      Mincemeat
      Pâté
      Salads
      Sandwiches
      Sauces
      Savories
      Snacks
      Soups
      Spreads (Food)
      Steaming (Cooking)
      Stew
      Stuffing (Food)
      Suppers
      Tarts

To locate information using Readers' Guide, students should follow this procedure:

1. Select a topic on which they want information available in periodicals.
2. Locate *Readers' Guide* in the library.
3. Gather the issues and bound volumes of *Readers' Guide* for the years to be included in the search for information.
4. Locate magazine articles on the topic.
5. Use the "See" and "See also" references to locate additional articles.
6. Prepare a bibliography card for each reference to be used. Preparation of bibliography cards is described in Chapter 8.

To locate magazines containing the articles they desire, students should follow this procedure:

1. Look in the card catalog by the title of the magazine to determine if the library has that magazine. In some cases students will have to go to a larger library to locate a specific magazine.
2. Locate the section of the library where the magazines are stored and look for the desired magazine by its title. Magazines are generally filed in alphabetical order on the shelves in the library. The latest issues are generally found in the magazine section in the Reading Room section of the library.
3. Use the volume number to locate the specific issue needed. Then use the page numbers to locate the article.
4. When confused, ask the librarian for help.

New York Times Index

When students with learning disabilities need more current information than that found in books or magazines, they will need to look for it in newspapers. Current information can usually be found in newspapers kept on file in the school or community library. Most school and community libraries subscribe to the local newspaper(s) as well as a few national newspapers. Issues of these newspapers are often maintained for up to a year. Older issues are available on microfilm.

Some major newspapers publish indexes to help readers locate articles which appeared in past issues. Students with learning disabilities should be taught how to use a newspaper index. Here are four of the most common newspapers for which there are indexes:

New York Times Index, 1913 to date (New York: New York Times Company). This index to articles that appeared in the *New York Times* is published twice each month and is accumulated into annual volumes. It is an excellent source of in-depth articles on almost every subject.

Wall Street Journal Index, 1958 to date (New York: Dow Jones). This is an index to articles that appeared in the *Wall Street Journal.* It is a particularly good source for students to look for business articles.

Washington Post Newspaper Index, 1972 to date (Wooster, Ohio: Bell and Howell). This is an index to articles that appeared in the *Washington Post.* It is a particularly useful source for articles about the U.S. government.

Index to the Christian Science Monitor International Daily Newspaper, 1960 to date (Boston: Christian Science Monitor). This is an index to articles that appeared in the Christian Science Monitor. It is a useful source for articles on topics of general human interest.

The *New York Times Index* is the most comprehensive and widely available newspaper index. Most libraries that have the *New York Times Index* also have a microfilm collection of this newspaper going back to 1913. The *New York Times Index* is organized according to subject, not by author or title. Each entry for an article includes a brief summary.

Examine this sample entry from the *New York Times Index* as you read about it.

[1]**Travel**

[2]•*Hawaii*

[3]Robert Trumbull article on travel attractions in Hawaii;

[4]illustrations[5] (L), Jl 12[6] 2:1[7]

1. **Travel** is the heading and can be identified as such by the bold print.

2. •*Hawaii* is a subdivision under **Travel.** This subdivision is identified by the dot in front of the word *Hawaii,* which is printed in italics.

3. This is an abstract or short comment on the article.

4. This shows that the article includes illustrations.

5. (L) indicates a long article of two columns or more, (M) a medium-length item up to two columns, and (S) a short item (usually a half column or less in length).

6. This indicates the month and date when the newspaper containing this article was published.

7. This indicates the page number and column number where the article appears. *Note:* Roman numerals are used to show section numbers for Sunday editions of the paper. A "p" in an entry stands for "page."

Figure 5.15 presents some items from the *New York Times Index* for your further examination.

■ OTHER IMPORTANT REFERENCES

Three additional sources of information include a range of useful reference materials. We categorize these as miscellaneous reference materials, government publications, and online databases.

Miscellaneous Reference Materials

Many other reference materials are available in the library. They are generally located in a specific area or room in the library and may not be checked out for home use. These references are not designed to be read from cover to cover but, rather, to be used selectively to locate information needed to answer a question or to identify an important fact or rule.

FIGURE 5.15 Items from the *New York Times Index*

Great Britain
Comment on bus tours, courses and other items of interest to travelers (S), Ja 4,X,12:3
Letter on Dona Guimaracs Nov 16 (1980) article on renting landmark homes in Britain (M), Ja 11,X,p27
Letters on Joan Cook Dec 14 (1980) article on joys of unplanned travel (S), Ja 11,X,p27
R W Apple travel article on 3-day tours of places associated with Sir Winston Churchill; illustrations; map (L), F 1,X,p1
Prof Roland V Layton Jr letter on Nov 30 (1980) article on travel attractions in London (S), F 8,X,p28
Letters from Philip Hall, L B Kaufman Jr and Lynne Vandewater on Feb 1 article; spokesman for British Information Service, NY, replies to Hall letter (S), Mr 8,X,p27
John M Gray article recounts 4-week budget vacation in Britain, trip made possible by staying in rented trailer or other non-luxurious accommodations; illustration; map; drawing (part 1 of 2-part section) (L), Mr 15,X,p1
Comment on growing number of organizations offering travelers opportunities to stay in private homes in Britain; some homes described (M), Ap 5,X,p7
William Borders article on travel attractions in London during summer; illustrations (L), My 10,X,p1
Article on array of tours available during week of Prince Charle's wedding date; illustrations; map; travel tips (L), My 10,X,p19
Nicholas A Ulanov article on travel attractions on Iona (Scotland); illustrations; maps (L), Je 28,X,p1
David Yeadon article on travel attractions in Dorset, where novelist Thomas Hardy set scene for his book, Tess of the D'Urbervilles; illustrations; maps (L), Jl 26,X,p1
Lrs on Nicholas Ulanov's June 28 article on Iona Island, Jl 26,X,p26
Letters on July 26 article on Dorset (S), Ag 16,X,p22
John Wain article on travel attractions in Wales; travel tips; illus; map (L), Ag 30,X,p1
Travel article on London focuses on city's art museums and galleries; illus; maps (L), O 11,X,p14; Paul Goldberger article on travel attractions in London; illus; maps (L), O 11,X,p15; Edmund Morris travel article on exploring London on moped; tips on renting moped (M), O 18,X,p28; article on travel attractions in London focuses on annual Lord Mayor's Procession through city; ilus (M), N 1,X,p42
Article offers tips to foreign travelers who get ill in GB (M), N 22,X,p5
Article on travel attractions in London; drawing; illus; map (L), D 20,X,p10

From *New York Times Index*, 1981, p. 1109.
Copyright © 1981 by The New York Times Company.
Reprinted by permission.

Some reference materials cover a wide variety of subjects, whereas others focus on one subject in depth. Some reference materials have the information right there; other references direct the reader to sources containing the information. In this section we identify a number of references that may be useful to students with learning disabilities.

Oxford English Dictionary. This reference is the most complete dictionary of the English language. It is useful for tracing the history of a word about which students want to know more than they can learn from an abridged dictionary. Definitions are provided in considerable detail. Quotations are used to show how words have been used in different ways over the years.

Dictionary of Slang and Unconventional English. This is a good reference for obtaining information on colloquialisms, catch-phrases, slang usage, nicknames, and other unconventional uses of language.

Roget's International Thesaurus. This is a source of synonyms, or alternative words for the same idea. It provides a range of words that can be used to express an idea more precisely.

World Almanac and Book of Facts. This is a source of information on a wide range of topics of general interest, including population, sports, government, and health.

Information Please Almanac, Atlas, and Yearbook. This is a source of information on many topics. It includes many graphs, charts, lists, and other visuals to provide information to the user.

Facts on File. This is a summary of many facts related to news events that occurred nationally and internationally.

A Handbook to Literature. This is a good source of information on the history of British and American literature. It clarifies important words and concepts.

Reader's Encyclopedia. This reference provides information on literature, music, and the arts. Brief statements are provided on authors, terms, expressions, plots, characters, places, events, and the general literary movement.

The New Illustrated Encyclopedia of World History. This reference lists chronologically events in history from prehistoric times to modern times. It is a good source for seeing how historic events relate to each other.

Current Biography. This is a good source of extensive information on people who appear in the news.

Who's Who in America. This reference contains biographies, mostly of living Americans who achieved prominence in some way. It also includes some biographies of non-Americans who became prominent in America. It is an interesting source of information on famous people.

International Who's Who. This reference contains biographies of people from throughout the world who have become prominent for their accomplishments.

Government Publications

The U.S. government is the largest publisher in the world. Since 1861 the Government Printing Office (GPO) has produced a vast array of publications ranging from popular pamphlets that are just one page long to technical works that may encompass thousands of pages. Government publications include official documents such as laws, court decisions, and census data. They also include reference books such as indexes, abstracts, and yearbooks.

Government publications are distributed at no cost to designated libraries and institutions. The 1,300 libraries receiving documents from the GPO are called *depository libraries.* Students with learning disabilities can locate the nearest depository library by asking the reference librarian at their school or local library.

Depository libraries house government publications as a separate collection, which is organized by use of the Superintendent of Documents (SuDocs) classification system. The SuDocs system is an alphanumeric system used by the GPO to assign call numbers to documents. In many libraries, government publications are listed in the card catalog by SuDocs numbers. When this is not the case, students will need to refer to the *Monthly Catalog of United States Government Publications* to locate documents. This catalog contains bibliographic entries that are arranged alphabetically according to the issuing government agency. Each issue of the catalog contains separate indexes for subjects, titles, keywords, and authors, as well as for series reports, contract numbers, stock numbers, and SuDocs numbers.

There are a number of other sources for locating government publications. These include the following:

Guide to U.S. Government Publications. This is an annual list of all the GPO serial publications. The major portion of this publication is an annotated list of classes.

List of Classes of United States Government Publications Available for Selection by Depository Libraries. This semiannual publication provides a list of currently available documents according to classification number. Two valuable indexes are an alphabetical listing of all government authors and a list of discontinued documents.

American Statistics Index: A Comprehensive Guide and Index to the Statistical Publications of the U.S. Government. This monthly publication is a comprehensive index to the voluminous statistics issued by the government. There is an annual cumulation.

Statistical Abstract of the United States. This is a publication of the U.S. Bureau of the Census, which provides statistical information on political, social, and economic topics.

Congressional Information Services Index to Publications of the United States Congress. This publication is a basic guide to congressional actions, including bills, laws, and hearings.

Publications Reference File. This is a bimonthly index to the publications available for purchase from the GPO. The index is in microfiche form.

Government Reports Announcements and Index. This bimonthly index cites government publications that are not routinely provided to depository libraries. All federally funded research done by private contractors is included here. The reports are organized by subject and are primarily scientific in nature.

Online Databases

Computer technology enables students with learning disabilities to acquire information by doing an online search. In an online search, a computer is used to retrieve information from databases far removed from the library in which the student initiates the search.

Online databases are available for a variety of subjects and provide information in the form of (1) indexes and abstracts covering such sources as periodical articles, books, and research reports; (2) full text of newspapers and periodicals; and (3) directories of various types.

There are hundreds of databases to which libraries can subscribe. Libraries must be selective regarding the databases to which they subscribe because of the cost involved. Some of this cost is passed on to users of the databases. The longer the search and the more information printed, the higher the cost to the user. It is important, therefore, for students to be very specific regarding the scope of their search. The process of organizing a search is fairly complex. We recommend that students with learning disabilities enlist the assistance of librarians who have training and specific responsibility for conducting online database searches. This will cut the cost of the search and increase the likelihood that relevant information will be obtained.

Databases that will be useful to students with learning disabilities include the following:

GPO Monthly Catalog. This database indexes the publications of the Government Printing Office.

Magazine Index. This is an index of more than 400 popular magazines.

National Newspaper Index. This database indexes the *Christian Science Monitor,* the *New York Times,* and the *Wall Street Journal.* Selected references from the *Washington Post* and the *Los Angeles Times* are also included.

Specific subject databases are available for Agriculture and Food Science; Arts and Humanities; Business and Economics: Computers; Criminal Justice; Education; Environment, Energy, and Natural Resources; Law and Public Affairs; Mathematics, Chemistry and Physics; Medicine and Biological Sciences; Science and Technology; and Social Sciences. There are a number of databases for each of these subjects. A comprehensive listing of specific subject databases is contained in *Books, Libraries, and Research,* third edition, by Hauer, Murray, Dantin, and Bolner (1987).

■ TEACHING PLAN

Here is a plan for teaching students with learning disabilities the three-step strategy for how to use the library.

1. Ask the students to tell what reference sources they are familiar with in the school library. List the references on the chalkboard for all to see. Add some of your own. Use Reproducible 5-1, "Three-Step Strategy for Using the Library," to introduce the three-step strategy for using the library. Have students take notes as you overview each step.

2. Distribute Reproducible 5-2, "Learning about the Dewey Decimal System." Have the students use 5-2 to learn about the ten primary classes of the Dewey Decimal System.

3. Distribute Reproducible 5-3, "Dewey Decimal System for Primary Classes and Subclasses." Have the students use 5-3 to learn about the subclasses into which each of the primary classes is divided.

4. Use Reproducible 5-4, "Dewey Decimal System Call Numbers," to teach students how to locate books in the library using the Dewey Decimal System. Carefully explain what each part of the call number stands for. Bring in several books to show how the call number is stamped on the spine of each book.

5. Distribute Reproducible 5-5, "Learning about the Library of Congress System." Use 5-5 to show how the Library of Congress System is organized using twenty primary classes.

6. Use Reproducible 5-6, "Library of Congress Call Numbers," to teach students how to locate books in the library using the Library of Congress System. Carefully explain what each part of the call number stands for. Bring in several books to show how the call number is stamped on the spine of each book.

7. Distribute Reproducible 5-7, "Locating Books Using Library of Congress Call Numbers." Explain to students that in order to locate books using the Library of Congress System call numbers, they will have to understand decimal order. Use the example to review decimal order. Then have the students complete the activity on their own. After they have completed the activity, review their answers.

8. Use Reproducible 5-8, "Learning about the Card Catalog," to introduce the card catalog to your students. Point out where the card catalog is located in your school library. Visit the library if possible. Have students who have used the card catalog tell about it. Bring out that there are three different types of cards found in the card catalog: *author, title,* and *subject.* Then have the students complete the activity.

9. Distribute Reproducible 5-9, "Author Card." Use 5-9 to familiarize students with the contents of the author card. Then have them answer the questions. Review the answers as a group activity before having students complete the page by making an author card.

10. Use Reproducible 5-10, "Title Card," in a similar way.

11. Use Reproducible 5-11, "Subject Card," in a similar way.

12. Distribute Reproducible 5-12, "Alphabetical Order in the Card Catalog." Explain that author cards are alphabetized by the last name of the first author, title cards by the first word in the title, and subject cards by the first word in the subject. Point out that words like *a, an,* and *the* are not used when placing titles in alphabetical order. Have students complete the alphabetizing activity.

13. Use Reproducible 5-13, "Learning about the Readers' Guide to Periodical Literature," to introduce students to this reference. Be sure students understand that this reference is used to locate articles in magazines. Use the example page from *Readers' Guide* to show the information found there. Be certain students understand they will find information listed under topics and subtopics. Explain what "See" and "See also" mean. If possible, bring in copies of single issues and bound volumes of *Readers' Guide* for the students to see.

14. Distribute Reproducible 5-14, "Reading an Entry in Readers' Guide." Use 5-14 to show students how to read an entry in *Readers' Guide.* Begin by reviewing how months of the year are abbreviated in the entries. Then use the sample entry to show students the information an entry contains. Finally, have students label the parts of an entry.

15. Use Reproducible 5-15, "Locating Information Using Readers' Guide," to identify the steps students should follow when using *Readers' Guide* to locate magazine articles. Have students take notes on each step as you present background information.

16. Use Reproducible 5-16, "Locating Magazines in Your Library," to have students familiarize themselves with the magazines available in their library.

17. Distribute Reproducible 5-17, "Learning about Newspapers and Their Indexes." Use the introductory paragraphs to point out that newspapers are the best source of

current information. Explain that actual copies of newspapers are usually kept in the library for one year and that older issues of some newspapers are kept on microfilm. Review the four newspaper indexes and then have students complete the activity.

18. Use Reproducible 5-18, "The New York Times Index," to familiarize students with the use of this index. Use the sample entry to explain what is found there. Then have students answer the questions about the next entry. Bring in a copy of the *Index* to show them. Also bring in a copy of the *New York Times* to show students the in-depth nature of its articles.

19. Use Reproducible 5-19, "Other Important References," to familiarize students with some other useful references they can use to locate information. Have students answer the questions about these references. Bring into class as many of these references as you can. Also bring in other references you believe are valuable.

20. Use Reproducible 5-20, "Government Document Searches," to acquaint students with another important source of information. Have the students visit the library and speak with the librarian to obtain answers to the questions.

21. Use Reproducible 5-21, "Using the Computer to Do Database Searches," to acquaint students with how computers can be used to obtain information. Have the students share any knowledge they have about using their home computers to obtain information. Have the students visit the library and speak with the librarian to obtain answers to the questions. If your school library has access to databases, arrange for a demonstration.

22. Distribute Reproducible 5-22, "What I Have Learned." Use this reproducible to evaluate how well your students have learned the information taught in this chapter. As needed, use any of the reproducibles to review what was presented in this chapter.

Three-Step Strategy for Using the Library

The library is probably the most interesting place in your school. It contains materials that will tickle your imagination, make you laugh or cry, or satisfy your thirst for information. But before you can enjoy the library, you need to know how to use it.

Here are the important steps in a strategy you need to follow when using a library. As your teacher discusses each step, write the important things you need to remember about each.

1. Find out how the library is organized:

   Dewey Decimal System

   Library of Congress System

2. Learn how to use these primary references for locating information:

   Card catalog

   Readers' Guide to Periodical Literature

   New York Times Index

3. Learn how to use these secondary references for locating information:

   Dictionaries

   Almanacs

   Encyclopedias

   Biographies

   Government publications

   Databases

Learning about the Dewey Decimal System ▬▬▬▬

Most school libraries are organized using the Dewey Decimal System. The system is designed to help you find books quickly and easily. The system consists of ten primary classes. Each primary class is organized by a set of numbers. Here are the ten primary classes and the numbers that go with each.

000–099	Generalities	500–599	Pure Science
100–199	Philosophy and Related	600–699	Technology (Applied Sciences)
200–299	Religion	700–799	The Arts
300–399	The Social sciences	800–899	Literature and Rhetoric
400–499	Language	900–999	General Geography and History, etc.

Under which numbers would you find books on the following topics:

1. the artist Picasso _____

2. chemistry _____

3. Christianity _____

4. French terms _____

5. the *Encyclopedia Britannica* _____

6. fall of the Roman Empire _____

7. the philosopher Plato _____

8. the playwright Shakespeare _____

9. social welfare _____

10. using robots _____

Dewey Decimal System for Primary Classes and Subclasses

The ten primary classes in the Dewey Decimal System are very broad. Because they are so broad, each primary class is divided into subclasses. Look at the ten primary classes and see how each is divided into subclasses. Notice how each subclass has its own number but keeps the same first number as its primary class. For example, the number for the primary class **language** is 400, and the number for the subclass "Classical & Greek" is 480.

PRIMARY CLASSES AND SUBCLASSES

000   Generalities
010   Bibliographies and catalogs
020   Library science
030   General encyclopedic works
040   Collected essays
050   General periodicals
060   General organizations
070   Newspapers and journalism
080   General collections
090   Manuscripts and book rarities

100   Philosophy and Related
110   Ontology and methodology
120   Knowledge, cause, purpose, man
130   Pseudo- and parapsychology
140   Specific philosophic viewpoints
150   Psychology
160   Logic
170   Ethics (moral philosophy)
180   Ancient, medieval, Oriental philosophy
190   Modern Western philosophy

200   Religion
210   Natural religion
220   Bible
230   Christian doctrinal theology
240   Christian moral & devotional theology
250   Christian pastoral, parochial, etc.
260   Christian social and ecclesiastical theology
270   History & geography of Christian church
280   Christian denominations and sects
290   Other religions and comparative religions

300   The Social Sciences
310   Statistical method & statistics

320 Political science
330 Economics
340 Law
350 Public administration
360 Welfare & association
370 Education
380 Commerce
390 Customs & folklore

400 Language
410 Linguistics & nonverbal language
420 English & Anglo-Saxon
430 Germanic languages
440 French, Provençal, Catalan
450 Italian, Romanian, etc.
460 Spanish & Portuguese
470 Italic languages
480 Classical & Greek
490 Other languages

500 Pure Science
510 Mathematics
520 Astronomy & allied sciences
530 Physics
540 Chemistry & allied sciences
550 Earth sciences
560 Paleontology
570 Anthropology & biological sciences
580 Botanical sciences
590 Zoological sciences

600 Technology (Applied Sciences)
610 Medical sciences
620 Engineering & allied operations
630 Agriculture & agricultural industries
640 Domestic arts & sciences
650 Business & related enterprises
660 Chemical technology, etc.
670 Manufactures processible
680 Assembled & final products
690 Buildings

700 The Arts
710 Civic & landscape art
720 Architecture
730 Sculpture & the plastic arts
740 Drawing & decorative arts
750 Painting & paintings
760 Graphic arts
770 Photography & photographs
780 Music
790 Recreation (Recreational arts)

800   Literature and Rhetoric
810   American literature in English
820   English & Anglo-Saxon literature
830   Germanic languages literature
840   French, Provençal, Catalan literature
850   Italian, Romanian, etc., literature
860   Spanish & Portuguese literature
870   Italic languages literature
880   Classical & Greek literature
890   Literatures of other languages

900   General Geography and History, etc.
910   General geography
920   General biography, genealogy, etc.
930   General history of ancient world
940   General history of modern Europe
950   General history of modern Asia
960   General history of modern Africa
970   General history of North America
980   General history of South America
990   General history of rest of world

Here are some very specific topics. For each specific topic, write the Dewey Decimal System number that shows where you would find information on this topic.

1. Why was the New Testament written? _____

2. The history of the *New York Times* _____

3. Engineering plans _____

4. Theories of psychology _____

5. Learning to speak Spanish _____

6. Educating young children _____

7. Newton's law of gravity _____

8. U.S. Civil War _____

9. The poems of Walt Whitman _____

10. Creating a sculpture _____

11. Why do you think Melvil Dewey divided his system into ten primary classes?

_____

12. Why did he add the subclasses? _____

Dewey Decimal System Call Numbers

When the library is organized using the Dewey Decimal System, books are located in the library by their Dewey Decimal System call number. Call numbers are obtained from either the author, title, or subject card in the card catalog. The call number you find for a book in the card catalog is also found on the spine of the book. For example, for a book by Berkman titled *Find It Fast*, the call number looks like this:

028.7
B513.f

The call number will tell you things about a book as well as help you find it in the library. Here is what it tells you about *Find It Fast:*

The number 028.7 tells you the book belongs to the 000–099 primary class, which is "Generalities." The number 028.7 tells you that within Generalities the book belongs to the subclass "Library science." The number 028.7 shows a further subdivision of the subclass Library science.

The second number is B513.f. The B513.f stands for the first letter in Berkman, which is the author's last name. The number B513.f is assigned to all books written by this author. The B513.f stands for the first letter in the title, *Find It Fast*.

Answer the questions about the information on the spine of this book.

1. What is the author's last name? _____

2. What is the title of the book? _____

3. What does the letter T stand for? _____

4. What does the letter u stand for? _____

5. Circle the number that shows the primary class   530.4

6. Circle the number that shows the subclass   530.4

7. What does the number 23 stand for? _____

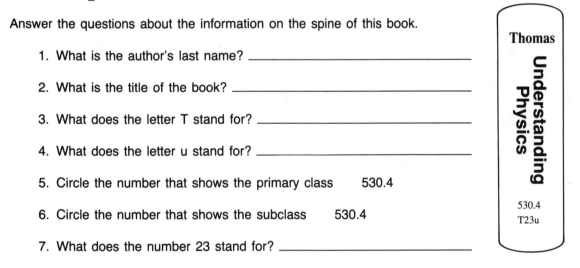

Thomas
Understanding
Physics
530.4
T23u

Learning about the Library of Congress System

The Library of Congress is located in Washington, D.C. A special system was developed to organize this library. This system is named the Library of Congress System.

Many large city libraries as well as college and university libraries are organized using the Library of Congress System. In this system, there are twenty primary classes. A single letter is used to designate each primary class. Combinations of letters, numbers, and decimals are used to show subdivisions within these twenty primary classes.

Look at the twenty primary classes of the Library of Congress System. Then answer the questions.

Primary Classes	Call Numbers Start with Letter
General Works	A
Philosophy, Psychology, Religion	B
Auxiliary Sciences of History	C
History: General and Old World	D
History: America	E–F
Geography. Anthropology. Recreation	G
Social Sciences	H
Political Sciences	J
Law	K
Education	L
Music	M
Fine Arts	N
Language and Literature	P
Sciences	Q
Medicine	R
Agriculture	S
Technology	T
Military Science	U
Naval Science	V
Bibliography. Library Science	Z

1. What primary class is identified by these letters?

   P _____

   C _____

   U _____

   D _____

   G _____

2. What letter goes with each primary class?

Law _____

Technology _____

Fine Arts _____

General History _____

General Works _____

Library of Congress Call Numbers

When a library is organized using the Library of Congress System, books are located by their Library of Congress call numbers. Call numbers are obtained from the author, title, or subject card in the card catalog. Letters, numbers, and decimals are combined to form call numbers for books. The call number is found on the spine of the book and looks like this. Each part has been labeled for you.

$$
\left. \begin{array}{l} \text{DA} \\ 754 \\ \text{.A1} \end{array} \right\} 1
$$

K4   **2**

1933   **3**

c2   **4**

1. Refers to primary class and subdivisions.

2. K4   The letter K refers to the first letter of the author's last name—for example, "Kane, Paul." The number 4 tells you that he is the fourth author whose last name begins with the letter K to have written a book in this primary class and subdivision.

3. Refers to year of publication.

4. Refers to the number of copies of this particular book in the library.

Label the parts of this Library of Congress call number:

E

279

.G3

P2

1988

c4

Locating Books Using Library of Congress Call Numbers

Look at these Library of Congress call numbers for three books. The books are in order according to their call numbers. Can you explain why they are in this order?

H	H	H
2479	2479	2479
.K3	.K39	.54

Since all three call numbers are for the H primary class and the 2479 subdivision, the numbers following the decimal point are used to place the call numbers in order. The second call number, **H2479.K39,** follows the first, **H2479.K3,** because the decimal **.39** follows **.3** in numerical order. In the same way, the third call number, **H2479.54,** follows the second, **H2479.K39,** because the decimal **.54** follows **.39** in numerical order.

Write the following seven call numbers in their correct order:

1. B _____
   346 _____
   .N23 _____

2. B _____
   346 _____
   .N237 _____

3. B _____
   346 _____
   .N24 _____

4. B _____
   346 _____
   .19 _____

5. B _____
   346 _____
   .78 _____

6. B _____
   346 _____
   .A4 _____

7. B _____
   346 _____
   .Z16 _____

Learning about the Card Catalog

Whether a library uses the Dewey Decimal System or the Library of Congress System, the best place to begin looking for a book in the library is in the **card catalog.** The card catalog is contained in file drawers in a number of large cabinets in the library. Usually the card catalog is in an easy-to-locate area in the library. All reference cards are filed in alphabetical order and stored in drawers in the card catalog. A card catalog looks like this:

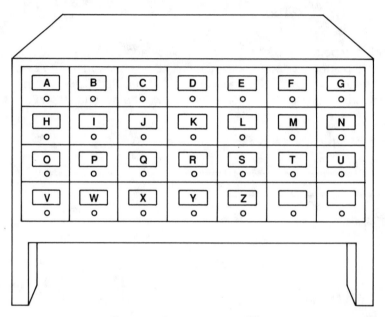

The card catalog contains three different reference cards for every book in the library. The cards are:

author card   This card is used to locate a book when you know the name of the author.

title card   This card is used to locate a book when you know the title of the book.

subject card   This card is used to locate a book when you know the subject.

Answer these questions:

1. When should you use a card catalog?

2. What three types of reference cards will you find in the card catalog?

3. How are the reference cards arranged in the card catalog?

4. Where is the card catalog located in your library?

Author Card

Here is an author card on which numbers have been added to show the information found on author cards.

Author Card

```
1  020.7   2  Michaels, Carolyn Leopold.
   M621L  3  Library Literacy Means Lifelong Learning. 4 Metuchen,
              N.J.
          5  Scarecrow Press,    6 1985.
          7  234 p.
          8  Bibliography:  pp 341–350
```

1. Call number. Always found in upper left-hand corner.

2. Author. Last name first.

3. Title. Sometimes the subtitle is also given.

4. Where published. City and state usually included.

5. Publisher

6. Year of publication

7. Number of pages in the book.

8. If needed, this is used to provide special information.

Look at the information on this author card. Answer the questions.

```
330.1  Fields, Mary Ellen.
F23E   Elementary Economics.
       Chicago, IL.
       Foxmore Press, 1989.
       127 p.
```

1. Who wrote the book? _____

2. In what year was the book published? _____

3. Where was the book published? _____

4. What is the title of the book? _____

5. What is the name of the publisher? _____

6. How many pages are there in the book? _____

7. What is the call number? _____

8. What, if any, special information was provided? _____

_____

Use this information to make an author card.

510.2, W13B.   Basic Mathematics.   Nashville, TN.

1988.   Trueblue Press.   George Williams, author.

243 p.

Title Card

Here is a title card on which numbers have been added to show the information found on title cards.

Title Card

```
1   150.2  2  Psychology and Daily Living.
    M68P   3  Mouly, George.
           4  Los Angeles, CA.
           5  Sunshine Press, 6 1990.
           7  365 p.
           8  Bibliography:  pp 123–125
```

1. Call number

2. Title of book

3. Author

4. Where published. City and state usually included.

5. Publisher

6. Year of publication

7. Number of pages in the book

8. If needed, this is used to provide special information.

Look at the information on this title card. Answer the questions.

```
340    Medical Law.
F96M   Forgan, James F.
       Tucson, AZ.
       Cactus Publishing Company, 1991.
       95 p.
```

1. Who wrote the book? _____

2. In what year was the book published? _____

3. Where was the book published? _____

4. What is the title of the book? _____

5. What is the name of the publisher? _____

6. How many pages are there in the book? _____

7. What is the call number? _____

8. What, if any, special information was provided? _____

_____

9. How is the title card different from the author card? _____

_____

10. Use this information to make a title card

   102p.   Earth Sciences for Today.   Paula Troy, author.
   552.6, T14E.   Star Press, 1990.   146 p.   Austin, TX.

Subject Card

Here is a subject card on which numbers have been added to show the information found on subject cards.

Subject Card

```
1  637.8  2  Agriculture
   M57M  3  Montigue, Sherry
         4  Modern Farming Techniques.
         5  Minneapolis, MN.
         6  Snowmass Publishing House, 7 1991.
         8  231 p.
         9  Maps:   pp 215–222
```

1. Call number

2. Subject

3. Author

4. Title

5. Where published

6. Publisher

7. When published

8. Number of pages in the book

9. If needed, this is used to provide special information

Look at the information on this subject card. Answer the questions.

```
610    Medical sciences
B35H   Bench, Tammy
       Headaches and Other Pains
       Detroit, MI.
       Motor City Press, 1989.
       125 p.
```

1. Who wrote the book? _____

2. In what year was the book published? _____

3. Where was the book published? _____

4. What is the title of the book? _____

5. What is the name of the publisher? _____

6. How many pages are there in the book? _____

7. What is the call number? _____

8. What, if any, special information was provided? _____

_____

9. What is the subject _____

10. How is the subject card different from the author and title card? _____

11. Use this information to make a subject card:

Botanical sciences.   How To Raise Yellow Roses.   90 p.

Steven Schaffer.   Madison, WI.   1990.   Household Press.

Includes 32 color illustrations of roses.   580 S35H

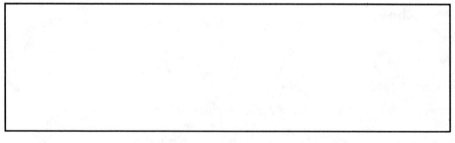

Alphabetical Order in the Card Catalog

You have learned that the card catalog contains author cards, title cards, and subject cards. These cards are arranged in alphabetical order in the card catalog.

Author cards are alphabetized by the last name of the author. Title cards are alphabetized by the first word in the title. Subject cards are alphabetized by the first word in the subject. Words like *the, a,* and *an* are not used when placing titles in alphabetical order.

Place the following in alphabetical order as they would appear in the author, title, or subject card catalog.

George Adams (author)

Exploring the Amazon River (title)

Mary Henderson (author)

Political science (subject)

Logic (subject)

How to Be a Better Student (title)

Music (subject)

Henry Teen (author)

A Guide to National Parks in the United States (title)

AUTHOR CARDS

1. _____

2. _____

3. _____

TITLE CARDS

4. _____

5. _____

6. _____

SUBJECT CARDS

7. _____

8. _____

9. _____

Learning about the *Readers' Guide to Periodical Literature*

The *Readers' Guide to Periodical Literature* will help you locate magazine articles on any topic you wish. *Readers' Guide* is an index to articles found in 175 of the most popular magazines. Many of these magazines will be found in your school or community library. For some of the magazines you may need to go to a college or university library or the main library in a large city.

Magazines are often called *periodicals,* which means "published at a regular interval." Some magazines are published weekly, some monthly, and still others several times a year. *Readers' Guide* can be used to locate magazine articles as far back as the year 1900.

Look at the page from the January 1990 issue of *Readers' Guide.* This page contains information on magazine articles about computers. Notice how many different topics there are about computers. The topics are printed using all capital letters. Also notice that there are subtopics. The subtopics are centered in each column of the page. For most topics there are several magazine articles.

Sometimes "See" or "See also" is written under a topic or subtopic. "See" gives you additional topics that *will* provide you with more information. "See also" gives you additional topics that *may* provide you with more information.

Readers' Guide to Periodical Literature
January 1990

COMPUTER CIRCUITS *See* Integrated circuits
COMPUTER CRIMES
   See also
      Computer viruses
      Desktop forgery
COMPUTER GAMES *See* Video games
COMPUTER GRAPHICS
   See also
      Desktop video
      TIGA (Texas Instruments' Graphics Architecture)
      VGA (Video graphics array)
The brains behind the graphics [graphics coprocessor boards] S. Apiki and others. il *Byte* 14:178–82+ N '89
Ultra Vision. J. Nimersheim. il *Compute!* 11:130+ N '89
        Programming
   See also
      Prograph (Computer program)
Create professional slides and presentations [Freelance Plus] R. Geist and H. Geist. il *Home Office Computing* 7:86–8 N '89
Homework [shape and color games for children] H. E. H. Aycock. il *Compute!* 11:114 N '89
New graphics program debuts in concert hall [acoustic design graphics program developed by Donald Greenberg and Adam Stettner] A. S. Moffat. il *Science* 245:1452 S 29 '89
PC Paintbrush IV. D. Atkin. il *Compute!* 11:119+ N '89
Quality CAD on a budget [DesignCAD] J. Devlin. il *Personal Computing* 13:200+ N '89
A simplified project manager with advanced capabilities [Project Scheduler 4] C. Hlavaty. il *Personal Computing* 13:195 N '89
TekColor lets you really see what you get [color-matching system for the Macintosh] J. Bertolucci and T. Thompson. il *Byte* 14:84+ N '89
Xerox Graph gives data its due [presentation graphics software] L. Kleinman. il *Personal Computing* 13:196+ N '89
        Standards
Clash of the graphics titans. R. Cook. il *Byte* 14 Special Issue: 143–4+ Fall '89
COMPUTER IMAGING CENTER *See* Fine Arts Museum of Long Island. Computer Imaging Center
COMPUTER INDUSTRY
   See also

      Apple Computer Inc.
      Computer service industries
      Data General Corp.
      Intel Corp.
      International Business Machines Corp.
      MIPS Computer Systems Inc.
      Wyse Technology
How computing changes everything: computing in America [cover story; special issue; with editorial comment by Fred Abatemarco] il *Personal Computing* 13:9; 21+ O '89
      Acquisitions and mergers
        International aspects
A Silicon Valley plum may drop into Taiwan's lap [Wyse Technology] D. J. Yang and M. Shao. il *Business Week* p38 D 4 '89
      Export-import trade
Responding to the Japanese 'threat'. P. Saffo. il *Personal Computing* 13:222 O '89
      Information services
   See also
      Gartner Group Inc.
      Management
View from the top. il *Personal Computing* 13:245+ O '89
      Marketing
IBM goes to war. J. Daly. il *Maclean's* 102:46–8 N 27 '89
What slump? F. Langa. il *Byte* 14:8 N '89
      Germany (West)
   See also
      Nixdorf Computer AG
      Japan
   See also
      Sony Corp.
Responding to the Japanese 'threat'. P. Saffo. il *Personal Computing* 13:222 O '89
      United States
See Computer industry
COMPUTER INPUT-OUTPUT EQUIPMENT
   See also
      Computer printers
      Computers—Buses
      Keyboards

Modems
Mouse (Computer equipment)
Speech processing systems
Video display terminals
Video monitors
The BIOS challenge. R. Vishney. *Byte* 14 Special Issue:72 Fall '89
COMPUTER LANGUAGES
See also
  Assembler language (Computer language)
  C (Computer language)
  CaPSL (Computer language)
  Compilers (Computers)
  Lisp (Computer language)
  Pascal (Computer language)
  PCL (Computer language)
  PostScript (Computer language)
  Structured Query Language (Computer language)
COMPUTER LITERATURE
See also
  Booksellers and bookselling—Computer literature
  Publishers and publishing—Computer literature
COMPUTER MUSIC *See* Computers—Musical use
COMPUTER NETWORK PROTOCOLS
See also
  NetBIOS (Local area network)
COMPUTER NETWORKS
See also
  Communications software
  File servers (Computers)
  Information systems
  Local area networks
Supercomputer policy under review [Office of Technology Assessment report] E. Marshall. *Science* 246:207 O 13 '89
COMPUTER OPERATING SYSTEMS
See also
  DOS operating systems
  Mach operating system
  OS/2 operating system
  UNIX operating system
COMPUTER PICTURE BOOKS FOR CHILDREN
Super Story Tree. C. Holzberg. il *Compute!* 11:122–3 N '89
COMPUTER PRINTERS

See also
  Dot matrix printers
  Laser printers
TekColor lets you really see what you get [color-matching system for the Macintosh] J. Bertolucci and T. Thompson. il *Byte* 14:84+ N '89
COMPUTER PROGRAMMING
See also
  Advertising mediums—Computer programming
  Communications software
  Compilers (Computers)
  Computer-aided software engineering
  Computer graphics—Programming
  Computer service industries
  Computer viruses
  Computers—Accounting use—Programming
  Computers—Architectural use—Programming
  Computers—Art use—Programming
  Computers—Business use—Programming
  Computers—Educational use—Programming
  Computers—Financial services use—Programming
  Computers—Investment use—Programming
  Computers—Mailing list use—Programming
  Computers—Musical use—Programming
  Computers—Photographic use—Programming
  Data structures (Computer science)
  Desktop publishing—Programming
  File organization (Computers)
  Floating-point arithmetic
  HyperCard (Computer program)
  Object-oriented programming
  Personal information management software
  Presentation Manager (Computer program)
  Prototyper (Computer program)
  Spreadsheets (Computer programs)
  VisiCalc (Computer program)
  Windows (Computer programs)
How computing changes everything: computing in America [cover story; special issue; with editorial comment by Fred Abatemarco] il *Personal Computing* 13:9, 21+ O '89
Anecdotes, facetiae, satire, etc.
Mice in the kitchen [Apple Computer] D. Gookin. *Compute!* 11:143 N '89

Complete the following:

1. Write the names of three topics found on this page. _____

_____

2. For the topic *Computer Graphics*, write the names of the subtopics. _____

_____

3. For the topic *Computer Industry* and its subtopics, how many different magazine articles

are listed? _____

4. Write the "See also" topics for the topic *Computer Industry*. _____

_____

Reading an Entry in *Readers' Guide*

Entries in *Readers' Guide* are written with some abbreviations. One common abbreviation is **il,** which tells you that there are illustrations in the article. The year is abbreviated as **'91** for "1991." The months of the year are abbreviated in the following way:

Ja	January
F	February
Mr	March
Ap	April
My	May
Je	June
Jl	July
Ag	August
S	September
O	October
N	November
D	December

Here is an entry from *Readers' Guide*. Study it to learn how to read a *Readers' Guide* entry. The parts have been labeled for you.

Title ⟶ Mice in the kitchen (Apple Computer)

Author ⟶ D. Gookin. **Compute!** 11: 143 N ⟍ '89 — Day of month

Magazine

Volume

Page

Month

Year

12

Label each of the parts of this entry.

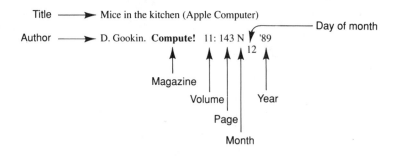

IBM goes to war. J. Daly. Maclean's

102:46–8 N 27 '89

Locating Information Using *Readers' Guide*

Here are the steps you should follow when using *Readers' Guide* to find magazine articles on a topic. As your teacher discusses each step, make notes that will help you use these steps.

1. Select a topic.

2. Locate *Readers' Guide* in the library.

3. Collect the issues you need for your search.

4. Locate magazine articles on your topic.

5. Use "See" and "See also" to locate additional magazine articles.

Locating Magazines in Your Library

Here are some popular magazines. Look for each in your library. For each magazine listed here, answer these questions:

1. Is it in the card catalog?

2. What is the date of the most current issue you can find?

3. Are there bound volumes of this magazine in your library?

Time	1. _____	2. _____	3. _____
Popular Mechanics	1. _____	2. _____	3. _____
Newsweek	1. _____	2. _____	3. _____
Car and Driver	1. _____	2. _____	3. _____
Jet	1. _____	2. _____	3. _____
Home Office Computing	1. _____	2. _____	3. _____
Current History	1. _____	2. _____	3. _____
National Geographic	1. _____	2. _____	3. _____
Scientific American	1. _____	2. _____	3. _____
Psychology Today	1. _____	2. _____	3. _____

Learning about Newspapers and Their Indexes

When you need more current information than you can find in books or magazine articles, you should look for the information in newspapers. Most school and community libraries subscribe to local newspapers as well as a number of national newspapers. Newspapers are usually kept in the library for up to one year.

For some newspapers, back issues more than one year old are available on microfilm. Some major newspapers publish indexes to help you locate articles that appeared in past issues. Here are four important newspaper indexes.

> *New York Times Index,* 1913 to date (New York: New York Times Company) This index to articles that appeared in the *New York Times* is published twice each month and is accumulated into annual volumes. It is an excellent source of in-depth articles on almost every subject.
>
> *Wall Street Journal Index,* 1958 to date (New York: Dow Jones). This is an index to articles that appeared in the *Wall Street Journal.* It is a particularly good source of articles about business.
>
> *Washington Post Newspaper Index,* 1972 to date (Wooster, OH: Bell and Howell). This is an index to articles that appeared in the *Washington Post.* It is a particularly useful source for articles about the U.S. government.
>
> *Index to the Christian Science Monitor International Daily Newspaper,* 1960 to date (Boston: Christian Science Monitor). This is an index to articles that appeared in the Christian Science Monitor. It is a useful source for articles on topics of general human interest.

Answer these questions:

1. To which types of newspapers do most libraries subscribe?

   _____

   _____

2. For how long do libraries keep newspapers? _____

3. In what form do libraries keep issues of newspapers that are more than one year old?

   _____

4. Which newspaper has been indexing its newspaper articles for the most years?

   _____

5. Which newspaper would be the best source of articles about business?

_____

6. Which newspaper would be the best source of articles about the U.S. government?

_____

7. Which newspaper provides articles on topics of general human interest?

_____

8. Which newspaper is an excellent source of in-depth articles on most subjects?

_____

The New York Times Index

The *New York Times* is probably the single best source of in-depth articles on almost every subject. Articles that have appeared in the *New York Times* have been indexed since 1913. Most libraries that have the *New York Times Index* also have a microfilm collection of this newspaper. This means you can locate and read articles that appeared in the *New York Times* from 1913 to the present.

To locate articles in the *New York Times Index,* you must look for the articles by subject and not by title or author. Once you locate the subject, you will find the articles about that subject that appeared in the *New York Times*. For each article, the index provides a variety of information.

Look at the sample entry from the *New York Times Index* for 1981. Read the explanation that goes with the entry.

1 Travel

2 •*Hawaii*

3 Robert Trumbull article on travel attractions in Hawaii;

4 illustrations **5** (L), **6** Jl 12 **7** 2:1

1. Tells the main heading. You can tell it is the main heading by the boldface type.

2. Identifies a subdivision. You can tell it is a subdivision by the large dot and italic type.

3. This is an abstract or short comment about the article that tells what it is about.

4. If an illustration appears in the article, the word *Illustrations* will be found here.

5. (L) means a long article of two columns or more; (M) means a medium-length item up to two columns in length; (S) means a short item, usually a half column or less in length.

6. Tells the month and date the article appeared in the *New York Times*.

7. Tells the page number and column number where the article appears.

Look at this entry from the *New York Times Index* for 1991. Then answer the following questions.

Automobiles

•*Race cars*

Bill Wildman's account of the Indianapolis 500 race.

illustrations (M), Je4,17:2

1. What is this article about?

2. Who wrote the article?

3. Under which heading does the article appear?

4. Under which subdivision does the article appear?

5. How long is the article?

6. What date did the article appear?

7. On what page would you look for the article?

8. In what column would you look to find the article?

Other Important References

The library has many other references you can use to locate information. These references are located in the reference section of your library. Some of the references tell you where to locate information. Others have the information you need right there. Here are some important references you should know about.

Oxford English Dictionary. This reference is the most complete dictionary of the English language. It will help you trace the history of a word about which you want to know more. The definitions are very complete. Sometimes quotations are used to show how a word is used in different ways.

Dictionary of Slang and Unconventional English. This is a good reference for obtaining information on colloquialisms, catch-phrases, slang usage, nicknames, and other unconventional uses of language.

Roget's International Thesaurus. This is a source of synonyms, or alternative words for an idea. It will give you a range of words you can use to express an idea more precisely.

The World Almanac and Book of Facts. This is a source of information on a wide range of topics of general interest, including population, sports, government, and health.

Information Please Almanac, Atlas, and Yearbook. This is a source of information on many topics. It includes many graphs, charts, lists, and other visuals to provide you with information.

Facts on File. This is a summary of many facts related to news events that occurred nationally and internationally.

A Handbook to Literature. This is a good source of information on the history of British and American literature. It clarifies important words and concepts.

Reader's Encyclopedia. This reference provides information on literature, music, and the arts. Brief statements are provided on authors, terms, expressions, plots, characters, places, events, and the general literary movement.

New Illustrated Encyclopedia of World History. This reference lists chronologically events in history from prehistoric times to modern times. This is a good source for seeing how historic events relate to each other.

Current Biography. This is a good source of extensive information on people who appear in the news.

Who's Who in America. This reference contains biographies, mostly of living Americans who achieved prominence in some way. It also includes some biographies of non-Americans who became prominent in America. It is an interesting source of information on famous people.

International Who's Who. This reference contains biographies of people from throughout the world who have become prominent for their actions and deeds.

Answer these questions:

Which reference would you use to locate information on the following:

1. To locate synonyms _____

2. To learn about a famous person in the news _____

3. To learn the history of a word _____

4. To learn about a famous American _____

5. To learn what a slang word means _____

6. To learn about important developments in American literature _____

7. To learn about the events of the American revolution _____

8. To learn about the plot of a famous novel _____

9. To learn about a famous scientist from Sweden _____

Government Document Searches

The U.S. government publishes materials on many subjects. Your library may have a special section where government publications are kept. Visit your library and ask the librarian the following questions to learn more about government publications available for your use. Write the librarian's answers here.

1. Where are the U.S. government publications kept in your school or community library?

2. Which librarian is assigned to help students use government publications?

3. Place a check(√) in front of each of the following that is found in your library.

   Monthly Catalog of United States Government Publications

   Guide to U.S. Government Publications

   List of Classes of United States Government Publications Available for Selection by Depository Libraries

   American Statistics Index: A Comprehensive Guide and Index to the Statistical Publications of the U.S. Government

   Congressional Information Services Index to Publications of the United States Congress

   Publications Reference File

   Government Reports Announcements and Index

   Statistical Abstract of the United States

4. For those found in your library, write a brief description of the information contained in the publication.

Using the Computer to Do Database Searches

Computers may be used to search for information that is not in your school or community library. This is done by accessing databases stored in computers at other locations. You may be able to obtain information from databases using a computer at your school or community library. Visit your school or community library and ask the librarian the following questions. Write the answers here.

1. Does this library have access to databases?

2. If yes, which ones?

3. If no, which is the closest library that does have access to databases? (If possible, visit this library to complete this page.)

4. Do you have any material that describes these databases?

5. Do I need authorization to use a database?

6. Do I have to pay to use the database? How much?

7. How long does it take to get the data?

8. Do I need special training?

9. Are there pamphlets or books that explain how to do a database search? If yes, list the titles here.

10. Is there someone who can explain how to use the database? What is this person's name?

What I Have Learned

Directions: Show what you have learned about using the library by writing an answer for each of the following.

1. What are the three steps in the strategy you learned for using the library?

2. What are the names of the two major systems used for organizing libraries?

3. What system is used to organize your school library?

4. What are the three primary references you need to know how to use?

5. Identify three secondary references that would be useful for obtaining information in the library.

6. What three types of reference cards are found in the card catalog?

7. How are the reference cards arranged in a card catalog?

8. What reference would you use to find information in magazines?

9. Name a major newspaper for which there is an index in your library.

Answers for Chapter 5 Reproducibles

5-1　Notes will vary.

5-2　1. 700–799.　2. 500–599.　3. 200–299.　4. 400–499.　5. 000–099.　6. 900–999.
7. 100–199.　8. 800–899.　9. 300–399.　10. 600–699.

5-3　1. 220.　2. 070.　3. 620.　4. 150.　5. 460.　6. 370.　7. 530.　8. 970.　9. 810.
10. 730.　11. To organize books according to their general content.　12. To organize
books according to their specific content.

5-4　1. Thomas.　2. *Understanding Physics.*　3. First letter in author's last name.　4. First
letter in title of book.　5. 5.　6. 3.　7. This number is assigned to all books written by this
author.

5-5　1. P = Language and Literature; C = Auxiliary Sciences of History; U = Military Science; D
= History: General and Old World; G = Geography. Anthropology. Recreation. 2. K, T, N,
D, A.

5-6　E, 279, .G3 = Primary class and subdivisions. P = first letter in author's last name. 2 =
second author whose last name begins with the letter *p* to have written a book in this
primary class and subdivision. 1988 = year of publication. C4 = Library has four copies of
this book.

5-7　1. B, 346, .Z16　2. B, 346, .19　3. B, 346, .N23　4. B, 346, .N237　5. B, 346, .N24
6. B, 346, .A4　7. B, 346, .78

5-8　1. To locate a book in the library.　2. Author, Title, Subject.　3. Alphabetical order.
4. Answers will vary.

5-9　1. Mary Ellen Fields　2. 1989　3. Chicago, IL　4. *Elementary Economics*　5. Foxmore
Press　6. 127　7. 330.1, F23E　8. None　9. 510.2　Williams, George
　　　　　　　　　　　　　　　　　　　　　　　　　　　　W13B　Basic Mathematics.
　　　　　　　　　　　　　　　　　　　　　　　　　　　　　　　　Nashville, TN
　　　　　　　　　　　　　　　　　　　　　　　　　　　　　　　　Trueblue Press, 1988.
　　　　　　　　　　　　　　　　　　　　　　　　　　　　　　　　243 p.

5-10　1. James F. Forgan.　2. 1991.　3. Tucson, AZ.　4. *Medical Law.*　5. Cactus Publishing
Company.　6. 95.　7. 340, F96M.　8. None.　9. The first entry is the title of the book.
10. 552.6　Earth Sciences for Today
　　　T14E　Troy, Paula
　　　　　　　Austin, TX
　　　　　　　Star Press, 1990.
　　　　　　　146 p.

5-11　1. Tammy Bench.　2. 1989.　3. Detroit, MI.　4. *Headaches and Other Pains.*　5. Motor
City Press.　6. 125 p.　7. 610, B35H.　8. None.　9. Medical Sciences.　10. The first
entry is the subject of the book.
11. 580　Botanical Sciences
　　　S35H Schaffer, Steven
　　　　　　　How to Raise Yellow Roses
　　　　　　　Madison, WI
　　　　　　　Household Press, 1990.
　　　　　　　90 p.
　　　　　　　Includes 32 color illustrations of roses.

5-12   1. George Adams.   2. Mary Henderson.   3. Henry Teen.   4. *Exploring the Amazon River.*   5. *A Guide to National Parks in the United States.*   6. *How to Be a Better Student.*   7. Logic.   8. Music.   9. Political Science.

5-13   1. Any 3 of the 16 topics shown in all capital letters.   2. Programming, Standards.   3. 6.
4. Apple Computer Inc.
Computer service industries
Data General Corp.
Intel Corp.
International Business Machines Corp.
MIPS Computer Systems Inc.
Wyse Technology

5-14   IBM goes to war. = Title
J. Daly. = Author
Maclean's = Magazine
102: = Volume number
46–8 = Pages
N = Month
27 = Day of month
'89 = Year

5-15   Notes will vary.

5-16   Answers will vary.

5-17   1. Local and national newspapers.   2. Up to one year.   3. Microfilm.   4. *New York Times.*
5. *Wall Street Journal.*   6. *Washington Post.*   7. *Christian Science Monitor.*   8. *New York Times.*

5-18   1. Indianapolis 500 Race.   2. Bill Wildman.   3. Automobiles.   4. Race cars.   5. 17.   6. June 4.   7. 2.

5-19.   1. *Roget's International Thesaurus.*   2. *Current Biography.*   3. *Oxford English Dictionary.*
4. *Who's Who in America.*   5. *Dictionary of Slang and Unconventional English.*   6. *Handbook to Literature.*   7. *The New Illustrated Encyclopedia of World History.*   8. *Reader's Encyclopedia.*   9. *International Who's Who.*

5-20.   Answers will vary.

5-21.   Answers will vary.

5-22.   1. (a) Find out how the library is organized.   (b) Learn how to use primary references.
(c) Learn how to use secondary references.   2. (a) Dewey Decimal System.   (b) Library of Congress System.   3. Answers will vary.   4. (a) Card Catalog.   (b) *Readers' Guide.*
(c) *New York Times Index.*   5. Any three of the following: dictionaries, almanacs, encyclopedias, biographies, government publications, databases. 6. (a) Author.   (b) Title.
(C) Subject.   7. Alphabetically.   8. *Reader's Guide.*   9. Answers will vary.

CHAPTER 6

Using Reference Books

■ Purposes

The purposes of this chapter are to:
1. teach students with learning disabilities strategies for using basic reference books.
2. provide reproducibles that can be used to help students learn to use basic reference books.

■ Titles of Reproducibles

■ RATIONALE

Students with learning disabilities cannot become independent learners if they remain solely dependent on their teachers and textbooks for information. It is important to make students with learning disabilities aware of the important reference books they can use on their own whenever they need information beyond that normally provided in class.

Mastropieri and Scruggs (1987) stated that students with learning disabilities must understand the different purposes that various reference books serve and must be able to identify the appropriate time to use each type of reference books. There are many reference books available to students. They range from general to specific and are available in school and public libraries. We recommend that students with learning disabilities be taught the use of the following basic reference books: dictionary, encyclopedia, thesaurus, almanac, and atlas.

■ BACKGROUND INFORMATION

In this section we provide information about the basic reference books. For each type of reference book, we present the steps that students with learning disabilities can use to obtain the information they need for different school purposes.

The Dictionary

Types of dictionaries. There are four types of dictionaries with which students with learning disabilities need to become familiar:

1. *Unabridged dictionaries.* These dictionaries contain entries for most of the common words in the English language. Although they do not contain all the words in the English language, they usually contain between 250,000 and 500,000 entries. An *entry* is a word, abbreviation, affix, or the like that appears in column format in the dictionary.

There are a number of publishing companies that publish and sell unabridged dictionaries. The most common are *Webster's Third New International Dictionary of the English Language, Unabridged,* and *The Random House Dictionary of the English Language.* You may have one or the other of these in your school library. Students will be able to identify an unabridged dictionary by its large size and by the appearance of the word *Unabridged* in the title. The unabridged dictionary found in the school library is the important one for students to be familiar with and know how to use.

The most complete dictionary of the English language is the *Oxford Dictionary of the English Language.* It contains more than one million entries and is continually being revised because new words are added to our language every day. Twenty-nine separate volumes form the current edition of the *Oxford Dictionary.*

2. *Abridged dictionaries.* These are shortened forms of unabridged dictionaries, usually containing between 50,000 and 100,000 entries. The major advantage of abridged dictionaries is their smaller size. They can be easily carried in a bookbag or pocket. Their major disadvantage is that they may not contain an uncommon entry about which a student needs to know.

Many abridged dictionaries are published in paperback form. They are relatively inexpensive and probably can be purchased by any student. Although an abridged dictionary will meet the needs of students with learning disabilities most of the time, students need to be taught to refer to an unabridged dictionary when an entry word does not appear in an abridged dictionary.

3. *Special dictionaries.* The explosion of knowledge and expansion of technical fields has produced many special words with meanings specific to their subject area. Although unabridged and even abridged dictionaries may contain an entry for such words, more complete definitions are usually provided in one of the special dictionaries. In addition, special dictionaries provide definitions for the jargon of a field.

An increasing number of special dictionaries are commonly found in such areas as medicine, psychology, education, business, and technology. Students need to be taught to determine if there is a special dictionary for subjects they are studying.

4. *Electronic dictionaries.* Today, students with learning disabilities also need to be familiar with the many different hand-size electronic dictionaries that are available. These electronic dictionaries are another form of an abridged dictionary; some are so small they fit in a shirt pocket. Those electronic devices that provide only synonyms or antonyms are more accurately referred to as electronic thesauruses.

Some of the most useful electronic dictionaries for students with learning disabilities have a "sounds like" function. This is particularly useful for students who spell words the way they sound and need this function to locate correct spellings of words.

Many students with learning disabilities do not realize the extensive amount of information contained in dictionaries. Students think that a dictionary is used only to determine what a word means, but dictionaries actually contain many types of standard information for each entry. Figure 6.1 shows a sample dictionary entry with the various types of information numbered.

At the bottom of each right-hand page in the dictionary is a short pronunciation

FIGURE 6.1 Sample dictionary entry

1 **remedy** 2 (rem̀ i dē) 3 n., tr. v. 4 (a) something that cures an illness. (b) something that corrects an evil. (c) legal redress. (d) legal means of correcting a wrong. 5. remedies, remedied, remedying. 6 L (f = remedi(um) 7 the doctor prescribed aspirin as a remedy for his headache. 8. Syn. cure. Ant. worsen (9)

1. correct spelling of entry word

2. phonetic respelling for pronunciation

3. parts of speech

4. definition in order of common use

5. variants of the word

6. etymology or origin of the word

7. correct usage in a sentence

8. synonym or antonym

(9) (illustration if appropriate)

key. This key contains letters, symbols, and words to help students pronounce words they do not know how to say. At the front of the dictionary there is a long pronunciation key to help students pronounce words for which the short pronunciation key is inadequate. The short pronunciation key will be adequate for the vast majority of words encountered by students with learning disabilities.

In addition to the standard information found in dictionaries, some dictionaries include special reference materials such as calendars, geographical names, signs and symbols, weights and measures, short biographies, and other useful information. The nature of the special reference materials varies from dictionary to dictionary.

Using the Dictionary. To use a dictionary efficiently, students with learning disabilities need to know about entries, guide words, root words, and how to locate a word quickly using knowledge of alphabetical order.

1. *Entries.* An entry is a word, term, phrase, abbreviation, or affix that appears in alphabetical order in the dictionary. Entries are printed in boldface type to make them stand out from the other information provided.

2. *Guide words.* The *opening guide word* is the first word listed in the alphabetical sequence of entries on a page in the dictionary. The *closing guide word* is the last entry on the page. Both the opening and closing guide words appear at the top of the page to show all entries that alphabetically fall between these guide words. By using guide words to locate an entry, students do not have to look at every entry on a page.

3. *Root word.* The root of any word is a word without any prefixes and suffixes. For example, the root word for *unpredictable* is *predict. Un* is the prefix and *able* is the suffix. Frequently a word with an attached prefix or suffix does not appear in a dictionary. Students need to be able to identify separately the root word and the prefix and/or suffix so they can learn the definition of the word. For example, the word *uncharacteristic* may not appear in the dictionary. The student can locate the definitions for *characteristic* and for the prefix *un* and combine them to derive the meaning of the word.

Students also need to know that for root words ending in *e,* the *e* is dropped when a suffix that begins with a vowel is added. For example, *smile + ing = smiling.* Students need to know that for some words that end in a single consonant, that consonant is doubled before adding a suffix that begins with a vowel. For example, *trip + ing = tripping.*

4. *Location of entry.* Students need to use their knowledge of alphabetical order to locate entries quickly. First they need to think of the dictionary as divided into thirds. Words beginning with the letters *a* through *g* make up the first third of the dictionary, *h* through *p* the middle third, and *q* through *z* the final third. Knowing this division enables students to turn quickly to the section of the dictionary where the word they are seeking will be located. Then students can use their knowledge of alphabetical order and the guide words to locate the entry they want.

The Encyclopedia

An encyclopedia is a special type of reference book that contains articles on a wide variety of subjects written by experts. The articles found in an encyclopedia offer students the opportunity to gain information on a subject quickly.

Because the encyclopedia contains so much information, it usually is published in a number of volumes. The volumes are arranged in alphabetical order so that a student who wants to obtain information about "baseball," for example, would look for this topic in the "B" volume. Letters are stamped on the spine of each volume to show the alphabetical range of information included in the volume. For example, if a volume is stamped with the letters T-U-V, it contains articles in subjects ranging from T through V. Guide words are printed at the top of each page to help users quickly locate their topic of interest.

Students should be taught that the encyclopedia is a great place to start learning about a subject. It allows students to go to one source and quickly learn many of the important facts about a topic. As students read the article about a subject, they will learn about important dates, people, events, and other information pertaining to the topic. Often the article is divided into subtopics, allowing students to focus on the particular part of the topic that is of most important at that time.

An encyclopedia may also provide a recommended outline for preparing a paper on a topic. Many articles contain a bibliography at the end listing authoritative books on the topic. Students who wish to go beyond the general information contained in the encyclopedia can use these books as important sources of additional information. Some encyclopedias also contain a list of "Additional Readings" that students can use to broaden their knowledge about a topic.

Encyclopedias have an index that can be used to locate information on a topic. The index is used to get information on one topic from several different articles throughout the encyclopedia. For example, information on the topic "gold" may be found under gold, minerals, mining, and money. By using the index, students are cross-referenced to other relevant topic headings such as minerals, mining, and money that they would not locate by just going to the entry "gold" itself.

The Thesaurus

A thesaurus is a reference book containing synonyms for commonly used words. It is an important reference for writing papers. Teachers have observed that students with learning disabilities usually write papers using only a limited variety of words. By using a thesaurus, students with learning disabilities can expand the number of different words they use in their writing, thereby making their papers more interesting to read.

A thesaurus also enables students to give more precision to their writing. For example, if a student wanted to write that the federal government took over a company that went bankrupt, the student might write that the government "grabbed" the company. Because *grabbed* indicates a forceful, physical occurrence, it may be more accurate to use a synonym from a thesaurus, such as *seized,* which implies that the government took control legally.

Like a dictionary, a thesaurus lists words alphabetically and provides guide words for locating entry words. A thesaurus also provides synonyms for various forms of a word. For example, synonyms are provided for the word *leave* as a noun ("vacation") or as a verb ("exit").

The Almanac

An almanac is a reference book that provides summaries, tables, charts, statistics, and other useful information on an extensive range of subjects. For example, in a recent edition of the *Information Please Almanac,* the editors highlighted the following features: what's happening in world affairs, the latest scientific information, the earth's vital statistics, maps and illustrations, sports, history, religion, taxes, cities and states, calendars, celebrities, travel, and much more. A number of special articles by experts were also included.

Almanacs are updated yearly. They contain an enormous amount of information presented in a variety of formats. Students with learning disabilities must be taught how to use the index included in the almanac. Further, students must be taught how to interpret the graphs, tables, charts, diagrams, and maps that appear in the almanac. Chapter 7 of this book contains ideas for teaching students how to use and interpret such visual aids.

The Atlas

An atlas is a book of maps. There are different types of atlases, each of which serves a different purpose. A geographical atlas provides maps that show the features of the earth's surface, such as oceans, lakes, rivers, mountains, and plateaus, and even more detail if necessary. A political atlas provides maps that show how the earth is divided into different countries, states, and important cities and other political regions. A road atlas contains maps that help people travel from one place to another. Many different types of atlases are available in a school or public library. Students should be taught to look for an atlas whenever they need information that is best presented through maps.

In Chapter 7 of this book we present information for teaching students with learning disabilities how to use and interpret maps.

■ TEACHING PLAN

Here is a plan for teaching students with learning disabilities how to use reference books.

1. Ask students to tell what they know about dictionaries, encyclopedias, thesauruses, almanacs, and atlases. Make a list of the facts the students present under each title on the chalkboard. Tell the students they will be studying these valuable reference books and learning how to use each.

   Distribute Reproducible 6-1, "Learning about Dictionaries." Have the students read to learn about unabridged, abridged, special, and electronic dictionaries. Then have them complete the questions. Show or have the students locate and examine samples of each type of dictionary. Create opportunities for the students to use each type of dictionary as part of class assignments.

2. Use Reproducible 6-2, "Information Found on a Dictionary Page," to acquaint students with the variety of information found on a dictionary page. Have the students read the instructional material and complete the activity on their own. Later, use the activity to discuss what is found on a dictionary page. Have students look at the page contents of their own dictionaries as well as others from the school library.

3. Use Reproducible 6-3, "Opening and Closing Guide Words," to familiarize students with the use of opening and closing guide words. Emphasize that opening and closing guide words help students locate entry words on dictionary pages. Then have the students complete the activity. Later, you may want to give your students some practice in using guide words to locate entry words in their own dictionaries.

4. Use Reproducible 6-4, "Locating Words Quickly in the Dictionary," to teach students how to use their knowledge of alphabetical order to locate entry words quickly. First, they need to understand how to open a dictionary to the approximate location of the entry word they want to find. Second, they need to understand how to use their knowledge of the alphabet to place words in order by second, third, and fourth letters. The activities on 6-4 will help them develop these understandings.

5. Use Reproducible 6-5, "Phonetic Respellings," to teach students how to use the short and long pronunciation keys found in their dictionary to pronounce words they do not know how to say. After the students have written the phonetic respellings of the words, help them use the two pronunciation keys found in their dictionaries to pronounce the respelled words.

6. Use Reproducible 6-6, "Choosing the Correct Definition," to show students how to choose a definition for a word. Explain to the students that before they choose a definition for a word, they must read each definition provided for that word to decide which definition best fits the context.

7. Use Reproducible 6-7, "Roots and Variants of Dictionary Entry Words," to explain how root words are identified. Students need to understand that sometimes they will not be able to locate a word in its inflected form in the dictionary. This activity will help them find root words among inflected and variant forms of words.

8. Distribute Reproducible 6-8, "Learning about Encyclopedias." Use the contents of this page to familiarize students with some of the characteristics of all encyclopedias. Then have the students complete the activity to practice selecting volumes of an encyclopedia for different topics.

9. Use Reproducible 6-9, "Different Encyclopedias," to introduce the students to four of the most useful comprehensive encyclopedias. If possible, bring a sample volume from each of these encyclopedias to show to the students. After reading about each, have the students answer the questions. Have the students further familiarize themselves with each encyclopedia by examining it in their school or community library.

10. Use Reproducible 6-10, "Helpful Aids Found in the Encyclopedia," to show students the different types of aids provided for them. Point out that major encyclopedias provide many useful aids to help students find, understand, and organize information on any topic. Then have students visit the library to answer the questions in 6-10.

11. Distribute Reproducible 6-11, "Learning about the Thesaurus." Use 6-11 to show students how a thesaurus is used to improve the effectiveness of communication in writing. Have the students complete the activity.

12. Use Reproducible 6-12, "Practice Using a Thesaurus," to show students how sentence meaning is changed by manipulating word choice. Encourage students to purchase a thesaurus if they do not already own one. Have them use their thesaurus in daily writing assignments.

13. Distribute Reproducible 6-13, "Learning about the Almanac." Use 6-13 to introduce students to this valuable source of statistical information and short articles on a variety of topics. Show the students an example of an almanac such as the *Information Please Almanac* or *The World Almanac and Book of Facts*. Have the students complete the activity by answering the questions about the table shown in Reproducible 6-13.

14. Distribute Reproducible 6-14, "Learning about the Atlas." Use 6-14 to introduce students to an atlas as a collection of maps that provide information on a variety of subjects. Emphasize that there are three different types of atlases: geographical, political, and road. Show samples of atlases available in your library. Demonstrate how an atlas can be used to learn about history, geography, and other subjects. Have the students complete the activity.

15. Distribute Reproducible 6-15, "What I Have Learned." Use this reproducible to evaluate how well your students learned what was taught in this chapter. Use any of the reproducibles as needed for review purposes.

Learning about Dictionaries

Dictionaries are handy references to information on words. Dictionaries will help you pronounce a word, discover its meaning, and learn how it is spelled. You need a good pocket dictionary you can carry with you and a more comprehensive dictionary for use where you study. From time to time you may need to go to the library to use an even more comprehensive dictionary to learn more about a word.

There are four basic types of dictionaries you should know about. Each has its own value, and knowing about them will help you decide when to use each one.

Unabridged Dictionary. Most unabridged dictionaries contain between 250,000 and 1,000,000 entries. An entry is a word, abbreviation, prefix, suffix, or word part that is listed and defined in the dictionary. The word *unabridged* appears in the title and means "not condensed or shortened." Unabridged dictionaries are very large books. Some unabridged dictionaries are several volumes long. The most complete unabridged dictionary of the English language is the *Oxford Dictionary of the English Language.* It contains more than 1,000,000 entries and has 29 separate volumes.

Abridged Dictionaries. Abridged dictionaries are shortened forms of unabridged dictionaries. The word *abridged* means "shortened by the omission of something." Abridged dictionaries omit words that are not used very often. They usually contain between 50,000 and 100,000 entries. Abridged dictionaries are smaller, lighter, and less expensive than unabridged dictionaries. Some abridged dictionaries are available in paperback form and are small enough to carry in your pocket.

Special Dictionaries. Special dictionaries are found in the fields of medicine, psychology, education, business, and technology. While an unabridged dictionary may have a definition for a technical word from one of these areas, the more complete technical definition is found in one of the special dictionaries.

Electronic Dictionaries. Until recently, nearly all dictionaries were found in book form. Today, hand-size electronic dictionaries that hold 100,000 or more entries are available. Some are so small they fit into a shirt pocket. Some electronic dictionaries provide definitions; others provide only synonyms or antonyms. Some also provide a voice pronunciation of each word. Their small size and the voice pronunciation feature make electronic dictionaries very useful. Someday these dictionaries will probably replace small paperback dictionaries as students' pocket dictionary of choice.

Answer these questions:

1. Which type of dictionary has the most entries? _____

_____

2. A paperback dictionary in book form is an example of which type of dictionary?

_____

3. Which type of dictionary is likely to become the pocket dictionary of the future?

_____

4. Why? _____

_____

5. Where should you look for the most complete definition of a technical word?

_____

6. What is the name of the most complete dictionary of the English language?

_____

7. How many volumes does this dictionary contain? _____

8. Which type of dictionary do you use most often? _____

_____

9. Locate an unabridged dictionary. Write the title, publisher, year of publication and number of pages here.

_____

_____

_____

10. Locate an abridged dictionary. Write the title, publisher, year of publication and number of pages here.

_____

_____

Information Found on a Dictionary Page

Read about the many types of information found on a dictionary page. Then identify each type of information by placing a number in the box near the information on the dictionary page provided.

1. *Guide words.* There are two guide words at the top of every dictionary page. The first guide word is called the *opening guide word* and tells the first word on the page. The second guide word is called the *closing guide word* and tells the last word on the page.

2. *Entry words.* These are the words listed and defined on the dictionary page. They appear in darker or bolder type on the dictionary page.

3. *Phonetic respelling.* After each entry word you will see a respelling for that entry. The respelling often uses different letters and symbols to show you how to pronounce the word. If you do not know what the letters or symbols mean, look at the *short pronunciation key* found at the bottom of every right-hand page.

4. *Part of speech.* Usually following the respelling you will find an abbreviation that tells the part of speech of the entry. Here are the abbreviations for the common parts of speech:

n = noun	pron = pronoun
v = verb	adv = adverb
adj = adjective	prep = preposition

5. *Definitions.* The definitions for each entry word are presented. The definitions are numbered to show the order of their common use. The most commonly used definition appears first, following the number 1. The next most common definition is numbered 2, and so on.

6. *Variants of the word.* Different forms of the word may also be presented as part of the entry. For example, for the word *define* you may also find the variants *defined* and *defining*.

7. *Origin or etymology.* In some dictionaries you will also find information that tells you where the word came from. For example, the letter G might be used to show that the word came from the Greek language, or L to show that it has a Latin origin.

8. *Correct usage in a sentence.* Sometimes a sentence containing the entry word is provided. The sentence shows how the word is used in a sentence. For example, to illustrate the meaning of the word *enforce* the following sentence might be provided:

   A police officer must *enforce* the law.

9. *Synonym or antonym.* Sometimes following the abbreviation *syn* a synonym for the entry word is provided. Sometimes following *ant* an antonym is provided.

10. *Illustration.* Sometimes drawings, pictures, or other types of visuals are presented to illustrate the word.

11. *Short pronunciation key.* This key to the pronunciation of words is usually found at the bottom of every right-hand page. The short pronunciation key contains letters, symbols, and words that will help you pronounce entries you do not know how to say. If the short pronunciation key does not help you pronounce an entry, then look at the long pronunciation key located in the front of your dictionary.

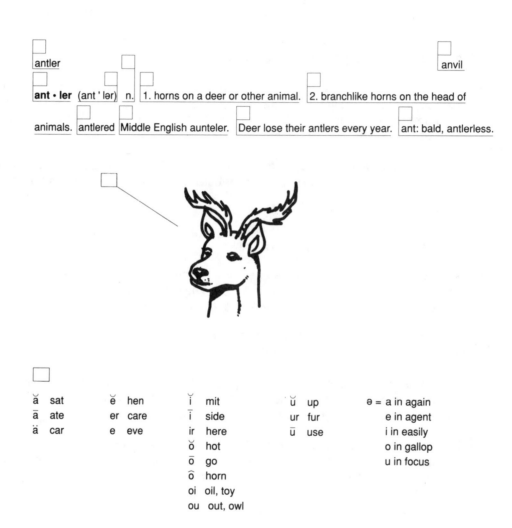

antler

anvil

ant • ler (ant ' lər) n. 1. horns on a deer or other animal. 2. branchlike horns on the head of animals. antlered Middle English aunteler. Deer lose their antlers every year. ant: bald, antlerless.

ă	sat	ĕ	hen	ĭ	mit	ŭ	up	ə = a in again
ā	ate	er	care	ī	side	ur	fur	e in agent
ä	car	e	eve	ir	here	ū	use	i in easily
				ŏ	hot			o in gallop
				ō	go			u in focus
				ô	horn			
				oi	oil, toy			
				ou	out, owl			

Opening and Closing Guide Words ━━━━━━━

At the top of every dictionary page you will find two very special words. They are called *guide words* because they guide you to the entry word you want to find. The first is called the *opening guide word* because it tells the first entry word to appear on the page. The second is called the *closing guide word* because it tells the last entry word to appear on the page. All the words that appear on a dictionary page are in alphabetical order, starting with the opening guide word and ending with the closing guide word.

When looking for an entry word, begin by comparing the entry word with the opening and closing guide words at the top of each dictionary page. When you find that the entry word you are looking for is alphabetically between these two guide words, you know the entry word will be on that page. Sometimes, however, the word you are looking for is not in the dictionary you are using. In these cases, you will need to look in a more comprehensive dictionary.

Use what you know about the alphabet to arrange each of the following pairs of guide words into alphabetical order. In each pair, one word is the opening guide word and the other word is the closing guide word. Write the two words.

Guide Words	Opening Guide Word	Closing Guide Word
1. tell ten	_____	_____
2. major mayor	_____	_____
3. defer deer	_____	_____
4. hard hang	_____	_____
5. party parliament	_____	_____
6. retreat restrain	_____	_____
7. small slow	_____	_____
8. town trade	_____	_____
9. centipede chain	_____	_____
10. faith faint	_____	_____

Locating Words Quickly in the Dictionary

To locate a word quickly in a dictionary you must know how to do two things:

> **First,** you must know how to open the dictionary to the approximate location for the word you want.

To do this, you must understand that a dictionary can be divided into three parts, as shown below. You must begin looking for an entry word by turning to the correct third of the dictionary.

Part 1. abcdefg

Part 2. hijklmnop

Part 3. qrstuvwxyz

Look at the words that follow. For each word, write 1, 2, or 3 to show in which third of a dictionary you would find the word.

1. trick	_____	2. awful	_____
2. jump	_____	4. umbrella	_____
5. empty	_____	6. rail	_____
7. youth	_____	8. open	_____
9. shown	_____	10. drop	_____
11. kelp	_____	12. lime	_____
13. zebra	_____	14. combine	_____

> **Second,** you must know how to use alphabetical order to determine where the entry word you want is located in relationship to other words.

Words are arranged alphabetically in a dictionary by all the letters in the word. When you have two words that begin with the same letter, you must alphabetize them by the second letter. When you have two words that begin with the same two letters, you must alphabetize them by the third letter. For example, **sample** and **salt** begin with the same two letters, so these two words are placed in alphabetical order by the third letter. *Salt* comes before *sample* because the *l* in *salt* comes before the *m* in *sample*. When two words begin with the same three letters, such as **thick** and **third,** you alphabetize them by the fourth letter. *Thick* comes before *third*. Sometimes you may even need to alphabetize by the fifth or sixth letter.

Look at the following six sets of words. Write the words in each set in alphabetical order.

15. ant _____

    all _____

    alter _____

    angle _____

16. ponder _____

    pound _____

    pollen _____

    pond _____

17. found _____

    fender _____

    feeder _____

    fold _____

18. casual _____

    case _____

    cap _____

    candy _____

19. melon _____

    melt _____

    meat _____

    melting _____

20. rent _____

    rear _____

    renter _____

    rents _____

Phonetic Respellings

Phonetic (fe net' ik) **respellings** are used in a dictionary to help you say a word. The phonetic respelling follows the entry word on the dictionary page. When you do not know how to pronounce a word, use the phonetic respelling along with the short pronunciation key to pronounce the word. Usually the short pronunciation key is found at the bottom of each right-hand page in the dictionary. If you still cannot pronounce the word, try using the phonetic respelling along with the long pronunciation key, which will be found at the front of the dictionary.

Use your dictionary to find the phonetic respelling for each of the following words. Copy the phonetic respelling for each word. Use the phonetic respelling and either the short or long pronunciation key found in your dictionary to pronounce each word.

eventually _____

plumber _____

familiar _____

sphere _____

pneumatic _____

goody _____

jargon _____

mire _____

intuition _____

mosaic _____

Choosing the Correct Definition

Many words in the English language have more than one meaning. This is why many entry words are followed by more than one definition. Each definition is numbered to separate it from the others. The first definition is the most commonly used meaning of the word, and the last definition is the least commonly used.

Read each sentence and think about what the highlighted word means in the sentence. Then read the definitions for the highlighted word. Use the meaning of the sentence to help you decide which definition best fits the sentence. Write the definition that best fits the meaning of the sentence.

1. The *palm* broke as I pulled on the oar.

   palm (pän) n.   1. bottom part of hand.   2. part of animal forefoot.   3. part of a glove.   4. blade of an oar.   5. linear measure 7–10 inches.   6. to conceal.   7. to pick up stealthily.

   _____

2. The policewoman gave the driver a *summons* for driving through the red light.

   summons (sum' nz) n.   1. a call to attend a meeting.   2. an official order to appear in court.   3. a traffic ticket.

   _____

3. Before leaving for the trip we placed our *dunnage* in the trunk of the car.

   dunnage (dun' ij) n.   1. baggage or personal items.   2. loose material wedged between objects.   3. a cover.

   _____

4. Mary went on an *odyssey* around the world.

   odyssey (od' i se) n.   1. a trip characterized by wandering.   2. poem attributed to Homer.   3. a dream.

   _____

5. Sir Henry is the *Grand* Duke of Windsor.

   grand (grand) adj.   1. standing out in size and beauty.   2. costly.   3. higher in rank than others.   4. amount of money.

   _____

6. After reviewing his class notes, Tom had a good *grasp* of what his teacher had talked about.

grasp (grasp) v.   1. grip of the hand.   2. control over.   3. ability to seize.
4. understanding.   5. take eagerly.

Roots and Variants of Dictionary Entry Words

Sometimes you cannot find a word in a dictionary because the word you are looking for has a prefix, a suffix, or both a prefix and a suffix. To find the word you want, you must first remove the prefix, suffix, or both. What remains is called the **root word.** Then you can look for the root word in your dictionary.

Write the root word for each of the following:

1. unafraid _____

2. nonabrasive _____

3. reappear _____

4. fairest _____

5. speaking _____

6. repainting _____

7. transportable _____

Sometimes the root word ends in *e* and the *e* is dropped when adding a suffix that begins with a vowel. For example, *bike + ing = biking, trade + ed + traded.* When this is the case, you must remember to add the *e* when writing the root word. Write the root word for each of the following:

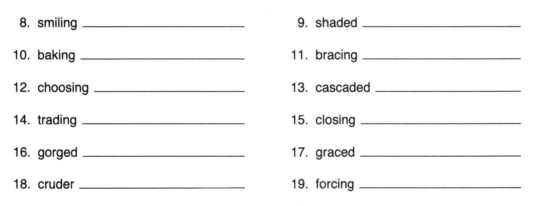

8. smiling _____

9. shaded _____

10. baking _____

11. bracing _____

12. choosing _____

13. cascaded _____

14. trading _____

15. closing _____

16. gorged _____

17. graced _____

18. cruder _____

19. forcing _____

Sometimes words that end in a single consonant have that consonant doubled before adding a suffix that begins in a vowel. For example: *run + ing = running, bat + er = batter.* When this is the case, you must remember to drop both the second consonant and the suffix when writing the root word.

Write the root word for each of the following:

20. canning _____

21. hugged _____

22. shipping _____

23. trotting _____

24. mobbed _____

25. sitter _____

26. tripped _____

27. mopping _____

28. putting _____

29. winner _____

30. jogging _____

31. sledding _____

Learning about Encyclopedias

An encyclopedia is a set of books containing articles on a wide range of subjects. The articles are arranged in alphabetical order. Each article is written by an expert who knows a great deal about the subject.

Look at the encyclopedia illustrated on this page. Notice that this encyclopedia has 22 different volumes. On the spine of each volume there is a letter or letters and a number. The letter is used to help you find the volume containing the topic you wish to know more about. The number is used when replacing the volume on the shelf. There is also an index that will help you find entries in the encyclopedia.

A	B	C-Ch	Ci-Cz	D	E	F	G	H	I	J-K
Encyclopedia	Encyclopedia	Encyclopedia	Encyclopedia	Encyclopedia	Encyclopedia	Encyclopedia	Encyclopedia	Encyclopedia	Encyclopedia	Encyclopedia
1	2	3	4	5	6	7	8	9	10	11

L	M	N-O	P	Q-R	S-Sn	So-Sz	T	U-V	WXYZ
Encyclopedia	Encyclopedia	Encyclopedia	Encyclopedia	Encyclopedia	Encyclopedia	Encyclopedia	Encyclopedia	Encyclopedia	Encyclopedia
12	13	14	15	16	17	18	19	20	21

Index
Encyclopedia
22

When looking for a person, look for the last name of the person and then the first name. For example, look for "Washington, George" not "George Washington." When looking for a topic, start by looking for the major word in your topic "Early American Indians," begin by looking for "Indian." Sometimes you may want to look in more than one volume to find information on a topic. For example, to find information on the topic "United States History," you should look under "United States" and "History."

Here is a list of topics you could learn more about using an encyclopedia. Write the letter(s) of the volume(s) in which you would look to learn more about each topic.

1. microbes _____

2. Disney World _____

3. Energy crisis _____

4. Thomas Jefferson _____

5. Mothers Against Drunk Drivers (MADD) _____

6. Potsdam conference _____

7. Russian Czars _____

8. spot welding _____

9. United Arab Republic _____

10. zinc _____

11. astrology _____

12. Making clothing in Colombia _____

13. Sir James George Taylor _____

14. Georgraphy of Europe _____

Different Encyclopedias

There are four major encyclopedias with which you should be familiar. All four are very useful, but they differ in the amount and type of information they provide about topics. Read to learn about each.

1. *Encyclopedia Britannica.* This is the most complete encyclopedia of world knowledge printed in the English language. It provides information on almost any imaginable topic. There is also a large index. The information is kept up to date with a separate yearbook.

2. *Encyclopedia Americana.* This is the most complete encyclopedia of American history and geography. Although the *Encyclopedia Americana* also contains information about the world there is a strong emphasis upon information about the United States. A separate yearbook keeps the information up to date.

3. *Collier's Encyclopedia.* This encyclopedia is written for elementary and high school students. The articles are easier to read and contain fewer facts than those found in the *Encyclopedia Britannica* or the *Encyclopedia Americana.* A yearbook helps keep the information up to date.

4. *World Book Encyclopedia.* This encyclopedia is written for elementary and high school students. The articles are shorter, contain fewer facts, and are easier to read than those found in the *Encyclopedia Britannica* or the *Encyclopedia Americana.* There are many visual aids that make the information easy to understand.

Now, answer these questions.

1. Which encyclopedia emphasizes United States history and geography?

   _____

2. Which encyclopedia contains the most complete presentation of information?

   _____

3. Which encyclopedias were written for elementary and high school students?

   _____

4. Which encyclopedia has many visual aids to help you understand the information it presents?

   _____

5. How do encyclopedias keep up to date?_____

   _____

Helpful Aids Found in the Encyclopedia ▬▬▬▬▬

The major encyclopedias provide useful aids to help you find, understand, and organize information on a topic. Here are some of the useful aids you should know about.

1. *Index.* All the major encyclopedias have an index. The index is found in a separate volume and is usually the last volume in the set. The index contains a comprehensive list of all the topics found in the encyclopedia.

2. *Study Guides.* Many encyclopedias contain study guides that will help you understand the information. Some study guides present detailed explanations of an important part of a topic. Some define words or clarify ideas. Others suggest books to read or other resources such as films, filmstrips, videotapes, audiotapes, and records.

3. *Suggested outlines for research papers.* At the end of some longer articles you can find a recommended outline for a research paper. Other references such as books, magazine articles, films, filmstrips, audiotapes, videotapes, and records related to the topic also may be listed.

4. *Visual aids.* Throughout each volume of the encyclopedia you will find pictures, maps, illustrations, graphs, and charts to help you understand and remember what you read. When you read be sure to refer to these visual aids. They will help you to more quickly understand and remember the information on your topic.

Go to your school library and examine all the different encyclopedias there for your use. Write the names of two encyclopedias here. Complete the following checklist for each by placing a √ in front of each feature found:

Name _____   Name _____

_____ Index   _____ Index

_____ Study guides   _____ Study guides

_____ Research outlines   _____ Research outlines

_____ Visual aids   _____ Visual aids

What other helpful features did you find in these encyclopedias?

_____

Which of the two encyclopedias did you like best?

_____

Why?_____

_____

Learning about the Thesaurus

A **thesaurus** (thi sor' əs) is a reference book that contains synonyms for commonly used words. The entry words are organized in alphabetical order. Following each entry word is its part of speech and a list of synonyms.

You can use a thesaurus to select words that help you precisely express your ideas when you are writing. Read the following to see how different synonyms change the meaning of the sentence.

The bank *took* control of the company.

The bank *grabbed* control of the company.

The bank *seized* control of the company.

A **thesaurus** is different from a **dictionary.** A thesaurus contains a large number of synonyms for each entry word. It also gives the part of speech for each synonym. Unlike a dictionary, it does not contain phonetic respellings, definitions, variants of the word, origins of the word, correct usage in sentences, antonyms, or illustrations. A thesaurus contains many more synonyms for commonly used words than a dictionary does. However, a dictionary contains a greater variety of information on each word.

Look at the sample entry for the word *raw* found in a thesaurus. It shows the entry word, part of speech, and a number of synonyms that can be used in place of the entry word.

raw   adj.   uncooked, crude, inexperienced, rude, coarse, obscene.

Locate a thesaurus in your school library. For each of the following sentences, find a synonym in the thesaurus that you can use in place of the highlighted word. Select the synonym that most precisely expresses the idea of the sentence. Write the synonym next to the sentence.

1. John will *gain* from the advice given to him.
2. Man has loved animals since the *start* of time.
3. Jane had a *fantastic* time at the rock concert.
4. It is important for teachers to *excite* their students to learn.
5. "Be careful or you will *tumble!*" His mother shouted.
6. Luis went to the grocery store to *obtain* a carton of milk.
7. Paula looked throughout the department store for new *garb* to wear to school.
8. The entire class *moaned* when the test was announced.
9. He was *undecided* about going to the party.
10. Sam was excited about moving into his new *dwelling.*

Practice Using a Thesaurus ▬▬▬▬▬▬▬▬▬▬▬▬▬▬▬▬▬

Read the following two sentences.

> Did you see Joe *eat* the food?
>
> Did you see Tom *devour* the food?

Notice how using the synonym *devour* instead of *eat* in the second sentence changes the meaning of the sentence. Although both *eat* and *devour* have the same general meaning, each has its own specific meaning. The word *eat* suggests consuming food in a slow and orderly manner using a knife and fork. The word *devour* suggests consuming food rapidly using one's hands to rip the food into pieces. Bill eats his food. Joe devours his food. Who would you bring home for dinner?

Read the following pairs of sentences. The first sentence has a highlighted word. In the second sentence that word has been replaced with a synonym found in a thesaurus. Read the two sentences and explain how the meaning of the sentence has been changed. You may need to go to a dictionary to look up the defintions of the words.

1. Mary is an *attractive* girl
   Mary is a *gorgeous* girl

   _____

2. *Write* your name on this page.
   Scribble your name on this page.

   _____

3. He found his new classmate to be *unfriendly.*
   He found his new classmates to be *hostile.*

   _____

4. Betty did her homework in a *careless* manner.
   Betty did her homework in a *listless* manner.

   _____

5. I have an *obsolete* car in my garage.
   I have an *antique* car in my garage.

   _____

6. She was *angry* when she saw her grade.
   She was *furious* when she saw her grade.

   _____

Learning about the Almanac

An **almanac** is a reference book that uses tables, charts, summaries, and other formats to provide the user with useful information on many subjects. A number of special articles written by experts are also included in an almanac. Almanacs are updated yearly so the information is very current.

Look at the table from a page in an almanac. The title tells the main idea of the table. The words and numbers in the table tell important details about the main idea. Use the table to answer the questions.

Highest and Lowest Fahrenheit Temperatures for Selected States

State	Hi Temp	Date	Lo Temp	Date
Alabama	112	1925	−27	1966
Alaska	100	1915	−80	1971
Arizona	127	1905	−40	1971
California	134	1913	−45	1937
Delaware	110	1930	−17	1893
Florida	109	1931	−02	1899
Hawaii	100	1931	14	1961
Kansas	121	1936	−40	1905
Michigan	112	1936	−51	1934
Missouri	118	1954	−40	1905
Nevada	122	1954	−50	1937
New York	108	1926	−52	1979
Ohio	113	1934	−39	1899
Oregon	119	1898	−54	1933
Texas	120	1936	−23	1933
Vermont	105	1911	−50	1933
Wyoming	114	1900	−63	1933

1. What does this table tell you about states?

   _____

2. Is information given for all the states in the United States

   _____

3. Which state has the highest recorded temperature?

   _____

4. Which state has the lowest recorded temperature?

   _____

5. What was the highest recorded temperature in Michigan?

   _____

6. What was the lowest recorded temperature in Ohio?

_____

7. In what year did Nevada record its highest temperature?

_____

8. In what year did Missouri record its lowest temperature?

_____

9. Which state recorded the greatest difference between its highest and lowest temperature?

_____

10. Which state has never recorded a temperature below 0?

_____

Learning about the Atlas

An **atlas** is a book of maps. There are different types of atlases and each is used for a different purpose. Read about the different types of atlases available in many libraries.

1. *Geographical atlas.* This type of atlas has maps showing the features of the earth's surface such as oceans, lakes, rivers, land masses, mountains, and plateaus. Some geographical atlases have maps showing even more details. Here is an example of a map from a geographical atlas.

NORTH AMERICA

0   200   400   600
SCALE OF MILES

Mountains—

211

2. *Political atlas.* This atlas has maps showing political boundaries. The maps in a political atlas show how the earth is divided into different countries, states, and even important cities. Some political maps show counties, smaller cities, and even towns and villages. Here is an example of a map from a political atlas.

UNITED STATES

0   200   400
SCALE OF MILES

National Boundaries ————
State Boundaries ————
State Capitals ————— ★

3. *Road atlas.* This atlas has maps showing the road system for a specific area. A United States road atlas will have a road map showing the major highways across the 50 states. It will also have road maps showing the highway and road system for each state and its large cities. Here is an example of a map from a road atlas.

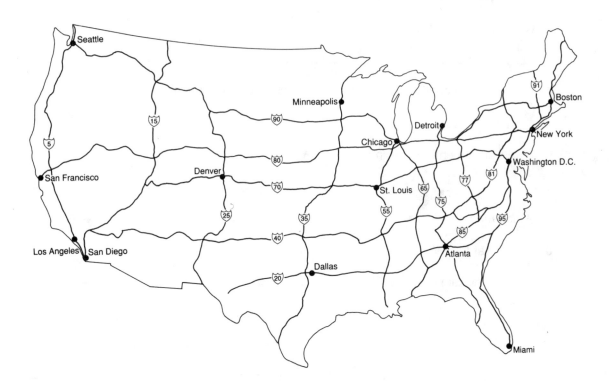

Answer these questions.

1. What is an atlas? _____

_____

2. What are the major types of atlases? _____

3. What information can you expect to get from a political map?

_____

4. Road map? _____

5. Geographical map? _____

6. Which atlas should you use to plan a long automobile trip?

_____

7. Which atlas should you use to identify major mountain ranges?

_____

8. Which atlas identifies the location of state capitals?

_____

9. Which map shows state boundaries? _____

10. Five Great Lakes? _____

11. Highway systems? _____

12. Major rivers? _____

13. Oceans? _____

14. Which of these atlases would you find most useful? Why? _____

_____

What I Have Learned

Directions: Show what you have learned about reference books by writing an answer for each of the following:

1. List the four types of dictionaries. Write a statement that tells something important about each.

    a.

    b.

    c.

    d.

2. List the four types of aids found in most encyclopedias. Write a statement that explains what each is used for.

    a.

    b.

    c.

    d.

3. Explain the difference between a thesaurus and a dictionary.

4. What is a good source of current information that is updated yearly?

5. List the three types of atlases. Write a statement that explains what each contains.

    a.

    b.

    c.

Answers for Chapter 6 Reproducibles

6-1 1. Unabridged. 2. Abridged. 3. Electronic. 4. Very small. 5. Special dictionary.
6. *Oxford Dictionary of the English Language.* 7. 29. 8–10. Answers will vary.

6-2

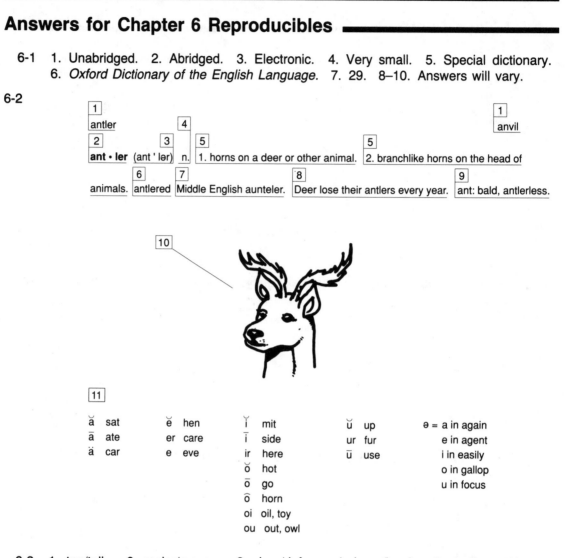

1								1
antler			4					anvil

2		3	5			5		
ant • ler (ant ' lər) n.			1. horns on a deer or other animal.			2. branchlike horns on the head of		

	6	7		8		9	
animals.	antlered	Middle English aunteler.		Deer lose their antlers every year.		ant: bald, antlerless.	

	ă	sat	ĕ	hen	ĭ	mit	ŭ	up	ə = a in again
	ā	ate	er	care	ī	side	ur	fur	e in agent
	ä	car	e	eve	ir	here	ū	use	i in easily
					ŏ	hot			o in gallop
					ō	go			u in focus
					ô	horn			
					oi	oil, toy			
					ou	out, owl			

6-3 1. ten/tell. 2. major/mayor. 3. deer/defer. 4. hang/hard. 5. parliament/party.
6. restrain/retreat. 7. slow/small. 8. town/trade. 9. centipede/chain. 10. faint/faith.

6-4 1. 3. 2. 1. 3. 2. 4. 3. 5. 1. 6. 3. 7. 3. 8. 2. 9. 3. 10. 1. 11. 2. 12. 2.
13. 3. 14. 1. 15. all, alter, angle, ant. 16. pollen, pond, ponder, pound. 17. feeder,
fender, fold, found. 18. candy, cap, case, casual. 19. meat, melon, melt, melting.
20. rear, rent, renter, rents.

6-5 Answers will vary with dictionary used by students.

6-6 1. blade of an oar. 2. a traffic ticket. 3. baggage or personal items. 4. a trip characterized by wandering. 5. higher in rank than others. 6. understanding.

6-7 1. afraid. 2. abrasive. 3. appear. 4. fair. 5. speak. 6. paint. 7. transport.
8. smile. 9. shade. 10. bake. 11. brace. 12. choose. 13. cascade. 14. trade.
15. chose. 16. gorge. 17. grace. 18. crude. 19. force. 20. can. 21. hug. 22.
ship. 23. trot. 24. mob. 25. sit. 26. trip. 27. mop. 28. put. 29. win. 30. job.
31. sled.

6-8   1. M.   2. D.   3. E.   4. J–K.   5. M.   6. P.   7. Ci–Cz.   8. W-X-Y-Z   9. U–V.   10. W-X-Y-Z.   11. A.   12. Ci–Cz.   13. T.   14. E.

6-9   1. *Encyclopedia Americana.*   2. *Encyclopedia Britannica.*   3. *Collier's* and *World Book.*   4. *World Book.*   5. Separate yearbook.

6-10 Responses will vary.

6-11 Answers will vary.

6-12 1. *Gorgeous* shows more beauty.   2. *Scribble* means the writing is not neat.   3. *Hostile* means the classmates were dangerous.   4. *Listless* means the homework was done with little effort.   5. *Antique* shows the car is old and of some value.   6. *Furious* shows rage and possible violence.

6-13 1. Highest and lowest temperatures in Fahrenheit degrees for selected states.   2. No.   3. California.   4. Alaska.   5. 112 degrees.   6. –39 degrees.   7. 1954.   8. 1905.   9. Alaska.   10. Hawaii.

6.14 1. Book of maps.   2. Geographical, political, road.   3. How the earth is divided into countries, states, and cities.   4. Shows the road system for a specific area.   5. Shows features of the earth's surface.   6. Road.   7. Geographical.   8. Political.   9. Political.   10. Geographical.   11. Road.   12. Geographical.   13. Geographical.   14. Student responses will vary.

6-15 1. (a) Unabridged. Contains many entries.   (b) Abridged. Shortened dictionary.   (c) Special. Provides technical definitions.   (d) Electronic. Small and may have voice pronunciation.   2. (a) Index. Lists all topics.   (b) Study Guides. Helps user understand the information.   (c) Outlines for research papers. Helps user write papers.   (d) Visual aids. Helps user quickly understand and remember information.   3. Dictionary: provides definitions for words; Thesaurus: provides synonyms for words.   4. Almanac.   5. Political: Shows how the earth is divided into countries, states, and cities. Road: Shows road system. Georgraphical: Shows features of earth's surface.

CHAPTER 7

Interpreting Visual Aids

■ Purposes

The purposes of this chapter are to:
1. teach students with learning disabilities strategies for interpreting the visual aids they will find in their textbooks.
2. provide reproducibles which can be used to help students learn how to interpret important visual aids.

■ Titles of Reproducibles

■ RATIONALE

Visual aids are an important means of communicating information in social studies, science, and mathematics. Alley and Deshler (1979) observed that because visual aids compress large amounts of information, it is important to teach students with learning disabilities how to interpret visual aids so they can better understand the information presented in their textbooks.

Textbook authors use visual aids to help explain important concepts to readers. Frequently students ignore the visual aids and concentrate on obtaining information solely from the printed text. This occurs when students are not aware of the importance of visual aids and have not been instructed in their use.

■ BACKGROUND INFORMATION

Visual aids consist of five major classes of devices used by authors to compress and explain information or concepts. The five classes are: maps, graphs, tables, diagrams, and charts.

Maps are representations of the earth's surface designed to show relationships. There are many types of maps. Students with learning disabilities should know how to use four types of maps: political, physical, road, and weather.

To understand a map, students need to know about the map legend, compass, and scale. The **legend** is usually found near the bottom of the map and provides the symbols necessary for interpreting the information found in the map. The **compass** tells directions on a map. The **scale** is used to tell distances in miles or kilometers.

Figure 7.1 shows a **political map** of South America. Political maps are used to show political or government boundaries. You can identify the different countries that make up the continent of South America as well as see their sizes and locations.

Figure 7.2 shows a **physical map** of South America. Physical maps are used to show the features of the earth's surface such as mountains, plateaus, deserts, and major bodies of water. No political boundaries are shown on a physical map.

Figure 7.3 shows a **road map**, which contains major highways and secondary roads for a geographical area. Major highways are identified by dark lines and secondary roads with lighter lines. Numbers are printed inside symbols to identify highways and roads.

Figure 7.4 shows a **weather map** similar to those students see in newspapers or on television. The weather map shows the major weather systems for a geographical or political area. Symbols are used to show rain, clear skies, cloudy conditions, snow, temperatures, and weather fronts.

Many times students will find maps that combine the features from political, physical, and road maps. Figure 7.5 shows a map of the state of California that combines features from these three types of maps. It has a legend, compass, and scale as aids to interpretation.

Graphs are used to show facts that are difficult to understand when presented in writing. Graphs come in many forms. The form used depends on the type of information the author wants to present. Here are four common types of graphs used in social studies, science, and mathematics.

Pictographs use pictures to show information. Each picture stands for an amount of something. In the pictograph in Figure 7.6 each football represents one win. To understand a pictograph, students must read the title and refer to the key.

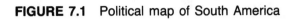

FIGURE 7.1 Political map of South America

FIGURE 7.2 Physical map of South America

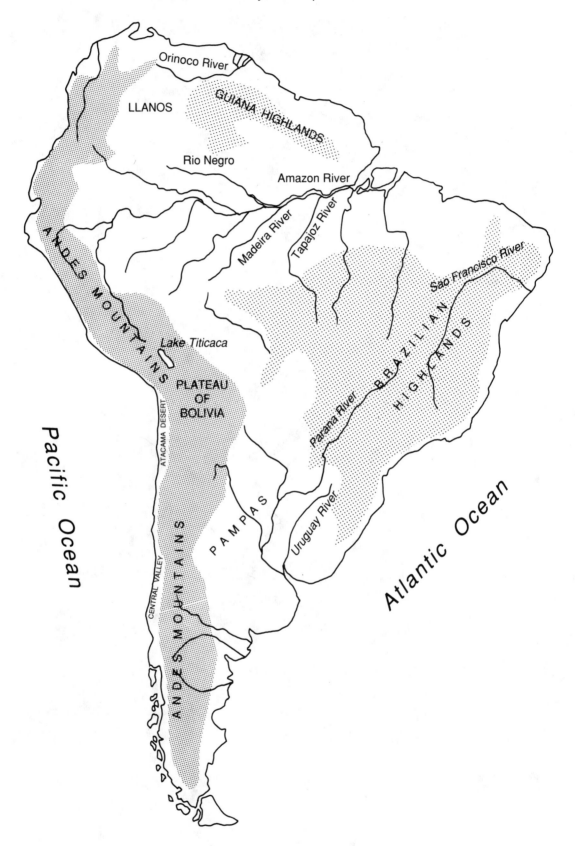

FIGURE 7.3 Road Map

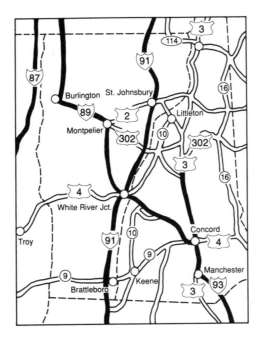

FIGURE 7.4 Weather Map

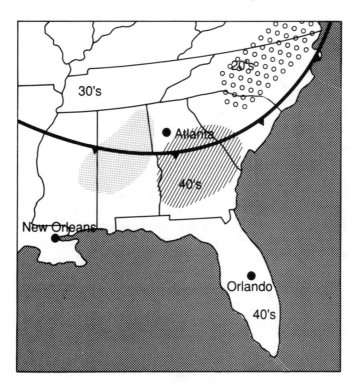

FIGURE 7.5 Map of California

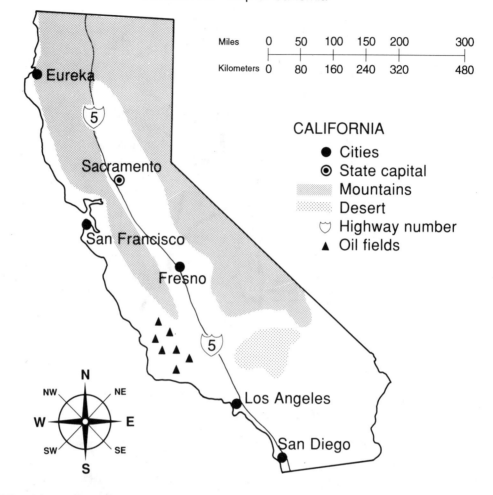

The title explains the purpose of the pictograph, and the key explains what each picture stands for in the pictograph.

Pie or circle graphs use the circle design to show the relationship between parts and the whole. Each part shows the amount or percentage of the whole it represents. All the parts must equal the total and add up to 100 percent.

To understand a pie or circle graph, students must read the title and examine the amount of each part. The title explains the purpose of the pie or circle graph, and the amount indicated for each part tells its relationship to the whole. Figure 7.7 is a pictograph showing how Luis uses his time on a typical school day.

Bar graphs use bars to show how one set of facts compares to another. A bar graph has a title at the top, labels on the left side and at the bottom, and a number line. To understand a bar graph, students must read the title, read all the labels, and examine the length of each bar in relation to the number line. By comparing the length of the bars, students can draw conclusions from the facts shown by the bars. Figure 7.8 is a sample of a bar graph.

Line graphs are generally used to show trends over a period of time. They have a title at the top and labels at the left side and the bottom. On the left side there is also a number line. Dots show how much there is of something. The dots are connected by a line to show a trend or how things are changing.

FIGURE 7.6 Pictograph

Games Won by NFL Teams

Dolphins	⬭⬭⬭⬭⬭⬭⬭⬭⬭⬭⬭
Bears	⬭⬭⬭⬭⬭⬭⬭⬭⬭
Giants	⬭⬭⬭⬭⬭⬭⬭⬭⬭
Cardinals	⬭⬭⬭⬭⬭⬭⬭
Saints	⬭⬭⬭
Rams	⬭⬭⬭⬭⬭⬭⬭⬭⬭⬭⬭

Key: ⬭ = game won

FIGURE 7.7 Typical day for Luis

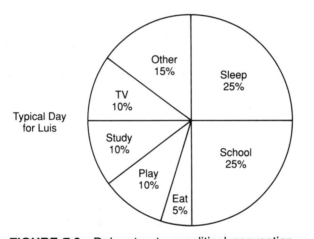

Typical Day for Luis

FIGURE 7.8 Delegates to a political convention

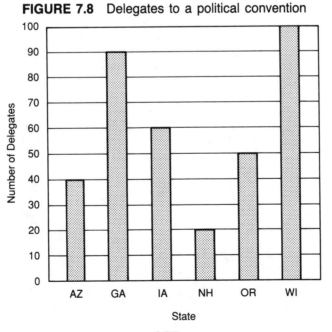

To understand a line graph, students need to begin by reading the title. Second, they need to read the label at the bottom to learn what the dots stand for. Third, they need to read the label on the left to learn what the numbers stand for. Fourth, they need to look at any one dot if they want to learn about a specific thing. Finally, they need to look at the line connecting the dots to see the trend or how things are changing. Figure 7.9 is a sample line graph.

Diagrams are used to show the parts of an object or thing. Diagrams may also be used to show how the parts go together or the object or thing works. Next to a diagram you will find a **key,** which explains the information in the diagram. Students need to use both the diagram and the key to make interpretations from a diagram. Figure 7.10 is a sample diagram.

Tables are used to show facts that would be difficult to understand quickly

FIGURE 7.9 Line graph

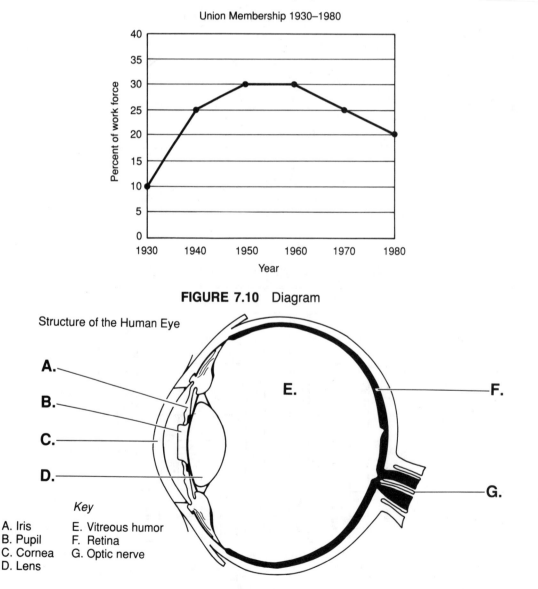

FIGURE 7.10 Diagram

Structure of the Human Eye

Key

A. Iris
B. Pupil
C. Cornea
D. Lens

E. Vitreous humor
F. Retina
G. Optic nerve

FIGURE 7.11   Table

Total Campaign Spending, 1952–1988

Year	Estimated Spending	Vote Cast for President	Cost per Voter
1952	$140 million	61.6 million	$2.28
1956	155 million	62.0 million	2.50
1960	175 million	68.8 million	2.54
1964	200 million	70.6 million	2.83
1968	300 million	73.2 million	4.10
1972	425 million	77.7 million	5.47
1976	$540 million	81.6 million	6.62
1980	1.2 billion	86.5 million	13.87
1984	1.8 billion	92.6 million	19.38
1988	3.0 billion	91.6 million	32.75

Source: Magruder, American Government (Englewood Cliffs, NJ: Prentice Hall, 1990). Used with permission.

and accurately if they were presented in writing. Tables are divided into columns. A table should have a title that explains its purpose. Likewise, each column should have a heading that explains its purpose. Within each column there may be numbers or words or a combination of both to show the information the author wants to present.

To understand a table, students must first read the title to learn what the table is about. Second, they should look at each column heading to learn what information the table contains. Third, students need to look in each column to get the specific facts. Figure 7.11 is a sample table.

Charts are used to show organization or a process by which something works or occurs. The **organizational chart** in Figure 7.12 shows the organization of the U.S.

FIGURE 7.12   Organizational chart

The Organization of the United States Government

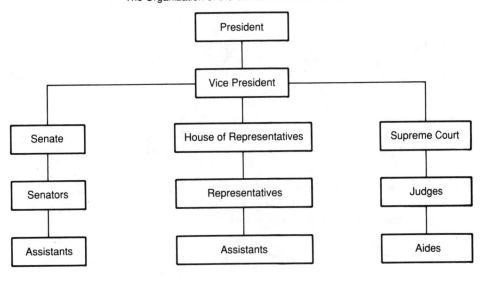

FIGURE 7.13 Flow chart

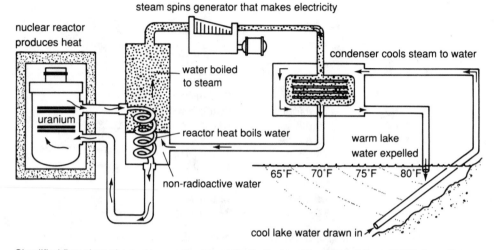

Simplified flow chart of a nuclear reactor. Laurel Cook, Boston, Ma. Adapted from *1990 Information Please Almanac* (Boston: Houghton Mifflin 1990), p. 377.

government. Information is presented in boxes, and lines are used to show how the boxes are related. By studying the chart, students can see how the government works.

A **flow chart** is used to show a process by which something works or occurs. Information is presented with drawings and a series of arrows. Statements are found next to the drawings to show what is occurring at that point. The arrows show the direction or order in which the process occurs. In the flow chart in Figure 7.13, drawings, statements, and arrows are used to explain how a nuclear reactor works.

■ TEACHING PLAN

Here is a plan for teaching students with learning disabilities strategies for interpreting visual aids.

1. Tell the students they will be learning how to interpret important visual aids they will find in their textbooks. Tell them these aids include maps, graphs, diagrams, tables, and charts. Distribute Reproducible 7-1, "Maps," to the students. Use 7-1 to introduce students to political and physical maps. Discuss each type of map and show its unique features. Then have the students complete the page activity.

2. Distribute Reproducible 7-2, "More Maps." Tell the students they will be learning about two more common types of maps: road maps and weather maps. Discuss each type of map and bring out its unique features. Have the students answer the questions.

3. Develop the understanding that every map has a map legend, which is used to explain the symbols appearing on the map. Use Reproducible 7-3, "Map Legend," to teach students how to use a map legend.

4. Bring out that maps have a compass which is used to tell directions on a map. Use Reproducible 7-4, "Map Compass," to teach students how to use a map compass.

5. Further explain that maps also have a scale, which is used to determine the distance between two points on a map. Point out that the scale is usually shown in both miles and kilometers. Use Reproducible 7-5, "Map Scale," to teach students how to use a map scale.

6. Distribute Reproducibles 7-6, "Map of California," and 7-7, "Putting It All Together with Maps." Review the use of a legend, compass, and scale. Have the students use the map of California on Reproducible 7-6 to answer the questions on 7-7.

7. Ask the students where they have seen a weather map (newspaper, magazines, television). Use this discussion to introduce the weather map. Use Reproducible 7-8, "Reading the Weather Map," to teach students how to interpret the weather map.

8. Tell students that another way to show information is with graphs. Explain that you will be teaching them about four common types of graphs: pictographs, pie or circle graphs, bar graphs, and line graphs. Emphasize that graphs show how two or more things go together. Use Reproducible 7-9, "Pictographs," to introduce students to pictographs. Clarify any questions the students may have. Then have them use the pictograph provided to answer the questions.

9. Distribute Reproducible 7-10, "Pie or Circle Graphs." Tell the students the term *pie graph* is often used because the end result looks like a pie divided into slices. Emphasize that the parts of every pie or circle graph must add up to 100 percent. Have students complete the activity.

10. Introduce bar graphs using Reproducible 7-11, "Bar Graphs." Explain that bars are used to show the relationship between two sets of facts. Show students the different parts of the bar graph. Then review the five steps students need to follow to use a bar graph. Finally, have students complete the page activity. After the activity has been completed, you might want to point out that bar graphs can also be laid out in a horizontal format.

11. Use Reproducible 7-12, "Line Graphs," to introduce the purpose and use of line graphs. Bring out that line graphs are used to show trends over a period of time. Explain the different parts of the line graph and the five steps students must follow to make interpretations. Then have the students answer the questions.

12. Tell students that still another way to show information is by using diagrams. Use Reproducible 7-13, "Diagrams," to familiarize students with these types of drawings. Bring out the fact that diagrams show how parts go together or how some thing works. Emphasize the importance of using the key to understand the information shown on a diagram. Then have students complete the page activity.

13. Tell students that tables are yet another way to show information. Distribute Reproducible 7-14, "Tables." Explain the importance of columns and column headings. Review the three steps for interpreting tables. Clarify any questions. Then have students complete the page activity.

14. Use Reproducible 7-15, "Organizational Charts," to introduce students to the use of organizational charts. Explain how boxes and lines are used to portray information. Have the students use the organizational chart provided to answer the questions.

15. Point out that another type of chart students will often see is the flow chart. Use Reproducible 7-16, "Flow Charts," to explain that flow charts are used to show a process by which something works or occurs. Point out the significance of the

arrows that appear on the flow chart. Clarify any questions about the flow chart and then have the students complete the activity.

16. Distribute Reproducible 7-17, "What I Have Learned." Use this reproducible to evaluate how well your students have learned the information taught in this chapter. As needed, use any of the reproducibles to review what was presented in this chapter.

Maps

Maps help you understand the relationships between things on the earth's surface. By studying a map, you gain a lot of information without doing much reading. Two important maps you should know how to interpret are political maps and physical maps.

A **political** map shows existing political or government boundaries. Lines are used to show the boundaries. Look at the political map of the continent of South America. Boundary lines are used to show the different countries that make up this continent. Sometimes you will find a political map of one country. Such a map will show boundaries inside that country. For example, a political map of the United States will show the boundaries of the states.

A **physical** map shows the features of the earth's surface such as mountains, highlands, plateaus, deserts, and major bodies of water. Look at the physical map of the continent of South America. Notice how the features are shown. Notice, too, that no political boundaries are shown on a physical map. You can learn a great deal about South America by studying a physical map of this continent. You can learn where the mountains are, the names of the major bodies of water, and whether there are any plateaus or deserts on this continent.

Answer these questions:

1. What types of information would you expect to find on a political map?

2. What types of information would you expect to find on a physical map?

3. Which type of map would you use if you wanted to identify the states that make up the United States?

4. Which type of map would you use if you wanted to identify major mountain ranges in Europe?

5. Which type of map would you use for a social studies report on the major oceans of the world?

6. Which type of map would you use for a report on the provinces of Canada?

Political Map of South America

Physical Map of South America

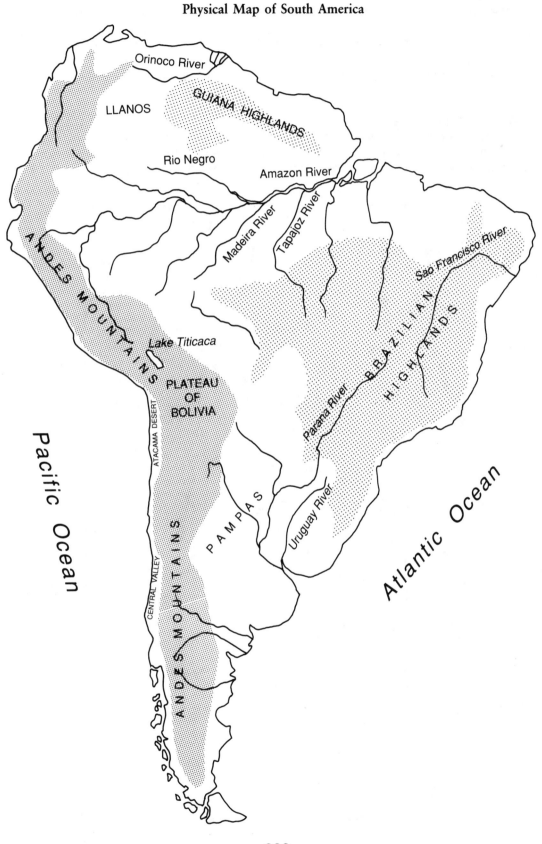

More Maps

Road maps and weather maps are two more important types of maps you need to know how to interpret.

A **road map** shows the major highways and the secondary roads for a geographical area. The major highways are identified with dark lines and secondary roads are identified with light lines. Both types of roads have symbols showing the number or name of the highway or road. Road maps are used to show how to get from one place to another. Here is a sample road map.

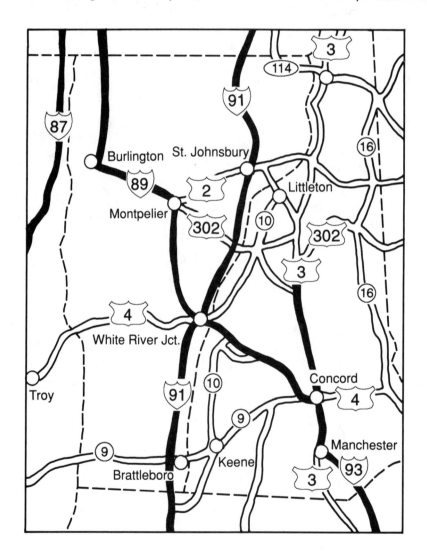

A **weather** map shows the major weather systems for a geographical or political area. Information is provided on rain, snow, cloud conditions, temperatures, and weather fronts. You use a weather map when you want to know the weather conditions where you live or in some other place. Here is a sample weather map.

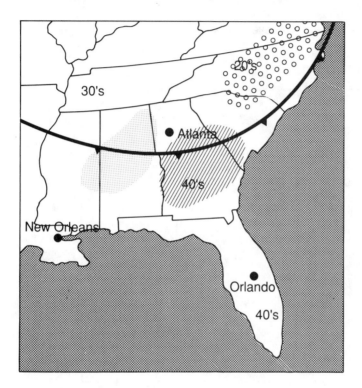

Answer these questions:

1. What information would you find on a road map?

2. What information would you find on a weather map?

3. Which type of map would you use to plan a trip by car?

4. Which type of map would you use to check ski conditions?

5. Which type of map would should be kept in the glove compartment of a car?

6. Which type is printed in most newspapers everyday?

7. Which type do you usually see on a television news show?

Map Legend

To read a map you need to use the **map legend.** The legend is usually located near the bottom of a map. It contains information that explains the symbols you see on a map. The legend on one map is different from the legend on another map because each map contains different kinds of information. The map legend is sometimes called by another name, the **map key.**

Here is a map with its legend. The legend tells you what the symbols on this map mean. This legend will help you only with this map. Use the map and legend to answer the questions that follow.

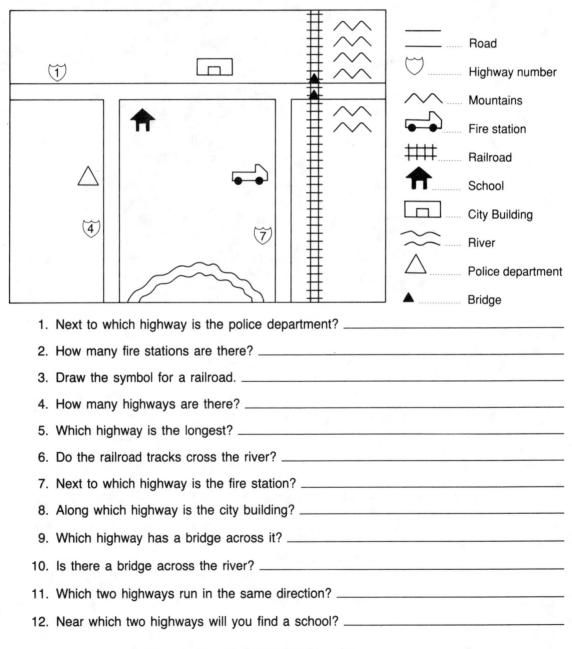

1. Next to which highway is the police department? _____

2. How many fire stations are there? _____

3. Draw the symbol for a railroad. _____

4. How many highways are there? _____

5. Which highway is the longest? _____

6. Do the railroad tracks cross the river? _____

7. Next to which highway is the fire station? _____

8. Along which highway is the city building? _____

9. Which highway has a bridge across it? _____

10. Is there a bridge across the river? _____

11. Which two highways run in the same direction? _____

12. Near which two highways will you find a school? _____

Map Compass

To tell directions on a map, you need to know how to use the **map compass.** Here is what a map compass looks like.

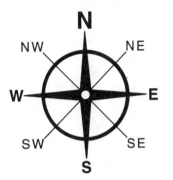

The map compass tells you north (N), south (S), east (E), west (W), and the directions in between: northeast (NE), southeast (SE), northwest (NW), and southwest (SW). Use the map of Ohio and the compass to answer the questions that follow.

Use the compass to tell in what direction you would travel to go from Columbus to the following cities?

1. Freemont _____

2. Portsmouth _____

3. Steubenville _____

4. Greenville _____

5. Cleveland _____

6. Defiance _____

7. Cincinnati _____

8. Athens _____

In what direction would you travel if you went from

9. Freemont to Portsmouth? _____

10. Greenville to Steubenville? _____

11. Cleveland to Cincinnati? _____

12. Defiance to Athens? _____

13. Cleveland to Defiance? _____

14. Athens to Cincinnati? _____

Map Scale

The **map scale** tells distance on a map. Sometimes it tells the distance only in miles, sometimes only in kilometers, and sometimes in both miles and kilometers. You can use the map scale to tell how far it is from one place to another.

Here is a map of Oregon containing cities and a map scale.

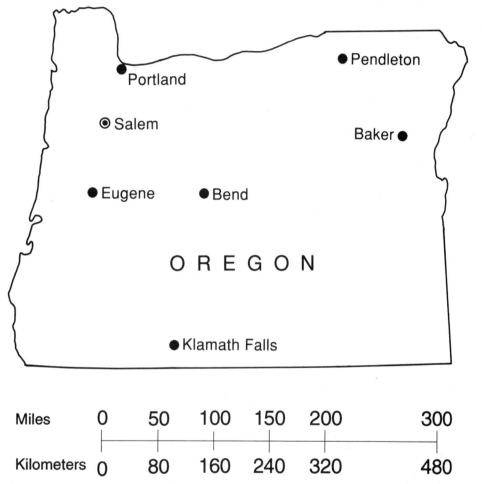

You can find the distance between any two cities by using the map scale. Place the edge of a piece of paper between any two cities shown on the map. Make a mark on the paper by each city. Then lay the paper on the scale to find out how far it is between the two marks. This will tell you how far it is between the two cities.

How far is it between

1. Salem and Klamath Falls in miles? _____

2. Portland and Bend in kilometers? _____

3. Eugene and Pendleton in miles? _____

4. Bend and Salem in kilometers? _____

5. Eugene and Pendleton in kilometers? _____

6. Baker and Portland in kilometers? _____

7. Which two cities are the closest? _____

8. What is the distance in miles between the two? _____

9. Which two cities are the farthest apart? _____

10. What is the distance in kilometers between the two? _____

Map of California

Sometimes map makers combine the features from different types of maps to make a map. Here is a map of California that combines the features from political, physical, and road maps. It has a legend, compass, and scale. Use the map to answer the questions your teacher will give you.

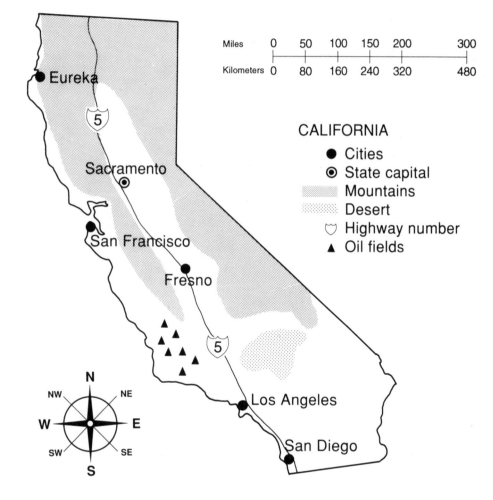

Putting It All Together with Maps ━━━━━━━━

Use the map of California to answer the following questions.

1. How many oil fields are shown on the map? _____

2. What two cities are they closest to? _____

3. What is the number of the highway running north and south? _____

4. What is the capital of the state of California? _____

5. Are there more mountains in the north or the south? _____

6. Is the desert in the north or the south? _____

7. How many cities are shown on the map? _____

8. Which two cities are the farthest apart? _____

9. How many miles apart are they? _____

10. Which two cities are the closest? _____

11. How many kilometers apart are they? _____

12. Which city is south of Los Angeles? _____

13. Which city is northwest of Sacramento? _____

14. In what direction would you travel to go from

    San Francisco to Fresno? _____

    Fresno to Sacramento? _____

    Eureka to San Francisco? _____

    Los Angeles to San Francisco? _____

    San Diego to Eureka? _____

    Los Angeles to Fresno? _____

15. In what direction would you travel if you went from San Diego to the mountains? _____

16. In what direction would you travel from the desert to the oil fields? _____

Reading the Weather Map

Maps can also be used to tell information about the weather. To read a weather map, you need a map legend. Look at the following weather map and map legend for the state of Kansas. Use both to answer the questions that follow.

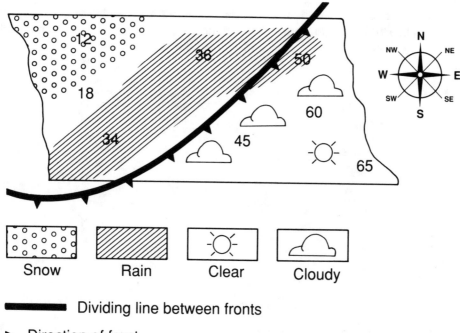

Snow	Rain	Clear	Cloudy

━━━━━ Dividing line between fronts

▶ Direction of front

Numbers show temperatures

What is the predicted weather for these areas of Kansas?

1. SE _____

2. NE _____

3. NW _____

4. SW _____

5. In which area is the coldest temperature? _____

6. In which area is the warmest temperature? _____

7. What will the weather be like in the SE area of Kansas in a day or two? _____

Pictographs

Graphs show how two or more things go together. Graphs make difficult and complex things easier to understand. There are four types of graphs you need to know how to interpret: pictographs, pie or circle graphs, bar graphs, and line graphs. All of these are used in social studies, science, and mathematics textbooks.

Pictographs use pictures to show information. Each picture stands for an amount of something. A pictograph has a title that tells you what it shows. It also has a key that explains what each picture stands for. Here is a pictograph. Study it and answer the questions.

Games Won by NFL Teams

Dolphins	⬭⬭⬭⬭⬭⬭⬭⬭⬭⬭⬭⬭⬭
Bears	⬭⬭⬭⬭⬭⬭⬭⬭⬭
Giants	⬭⬭⬭⬭⬭⬭⬭⬭⬭⬭⬭
Cardinals	⬭⬭⬭⬭⬭⬭⬭
Saints	⬭⬭⬭
Rams	⬭⬭⬭⬭⬭⬭⬭⬭⬭⬭⬭

Key: ⬭ = game won

1. Which team won the most games? _____

2. Which team won the fewest games? _____

3. How many games did the Cardinals win? _____

4. How many games did the Bears win? _____

5. How many more games did the Bears win than the Cardinals? _____

6. Which two teams won the same number of games? _____

7. How many teams won more games than the Bears? _____

8. How many teams won fewer games than the Giants? _____

9. What does ⬭⬭ stand for? _____

10. Where did you look to find out what ⬭⬭ stands for? _____

11. What is the title of this pictograph? _____

244

Pie or Circle Graphs ━━━━━━━━━━

Some graphs use a circle to show the relationship between the parts of something and the whole thing. This type of graph is called either a **pie graph** or a **circle graph.** The name *pie graph* is used because the graph looks like a pie divided into slices. Each part of a pie or circle graph shows how much of the whole it stands for. The parts must equal the whole and must add up to 100 percent.

Study the following pie or circle graph and answer the questions.

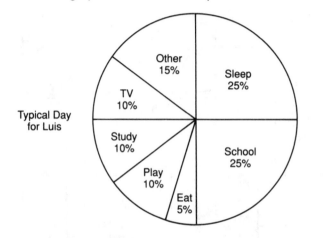

What percentage of the day does Luis spend:

1. sleeping? _____

2. studying? _____

3. in school? _____

4. watching TV? _____

5. playing? _____

6. both at school and studying? _____

7. playing and watching TV? _____

8. What does Luis spend 5% of his day doing? _____

9. 25% doing? _____

10. 15%? _____

11. Does Luis spend more time sleeping than watching TV, studying, and playing combined?

12. Does Luis spend more time at school than he does sleeping? _____

Bar Graphs ▬▬▬▬▬▬▬▬▬▬▬▬▬▬▬▬▬▬▬▬▬▬▬▬▬▬▬▬

Bar graphs use bars to show the relationships between sets of facts. The bar graph has a title at the top and labels on the left-hand side and bottom. On the left side of the graph there is a number line. The height of each bar shows how much the bar stands for. Look at the following bar graph.

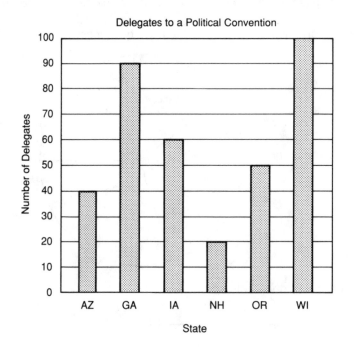

Delegates to a Political Convention

To read a bar graph you need to do the following:

1. Read the title to learn what it is about.

2. Read the label at the bottom to learn what the bars stand for.

3. Read the label on the left to learn what the numbers stand for.

4. Look at the height of any one bar to learn about a specific thing.

5. Look at the height of two or more bars to make comparisons between things.

Answer these questions:

1. What is this bar graph about?

2. What do the bars stand for?

3. What do the numbers stand for?

4. How many delegates came from Iowa (IA)?

5. How many from Oregon (OR)?

6. From Wisconsin (WI)?

7. Which state sent the most delegates?

8. Which state sent the fewest delegates?

9. Did New Hampshire (NH) send more delegates than Arizona (AZ)?

10. Did Georgia (GA) send more than Oregon (OR)?

11. How many more delegates did IA send than NH?

12. How many delegates came from GA and AZ combined?

Line Graphs

Line graphs are used to show trends over a period of time. The line graph has a title at the top and labels on the left-hand side and the bottom. On the left side of the line graph there is a number line. Dots are used to show how much there is of something. The dots are connected by a line. The line shows how a trend is developing or how things are changing. Look at the following line graph.

Union Membership 1930–1980

To read a line graph you need to do the following:

1. Read the title to learn what it is about.

2. Read the label at the bottom to learn what the dots stand for.

3. Read the label on the left to learn what the numbers stand for.

4. Look at any one dot to learn about a specific thing.

5. Look at the line to see the trend or how things are changing.

Answer these questions:

1. What is this line graph about?

2. What do the dots stand for?

3. What do the numbers on the left side stand for?

4. What percentage of the work force belonged to unions in 1930?

5. In 1950?

6. In 1970?

7. In 1980?

8. What happened to union membership between 1930 and 1950?

9. Between 1950 and 1960?

10. Between 1960 and 1980?

11. In what ten-year period was there the greatest increase in union membership?

12. In what year did union membership begin to drop?

Diagrams

Diagrams are drawings of some object or thing. A diagram shows the parts of the object or thing. Often a diagram shows how the parts go together or how the object or thing works. Next to the diagram is a key. The key helps you understand the diagram. Look at the following diagram and key. Use the diagram and key to answer the questions.

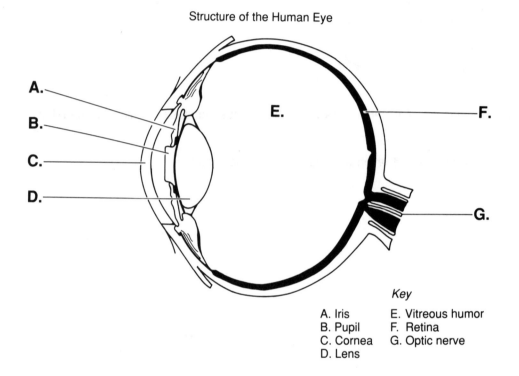

Structure of the Human Eye

Key

A. Iris E. Vitreous humor
B. Pupil F. Retina
C. Cornea G. Optic nerve
D. Lens

1. What is the title of this diagram?

2. What can you learn from studying this diagram?

3. How many parts of the eye are labeled?

4. What is the largest part?

5. What part is directly in front of the vitreous humor?

Tables

Tables are used to show facts that would be difficult to understand quickly and accurately if they were presented in written form. A table has a title that explains its purpose. In the table you will find columns. Each column has a heading that tells what facts you will find in that column. Look at the following table.

Total Campaign Spending, 1952–1988

Year	Estimated Spending	Vote Cast for President	Cost per Voter
1952	$140 million	61.6 million	$2.28
1956	155 million	62.0 million	2.50
1960	175 million	68.8 million	2.54
1964	200 million	70.6 million	2.83
1968	300 million	73.2 million	4.10
1972	425 million	77.7 million	5.47
1976	$540 million	81.6 million	6.62
1980	1.2 billion	86.5 million	13.87
1984	1.8 billion	92.6 million	19.38
1988	3.0 billion	91.6 million	32.75

Source: Magruder, *American Government* (Englewood Cliffs, NJ: Prentice Hall, 1990). Used with permission.

To read a table you need to do the following:

1. Read the title to learn what the table is about.

2. Look at each column heading to learn what information the table contains.

3. Look in each column to get specific facts.

Answer these questions:

1. What is the title of this table?

2. What information is provided in the second column?

3. In the third column?

4. In the fourth column?

5. In which column should you look to find the number of people who voted for a president?

6. In what year was the most money spent on campaigns?

7. In what year was the cost per voter the least?

8. In what year did campaign spending first go over $1 billion?

9. What is the first year for which information is given on cost per voter?

10. What did you learn from this table?

Organizational Charts

Organizational charts are used to show how things are organized. Information is presented in boxes. Each box is labeled to show what it represents. Lines are used to show how the boxes are related.

Look at the following organizational chart. It shows how the U.S. government is organized to do its work. The boxes contain facts about the government. The lines show how the facts go together. By studying the chart you can see how the government works.

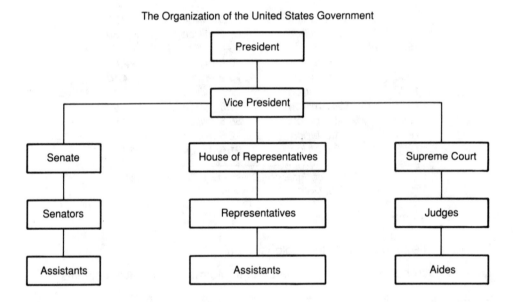

The Organization of the United States Government

Use the chart to answer these questions:

1. Who is the highest ranking official in the United States government?

2. Who works in the Senate?

3. Who works in the House of Representatives?

4. Who works in the Supreme Court?

5. What official is directly below the president?

6. Where do aides work?

7. For whom do assistants work?

Flow Charts

Flow charts are used to show a process by which something works or occurs. Information is presented with drawings and a series of arrows. Statements are found next to the drawings to show what is occurring at that point. The arrows show the direction or order in which the process occurs.

Look at the following flow chart, which shows how a nuclear reactor works. Read the title and the statements, and study the drawings. Then use the arrows to learn the process.

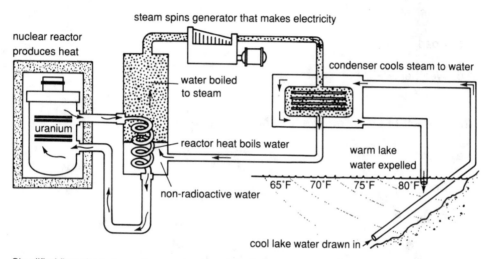

Simplified flow chart of a nuclear reactor. Laurel Cook, Boston, Ma. Adapted from *1990 Information Please Almanac* (Boston: Houghton Mifflin 1990), p. 377.

Answer these questions:

1. What is the title?

2. What process is being shown?

3. What creates the heat in the nuclear reactor?

4. What is the heat used for?

5. What spins the generator?

6. What makes the electricity?

7. What changes the steam back to water?

8. Where does the water come from for the cooling process?

9. Where does the warm water go?

What I Have Learned ━━━━━━━━━━━━━━━━

Directions: Show what you have learned about interpreting visual aids by writing an answer for each of the following:

1. Tell what each type of map shows:

   a. Political

   b. Physical

   c. Road

   d. Weather

2. What is each of the following used for on a map?

   a. Legend

   b. Compass

   c. Scale

3. What is used to show how much there is of something in a pictograph?

4. What is another name for a circle graph?

5. What does the height of the bar show in a bar graph?

6. What type of graph is used to show trends over a period of time?

7. What type of drawing shows the parts of some object or thing?

8. What is used to show facts in columns?

9. What type of chart is used to show how things are organized?

10. What type of chart is used to show how something works?

Answers for Chapter 7 Reproducibles

7-1   1. Shows political and government boundaries.   2. Shows features of the earth's surface.   3. Political map.   4. Physical map.   5. Physical map.   6. Political map.

7-2   1. Major highways and secondary roads. Major weather systems.   3. Road map.   4. Weather map.   5. Road map.   6. Weather map.   7. Weather map.

7-3   1. 4.   2. 1.   3.   .   4. 3   5. 1.   6. Yes.   7. 7.   8. 1.   9. 1.   10. No.   11. 4,7. 12. 1,4.

7-4   1. N.   2. S.   3. E.   4. W.   5. NE.   6. NW.   7. SW.   8. SE.   9. S.   10. E. 11. SW.   12. SE.   13. W.   14. W.

7-5   1. 200.   2. 210.   3. 240.   4. 160.   5. 390.   6. 390.   7. Eugene and Bend.   8. 90. 9. Klamath Falls and Pendleton.   10. 455.

7-6   No writing required.

7-7   1. 4.   2. Los Angeles and Fresno.   3. 5.   4. Sacramento.   5. North.   6. Southeastern.   7. 6.   8. Eureka and San Diego.   9. 675.   10. San Francisco and Sacramento. 11. 140.   12. San Diego.   13. Eureka.   14. SE, NW, SE, NW, NW, NW.   15. N. 16. W.

7-8   1. Clear.   2. Cloudy.   3. Snow.   4. Rain.   5. NW.   6. SE.   7. Cloudy, possible rain turning to snow, colder.

7-9   1. Dolphins.   2. Saints.   3. 7.   4. 9.   5. 2.   6. Giants and Rams.   7. 3.   8. 3. 9. Game won.   10. Key.   11. Games won by NFL teams.

7-10   1. 25%.   2. 10%.   3. 25%.   4. 10%.   5. 10%.   6. 35%.   7. 20%.   8. Eating. 9. Sleeping and going to school.   10. Other.   11. No.   12. No.

7-11   1. Number of delegates from different states attending a political convention.   2. States. 3. Number of delegates.   4. 60.   5. 50.   6. 100.   7. Wisconsin.   8. New Hampshire. 9. No.   10. Yes.   11. 40.   12. 130.

7-12   1. Union membership during the years 1930–1980.   2. Years.   3. Percentage of work force belonging to unions.   4. 10%.   5. 30%.   6. 25%.   7. 20%.   8. Increased. 9. Stayed the same.   10. Decreased.   11. 1930–1940.   12. 1970.

7-13   1. Structure of the human eye.   2. Names of parts of the human eye.   3. 7.   4. Vitreous humor.   5. Pupil.

7-14   1. Total campaign spending, 1952–1988.   2. Estimated spending.   3. Votes cast for president.   4. Cost per voter.   5. 3rd column, "Votes Cast for President."   6. 1988. 7. 1952.   8. 1980.   9. 1952.   10. Each year more money was spent on presidential campaigns. The number of voters increased until 1984. In 1988 the number of voters dropped. The cost per voter keeps increasing.

7-15   1. President.   2. Senators and assistants.   3. Representatives and assistants. 4. Judges and aides.   5. Vice-president.   6. Supreme Court.   7. Senators and representatives.

7-16   1. Simplified flow chart of a nuclear reactor.   2. The process of using a nuclear reactor to generate electricity.   3. Uranium.   4. Boil water.   5. steam.   6. Generator. 7. Condenser.   8. From the lake.   9. Back to the lake.

7-17 1. (a) Political or government boundaries. (b) Features of the earth's surface. c) Major highways and secondary roads. (d) Major weather systems. 2. (a) To explain the symbols on a map. (b) Tells directions on a map. (c) Tells distance on a map. 3. Pictures. 4. Pie graph. 5. How much of something. 6. Line graph. 7. Diagram. 8. Table. 9. Organizational chart. 10. Flow chart.

CHAPTER 8

Writing a Research Paper

■ Purposes

The purposes of this chapter are to:
1. teach students with learning disabilities a strategy for writing a research paper.
2. provide reproducibles that can be used to guide students through the process of writing a research paper.

■ Titles of Reproducibles

■ RATIONALE

Teachers realize how important it is for students to learn how to write research papers. Devine (1981) pointed out that even students in elementary school need opportunities to search out information and ideas and present them in writing. As students with learning disabilities progress through school, they will increasingly be required to write research papers. As they do so, they will need to integrate many of the study strategies we present throughout this book, including using the library to locate information (Chapter 5), using reference materials (Chapter 6), and managing time effectively (Chapter 10).

As you probably know from your own experience as a student, writing a research paper is a complex task. Hoover (1988) pointed out that writing a research paper involves a range of skills necessary to organize one's ideas and present them on paper in a meaningful and appropriate manner. This is no simple task for any student. For students with learning disabilities, it is a formidable task. Pope (1982) observed that these students do not know where to begin a paper or how to organize it. They may feel that they do not know enough about a subject to write about it, and that they do not know how to find out more about the subject. Consequently, students with learning disabilities initially need a great deal of guided practice through every step of preparing a research paper (Mastropieri & Scruggs, 1987). After the students have prepared a few papers with teacher involvement, however, they should be able to write papers independently.

Teachers should be particularly aware of a special problem that arises as they teach students with learning disabilities a strategy for writing research papers. This is the problem of plagiarism. Mastropieri and Scruggs (1987) noted that students with learning disabilities are likely to be discouraged and frustrated at the prospect of writing a research paper. Consequently, they may be tempted to copy entire sections from articles and books. It is important, therefore, to familiarize students with the ethical and legal implications of plagiarism, and to teach them how to paraphrase and cite the works of others rather than simply copy them.

■ BACKGROUND INFORMATION

A research paper is prepared using factual information obtained from a number of sources. The length of the research paper and the minimum number of sources students can use to prepare such a paper is determined by the teacher.

Strategy for Writing a Research Paper

There are ten steps students with learning disabilities need to follow when writing a research paper:

1. Choosing a topic

2. Locating sources of information

3. Preparing bibliography cards

4. Preparing note cards

5. Preparing the outline for the paper

6. Writing the paper

7. Preparing footnotes

8. Preparing the bibliography

9. Preparing the title page and table of contents

10. Final proofing

In this section we provide information on each of the ten steps in the strategy for writing a research paper.

Step 1   Choosing a Topic. Students with learning disabilities find it difficult to choose a topic. For some students with learning disabilities, it is probably best for the teacher to provide a list of topics from which students can choose a topic. For students who choose their own topics, we present four questions they can use to determine if they have chosen an appropriate topic.

1. *Is the topic too broad or too narrow?*

Frequently students with learning disabilities choose topics that are too broad, such as "The Effects of Pollution on the Lives of People Throughout the World." Broad topics require extensive research that would take more time than most students have to complete their assignments. Broad topics also make it difficult to cover a topic adequately in the maximum number of pages a teacher assigns for the project.

Students with learning disabilities sometimes choose topics that are too narrow, such as "The Effects of Pollution on Mallard Ducks." It is very difficult to find a variety of information on a narrow topic, particularly given the limited resources available in most school libraries. Students with narrow topics usually must go to regional or university libraries to locate the information they need on their topics. When students cannot find enough sources, they frequently resort to using opinions in their research papers.

2. *Is there enough factual information on the topic?*

Each student must determine if adequate information is available on a topic to allow him or her to write a research paper of the length required. For example, if the teacher requires that the paper be 10 to 15 pages in length and contain between 15 and 20 references, each student must go to the library and determine if there are at least 15 to 20 suitable references available on their topic. Each student also must determine if the references contain sufficient information to write a paper between 10 and 15 pages in length.

3. *Are you interested in this topic?*

It is important that a student have a strong interest in the selected topic or the quality of the writing will deteriorate toward the end of the paper. A research paper takes a long time to prepare and write, and it is important that each student have a strong interest in the topic in order to sustain effort.

4. *Has the topic been approved by your teacher?*

Each student should meet individually with the teacher who will review the topic on which the student proposes to write a research paper. At this meeting the teacher can decide whether the topic chosen by the student is appropriate for a research paper. The teacher can also help the student refine the topic, can review the list of references, and can verify the student's interest in the topic.

Once the teacher has approved a topic, the student should record the approved topic and date in a notebook called a Research Log. The Research Log may be kept on the teacher's desk or in a designated research area in the classroom. It is a good idea for the teacher to validate every entry by placing his or her initials after the entry in the Research Log.

Step 2.   Locating Sources of Information. The best place to start looking for information is the school library, and the best person to consult there is the librarian. There are a number of different sources of information from which factual information can be obtained. The school librarian can help students locate sources of information if students cannot do so independently.

Reference books. Encyclopedias, almanacs, books of facts, and dictionaries are good sources of factual information. They may give students ideas on how to organize their papers as well as provide useful facts.

Magazines. These are also a good source of information. Magazines often contain longer articles on a topic and help students make their papers more interesting.

Newspapers. These are the best source for the most current information on a topic.

Books. These are the best source for extensive background information on any topic.

Television, radio, videotapes, audiocassettes. These sources should also be used to obtain information for reports. Students should be encouraged to get information by watching and listening as well as by reading.

Experts. People with extensive knowledge of a subject are another good source of information for a research paper. Facts provided by experts are sometimes not available from any other source.

Step 3.   Preparing Bibliography Cards. Once the sources of information have been identified, students should prepare a separate bibliography card for each source. A bibliography card identifies the source from which the information is obtained for the research paper. Figure 8.1 presents sample bibliography cards for the common sources used by students to write research papers. The school or local library will have references to guide students in the preparation of bibliography cards for less common sources.

After all the bibliography cards have been prepared, they should be placed in alphabetical order by the author's last name and numbered from 1 through whatever number of cards there are in the set. The numbers should be written in the top

FIGURE 8.1 Bibliography cards

BIBLIOGRAPHY CARD FOR A REFERENCE BOOK

"Water Pollution,"

Encyclopedia Americana,

Volume 24, p. 213.

BIBLIOGRAPHY CARD FOR A MAGAZINE ARTICLE

Rockman, Julie. "Examining the Shores of the Great Lakes." Preserving Mother Nature.

October 1991, pp. 3–6.

FIGURE 8.1 Continued

BIBLIOGRAPHY CARD FOR A NEWSPAPER ARTICLE

"Pollutants Destroying the Great Lakes,"

Detroit Free Press,

October 14, 1991, p. 5.

BIBLIOGRAPHY CARD FOR A BOOK

Hanson, Tom. Water Pollution.

Appleton Press Publishers,

Great Falls, Iowa, 1991.

FIGURE 8.1 Continued

BIBLIOGRAPHY CARD FOR A FILM, TAPE, OR TELEVISION
OR RADIO PROGRAM

Cruising the Waters of Lake Michigan.

Videotape, 1989. 60 minutes, VHS.

Distributed by NBC Educational Services,

New York.

BIBLIOGRAPHY CARD FOR AN EXPERT

Jason, Beth. Water Supervisor,

Marquette, Michigan 49780

Personal conversation, October 20, 1991.

right-hand corner of each card and circled for easy identification. The numbers are used to keep the bibliography cards in alphabetical order as well as for referencing note cards.

Step 4. Preparing Note Cards. Notes should be written on index cards that are either 4×6 inches or 5×8 inches in size. The larger card size works best for students with learning disabilities, who may have difficulty writing legibly or writing in small spaces. Figure 8.2 shows a note card that goes with one of the previously presented bibliography cards.

The number written on the bibliography card should also be written in the top right-hand corner of each corresponding note card. It is likely that students will use several note cards to record notes from a particular source. To keep the note cards in order, students should be directed to write the bibliography card number followed by a dash and the number of the note card. For example, "4-1" indicates bibliography card number 4, note card number 1. Similarly, "4-4" indicates bibliography card number 4, note card number 4. The number should be circled for easy identification and to keep it distinct from other numbers written on the card.

Important notes from the sources of information should be written on the note cards. Notes should be paraphrased or written in the students' own words. All quotations should be in the author's exact words and included within quotation marks. Page numbers should follow every quote. Because students at this point have only a general sense of their topic, they should be encouraged to make notes on all the information in each reference.

It is important to emphasize the need for legible writing on the note cards. Illegibly written words or sentences usually require students to return to the original source to figure out what their notes mean. Students who have difficulty writing legibly should be encouraged to prepare their note cards using a typewriter or word processor. Some students with learning disabilities may need to orally record their notes using a tape recorder or dictaphone.

Step 5. Preparing the Outline for the Paper. Once all the notes necessary for writing the paper have been gathered, students must organize them to write their papers. The best way to organize the information is by preparing an outline, consisting of topics, subtopics, details, and subdetails. It is generally best to prepare the outline using phrases and key words instead of complete sentences.

The outline should follow this format:

Title

I. Roman numerals for topics.

  A. Capital letters for subtopics

    1. Arabic numerals for details

      a. Small letters for subdetails

FIGURE 8.2 Note card

BIBLIOGRAPHY CARD   13

Maxson, Bill. Can't Drink the Water or Eat the Fish. Dwag Press,

South Bend, Indiana, 1990.

NOTE CARD   13-1

"The water contains mercury and other chemicals." p. 23
Many fish are dying.
Fishing industry is hurting. People are worried about their jobs.
New, tough laws are making things better.
The lakes will be safe again and soon.

A sample outline looks like this:

Famous People During the Civil War

I. Men

A. Government

B. Business

C. Military

   1. Army

   2. Navy

      a. U.S. citizens

      b. From foreign countries

II. Women

  A. Government

  B. Social leaders

  C. Teachers

  D. Nurses

Step 6. Writing the Paper. Research papers should be written more than once to present the information in the best form possible. Each writing of the paper is called a *draft*. The first draft is called the *rough draft* because the writing is in rough or unfinished form. Ideas may be unclear, information may be incomplete, wrong words may be used, and words may be misspelled. These are the things that are corrected when the rough draft is reread and edited.

Before writing the rough draft, students need to organize their note cards to correspond to the outline. Then, using the outline as a guide, students select notes from their note cards and begin writing. The notes should be used to guide the writing and not copied directly into the paper except where students intend to use a direct quotation.

The paper should be organized into a working title, introduction, body, and conclusion.

The *working title* is usually the first title selected for a research paper. Generally, the working title needs to be revised after the paper has been written to reflect the information that actually appears in the paper.

The *introduction* should tell the reader what the research paper is about. It should contain an overview of the topic and get the reader interested in what the writer has to say.

The *body* contains the important information and ideas from the note cards. Students should use the outline prepared in step 5 as they write their papers. Side headings should be used to help the reader understand the organization of the paper.

The *conclusion* is the ending of the paper. It is where the writer indicates the essential meaning of all the information presented.

When writing the paper, students must number each page to keep the pages in order. It is a good idea to circle the page number to keep it separate from other numbers in the research paper. All visuals such as graphs, charts, and maps should be inserted during the first draft. All quotations should be clearly marked with quotation marks.

When students have finished their first drafts, they should use the Revising Checklist that follows to determine which changes they should make to improve their papers.

Revising Checklist

1. Does the introduction clearly introduce the topic?

2. Are side headings used to help the reader understand the paper?

3. Does the body contain all the facts needed?

4. Is each paragraph written with a main idea?

5. Does every sentence and paragraph add something to the paper?

6. Did I choose the best words to explain the ideas?

7. Does the conclusion follow from the facts?

8. Have I corrected all the misspelled words?

9. Have I capitalized all the appropriate words?

10. Have I used quotation marks to identify all quotations?

11. Have I reread the paper at least three times looking for ways to make it better?

12. Did I number all the pages?

Once all the changes have been made in the first draft, the second draft should be written. When the second draft is completed, the Revising Checklist should be used again to determine if there are changes that will improve the paper. It is not uncommon for students to write three or even more drafts of a research paper. When all the questions in the Revising Checklist have been answered satisfactorily, students have the final drafts of their papers.

Step 7. *Preparing Footnotes.* It is important for students to understand that the sources from which quotations or major ideas were taken must be given appropriate credit. In a research paper, credit is given by using footnotes. The footnotes can be placed at the bottom of the page on which the information appears. It is also acceptable to write all the footnotes on a separate page that is placed at the end of the paper. Figure 8.3 presents a sample of text from a research paper and the two corresponding footnotes that would appear at the end of that page.

When footnotes are listed at the end of a paper, the same format is used for writing the footnotes. However, the footnotes are written on a separate sheet of paper and placed before the bibliography in the paper. Footnotes, whether they appear at the bottom of a page or as a collection on a separate page, are used to designate information cited in the paper.

FIGURE 8.3 Footnotes

The most common shoe size for men is size nine and for women it is size seven.[1] According to Donald Blake in the *Shoe Manufacturer's Journal,* "men and women are growing bigger feet."[2]

---

1. Phil Harris, *Shoe Sales.* p. 34.

2. Donald Blake, "Feet Are Getting Bigger," *Shoe Manufacturer's Journal,* Volume 11, September 1990, p. 56.

Step 8. Preparing the Bibliography. Students need to know that a bibliography is an alphabetical list of all the sources of information they consulted to prepare the research paper. Even if specific information from a reference is not included in a paper, the reference must still be included in the bibliography. The bibliography appears at the end of the paper.

To prepare a bibliography, students must have all their bibliography cards in alphabetical order by the last name of the author. The students should be told to disregard less important words like *the, an,* and *a* in titles. Then students should head a piece of blank paper with the word BIBLIOGRAPHY in all caps and centered on the page. Next students should write or type each reference being sure the references are listed in alphabetical order. For each entry, the second and following lines should be indented five spaces from the first line. Figure 8.4 presents a sample bibliography for a research paper on the topic, *Rulers of Russia.* This bibliography is also used for Reproducible 8-13.

There are different ways of citing information in a bibliography. From the many style manuals available, teachers should select the format they believe will be easiest for their students to use.

Step 9. Preparing the Title Page and Table of Contents. Every research paper must have a title page. The title should reflect the topic of the paper. It should also capture the interest of readers. The title page is the first page of the research paper.

On a blank sheet of paper, students should write or type their title about three inches from the top of the paper. The title should be centered and written or typed in all capital letters. About six inches from the top of the paper and centered, the word "by" should be written or typed. Two lines below this and centered should appear

FIGURE 8.4 Bibliography

BIBLIOGRAPHY

Bos, Candy. Director of the Miami Historical Center, Miami, Florida 33122. Personal letter, May 25, 1990.

"Government in the Early Years of the USSR." San Francisco Daily News, June 15, 1990, p. 20.

Mann, Mark. "The Mongols Take Over Russia." Historical Review, April 1990, pp. 10–12.

"Russian Tzars." Encyclopedia Britannica, Volume 23, pp. 367–382.

Striker, Sally. "Beautiful Icons." Modern Art, July 1990, pp. 23–27.

Thompson, Mary Ellen, Russian Language Teacher, Willow School, Minneapolis, Minnesota 48767. Personal conversation, June 4, 1990.

Touring the Kremlin. Videotape, 1988. 60 minutes. Distributed by International Video Productions, Dallas, Texas.

Zayre, Albert. The Russian State. New York: Williams House Publishers, 1990.

the student's name. Two lines below the student's name and centered should appear the date on which the paper was submitted to the teacher. Figure 8.5 shows a correctly formatted title page. This is the second page of the research paper.

To prepare a table of contents, students will need another blank sheet of paper. Students begin by writing or typing the words "Table of Contents," centered about

FIGURE 8.5 Title page

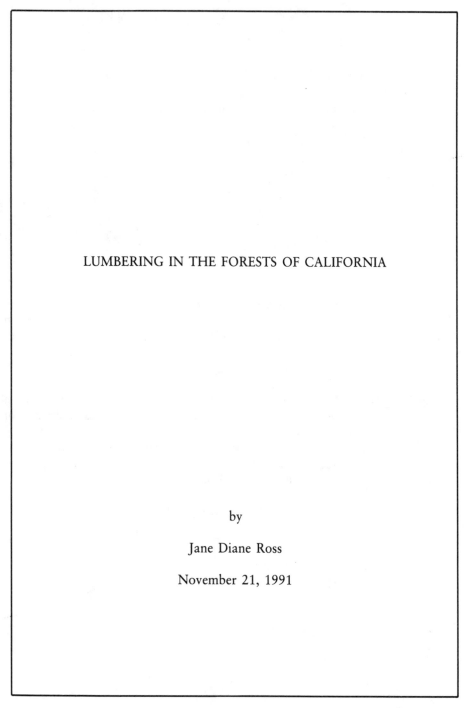

LUMBERING IN THE FORESTS OF CALIFORNIA

by

Jane Diane Ross

November 21, 1991

FIGURE 8.6 Table of contents

Table of Contents

	Page
Introduction	1
A Land of Many Trees	2
Rapid Growth in Population	6
More Housing Needed	8
Saving the Forest	12
Conclusion	15
Bibliography	17

three inches below the top of their papers. Each major section of the paper becomes one of the entries in the table of contents. Each entry, along with the page number on which it begins, is placed in the table of contents. Only the major words in each entry should be capitalized. Students should leave a double space between entries. Figure 8.6 shows a correctly formatted Table of Contents.

Step 10. **Final Check.** Before submitting their papers, students should do a final check. Figure 8.7 provides a checklist students can use for the final check of their papers before submitting them to their teacher.

When students can answer "yes" to each of these questions, they are ready to submit their research papers to their teacher. Students should submit the original to their teacher and keep a second copy for themselves.

FIGURE 8.7 Checklist

FINAL CHECKLIST

	Yes	No
1. Do I have a title page?	———	———
2. Do I have a table of contents?	———	———
3. Are the pages numbered correctly?	———	———
4. Have I included all the footnotes?	———	———
5. Do I have a bibliography?	———	———

■ TEACHING PLAN

Here is a plan for teaching students with learning disabilities a strategy for writing research papers. It is a good idea to have students actually write a research paper as you guide them through the strategy.

1. Write the words "Research Paper" on the chalkboard and ask students to tell what they know about research papers. Bring out the idea that research papers are written using facts found by students after they have researched a topic. Distribute copies of Reproducible 8-1, "Preparing the Research Paper." Explain the steps in the process of writing a research paper. Students can use the space below each step to record notes as you explain each step.

2. Distribute copies of Reproducible 8-2, "Choosing a Topic." Use the introductory text to explain the difference between topics that are either too broad or too narrow and those that are suitable. Use the activity to provide students with practice identifying topic statements that are *broad, narrow,* or *suitable.*

3. Distribute copies of Reproducible 8-3, "Practice Writing Topic Statements." The page consists of topic statements that are either too broad or too narrow. Have the students rewrite each statement to make it appropriate for a research paper.

4. Distribute copies of Reproducible 8-4, "Knowing If You Have Chosen a Good Topic." Students are directed to write at least two topics. Have each student use the four questions to evaluate and choose one of the topics as the topic on which they would like to write a research paper.

5. Distribute copies of Reproducible 8-5, "Locating Sources of Information." Use 8-5 to acquaint your students with some common sources of factual information. Students complete 8-5 by locating one example of each of eight different sources from which they can obtain information for writing research papers. If you are having the students write a research paper while going through these activities, establish the minimum number of sources your students must use for writing their research papers.

6. Distribute copies of Reproducible 8-6, "Learning about Bibliography Cards." Use the introductory paragraph to explain why it is important to prepare bibliography cards. Use the sample bibliography cards to explain how bibliography cards are prepared for the most common references. Explain what information is found on each card and how it is presented. For less common references you will need to provide the format.

7. Distribute copies of Reproducible 8-7, "Preparing Bibliography Cards (Part 1)." Have students use the sample bibliography cards on Reproducible 8-6 to prepare bibliography cards for three common references.

8. Distribute copies of Reproducible 8-8, "Preparing Bibliography Cards (Part 2)." Have students use the sample bibliography cards on Reproducible 8-6 to prepare

bibliography cards for three more references. If your students are writing a research paper, tell them to use the models in 8-7 and 8-8 to prepare bibliography cards for their research papers.

9. Distribute copies of Reproducible 8-9, "Preparing Note Cards." Use 8-9 to explain how note cards are prepared. If your students are writing a research paper, have them prepare note cards for their sources of information.

10. Distribute copies of Reproducible 8-10, "Preparing the Outline for the Paper." Use 8-10 to explain the format of an outline and how note cards are used to prepare an outline. If your students are writing a research paper, have them prepare outlines for their research papers. Approve the outlines before having students proceed to the next step.

11. Distribute copies of Reproducible 8-11, "Writing the Research Paper." Use 8-11 to explain how students would write the first draft of their papers. Help the students understand what information belongs in each section of the paper: *introduction, body,* and *conclusion.* Show them how to use the *Revising Checklist* to improve their rough draft and subsequent drafts of the research paper. If your students are writing a research paper, have them prepare the rough draft.

   Students can work in cooperative groups to revise their research papers. In this way students can help each other revise their papers. All revising should be done by the writer of the paper. The other students serve only as consultants to the writer.

12. Distribute copies of Reproducible 8-12, "Preparing Footnotes." Use the information and example in 8-12 to explain and demonstrate how footnotes are prepared. If your students are writing a research paper, have them prepare footnotes for their papers.

13. Distribute copies of Reproducible 8-13, "Preparing the Bibliography." Use the information to explain how the bibliography is prepared. An activity is provided that gives students an opportunity to prepare a bibliography. If your students are writing a research paper, have them prepare the bibliography for their research papers.

14. Distribute copies of Reproducible 8-14, "Preparing the Title Page and Table of Contents." The sample title page and table of contents included in 8-14 can serve as models when students prepare research papers.

15. Distribute copies of Reproducible 8-15, "Final Proofing." Discuss how students can use the Final Checklist to make sure their research papers are in the correct form to hand in to teachers. If your students are writing a research paper, have them use the Final Checklist before submitting their papers to you. You will find the Revising Checklist (Reproducible 8-11) and the Final Checklist useful for evaluating research papers written by your students. Students who use these checklists profit from the self-monitoring and self-evaluation involved.

16. Distribute Reproducible 8-16, "What I Have Learned." Use this reproducible to evaluate how well your students have learned the information taught in this chapter. Use any of the reproducibles as needed to review what was presented in this chapter.

Preparing the Research Paper

Here are the important steps to follow to write a research paper. As your teacher discusses each step, write down the important things you need to remember about each step.

Step 1. Selecting a topic

Step 2. Locating sources of information

Step 3. Preparing bibliography cards

Step 4. Preparing note cards

Step 5. Preparing the outline for the paper

Step 6. Writing the paper

Step 7. Preparing footnotes

Step 8. Preparing the bibliography

Step 9. Preparing the title page and table of contents

Step 10. Final proofing

Choosing a Topic

The first step in writing a research paper is to choose a topic. Your topic should not be too broad or too narrow. If your topic is too broad, you will not be able to complete the research paper in the number of pages assigned by your teacher. If your topic is too narrow, you will not find enough information. Be sure to select a topic in which you are interested.

Read each of the following topic statements. One is too broad, one is too narrow, and the other is suitable. Read to learn why.

> The effects of pollution on the lives of people throughout the world.

This statement is too broad because it would take too long to obtain information on people who live in every country in the world.

> The effects of pollution on mallard ducks.

This statement is too narrow because it limits the topic only to mallard ducks. Although there may be a lot of information available on pollution, there is probably very little on how pollution affects mallard ducks.

> The effects of pollution on people who get their water from the Great Lakes.

Here is a topic that is suitable for a research paper. The topic is limited to water pollution and to the Great Lakes. There will be sufficient information in your library on both pollution and the Great Lakes.

Read each of the following topic statements. For each, tell if the topic is too broad, too narrow, or suitable. Explain your answer.

1. Agriculture in America _____

   _____

2. Raising soybeans in southwest Arkansas. _____

   _____

3. Soybean production in the United States. _____

   _____

4. The uses of computers. _____

   _____

5. Using computers to learn to spell state capitals. _____

   _____

6. Using the computer to improve spelling skills. _____

   _____

Practice Writing Topic Statements

Here are some topic statements. In each case, the topic statement is either too broad or too narrow. Rewrite each to make it a suitable topic statement for a research paper.

1. The rise and fall of the Roman Empire.

_____

_____

2. Famous world leaders.

_____

_____

3. How rainfall affects the growth of red roses.

_____

_____

4. The use of eyeglasses for reading _Newsweek_ magazine.

_____

_____

5. Getting along with people.

_____

_____

6. Beethoven's influence on Michael Jackson.

_____

_____

7. The weather on Mt. Everest.

_____

_____

8. Marriage in early America.

_____

_____

Knowing If You Have Chosen a Good Topic ━━━━━━━

Here are some important questions you should answer about any topic you choose. These questions will help you know if the topic you have chosen is a good one.

Write at least two topics about which you would like to write a research paper.

1. _____

2. _____

3. _____

Now answer these these questions for each topic you wrote.

• Is the topic too broad, too narrow, or suitable?

Remember, if the topic is too broad or too narrow you will find it difficult to complete the paper within the number of pages assigned by your teacher.

• Is there enough factual information available to you on the topic?

Check in the library to see if there are enough references available to get the factual information you need on the topic. Make sure you have at least as many references as required by your teacher.

• Are you interested in this topic?

Be sure to select a topic in which you are interested. It takes a lot of time to do the research and writing. If you are not interested in the topic, you will probably not do a very good job of writing the paper.

• Will your teacher approve the topic?

Show your written topic statement to your teacher and ask for approval. Do not begin to work on a topic unless your teacher has approved it. Your teacher will probably have a book in which all the research topics are recorded by students in the class. Usually teachers will not allow more than one student to work on the same topic.

On which one of your topics would you like to write a research paper?

_____

_____

Why did you choose this one?

_____

_____

Locating Sources of Information

Your school or community library is the best place to begin looking for the information you need to complete your research paper. The librarian can help you locate sources of information on your topic if you do not know how to do so on your own. Here are a number of different sources of information you should consider using as you write your research paper.

Reference books. Encyclopedias are good sources of information on most topics. The articles in encyclopedias are written by experts. Frequently additional articles are recommended; sometimes even a recommended outline for a research paper is provided. The encyclopedia is probably the best place to start reading on your topic. Other useful first references are almanacs, books of facts, and dictionaries.

Magazines. These are good source of interesting information on topics. Articles from magazines can help you develop an interesting as well as factual research paper.

Newspapers. These are the most current source of printed material you will probably find on any topic.

Books. These are the best source of extensive background information on any topic.

Television, radio, films, audiocassettes. All these sources should also be examined for useful information

Experts. People who know a great deal about a topic are called experts. Experts often can provide information not available from other sources.

Write the topic you chose on Reproducible 8-4 on the following line:

_____

For this topic, find one example of each of the following sources of information. Write the name of each source.

Encyclopedia _____

Another reference book _____

Magazine _____

Newspaper _____

Book _____

Television or radio program _____

Videotape or audiocassette _____

Expert person _____

Learning about Bibliography Cards

You must prepare one bibliography card for every reference you use to write a research paper. Bibliography cards are usually 5″ by 8″ index cards. Look at the following bibliography cards for different types of references. Notice the information contained on each type of bibliography card. Also pay attention to how the information is capitalized and punctuated.

BIBLIOGRAPHY CARD FOR A REFERENCE BOOK

"Water Pollution,"

Encyclopedia Americana,

Volume 24, p. 213.

BIBLIOGRAPHY CARD FOR A MAGAZINE ARTICLE

Rockman, Julie. "Examining the Shores of the Great Lakes." Preserving Mother Nature.

October 1991, pp 3–6.

BIBLIOGRAPHY CARD FOR NEWSPAPER ARTICLE

"Pollutants Destroying the Great Lakes,"

Detroit Free Press,

14 October, 1991, p. 5.

BIBLIOGRAPHY CARD FOR A BOOK

Hanson, Tom. Water Pollution.

Appleton Press Publishers,

Great Falls, Iowa, 1991.

BIBLIOGRAPHY CARD FOR A FILM, TAPE, OR TELEVISION OR RADIO PROGRAM

Cruising the Waters of Lake Michigan.

Videotape, 1989. 60 min., VHS.

Distributed by NBC Educational Services, New York.

BIBLIOGRAPHY CARD FOR AN EXPERT

Jason, Beth. Water Supervisor,

Marquette, Michigan 49780

Personal conversation, 20 October 1991.

Preparing Bibliography Cards (Part 1)

Using the sample bibliography cards on Reproducible 8-6 as your guide, prepare a bibliography card for each of the following references:

1. Book titled <u>Water All Around Us.</u> Jake Brown is the author. University of Michigan Press, Lansing, Michigan, is the publisher. Published in 1989.

2. Magazine article entitled, "Stop Polluting My Drinking Water." Francis Duda is the author. The article appeared in the <u>Great Lakes Monthly Magazine</u> on page 44 of the September 25, 1990, issue.

3. Article entitled, "Polluting America's Great Lakes," found on pages 45–46 of the <u>World Book Encyclopedia,</u> Volume 18.

Preparing Bibliography Cards (Part 2)

Using the sample bibliography cards on Reproducible 8-6 as your guide, prepare a bibliography card for each of the following references:

1. Conversation with Kathy Clark, Director of Public Works, Chicago, Illinois, on September 16, 1991.

2. Audiocassette tape made in 1990, entitled Boating the Great Lakes, that is 30 minutes long and distributed by LTM Audiotapes, Milwaukee, Wisconsin.

3. Newspaper article entitled "What I Saw on the Beach Made Me Sick," found on page 24 of the Minneapolis Times on October 1, 1991.

Preparing Note Cards ━━━━━━━━━

When you have finished preparing your bibliography cards, you are ready to take notes from your sources. Use 5″ × 8″ index cards to take notes on the information from the sources you have found. Write the number of the bibliography card in the upper right-hand corner of each note card that goes with it. Use a dash and a second number to show the number of note cards. For example, 4-2 means bibliography card number four and note card number two. Circle the number to keep it separate from other numbers on your note card.

Write your notes in your own words. Be sure to place quotation marks around all quotes. Write the page number on which each quote appears.

Here is an example of a bibliography card and a note card that goes with it.

BIBLIOGRAPHY CARD   13

Maxson, Bill. Can't Drink the Water or Eat the Fish. Dwag press,

South Bend, Indiana, 1990.

NOTE CARD   13-1

"The water contains mercury and other chemicals." p. 23

Many fish are dying.

Fishing industry is hurting. People are worried about their jobs.

New, tough laws are making things better.

The lakes will be safe again and soon.

Complete the note card that goes with this bibliography card.

BIBLIOGRAPHY CARD   7

Zayre, Terry.

"The Great Lakes are Healing,"

Science Today. July 1991, p. 56–59.

Here is the information from this book on the topic:

Everyone has heard of the Great Lakes. They border a number of states in the United States and a number of provinces in Canada. They are the largest source of fresh water in the world.

Things are getting better in the Great Lakes since many industries have stopped discharging polluted water directly into the lakes. The water is safe to drink and the fish are once again safe to eat. It took 10 years to turn things around but it has finally happened.

It took cooperation between government and industry to solve the problem. Now everyone has to be responsible for keeping the lakes clean and healthy. The Great Lakes are an important source of water, food, and recreation for many Americans and Canadians.

NOTE CARD

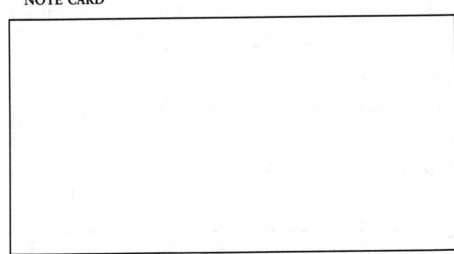

Preparing the Outline for the Paper

An outline is a plan for writing a paper. When you have obtained enough notes to write a paper, you must organize the notes into an outline. Study the outline at the bottom of this page as you read the information in the box about outlines.

> Organize your notes into main topics, subtopics, details, and subdetails. Begin by writing the working title of your paper near the top on a blank piece of paper. Then write the Roman numeral I and after it the first main topic. Use capital letters before each subtopic that goes with the main topic. Use Arabic numerals before each detail that goes with the subtopic. Use small letters before each subdetail. Repeat this for each main topic until you have completed your outline.
>
> You can write the main topics, subtopics, details, and subdetails as sentences, phrases, or single words. Do whatever will help you recall the important ideas in your outline.

Outline

The effects of pollution on people who get their water from the Great Lakes.

I. Water for drinking

    A. Mercury

    B. Iron ore

    C. Paper industries

        1. Getting the wood to the paper mills

            a. truck

            b. railroad

            c. floating logs down rivers

        2. Chemicals used to make paper

    D. Tourists add to the problem

II. Fish for eating

    A. Chemical contamination

    B. Fewer fish

    C. Takes years to reproduce

III. Recreation

    A. There will be less fun in the sun if something isn't done soon.

    B. Recreational boaters cause some of the problem.

    C. People are scared to swim in the water.

Answer these questions about the outline:

1. What is the working title for this research paper?

2. List the main topics found in this outline.

3. How many subtopics are found for the main topic "Fish for eating"?

4. Write the two details that go with the subtopic "Paper industries."

5. Write the three subdetails found in the outline.

6. Why should you prepare an outline before writing a research paper?

Writing the Research Paper

Using the outline as a guide, you would write the rough draft of a research paper. Your teacher would tell you how many pages the paper should be and how many references you would need to use. Use regular loose-leaf, lined paper for writing a rough draft. Leave at least one-inch margins at the top, bottom, left, and right of each page. Write on every other line. This will leave plenty of room for revising the rough draft.

Organize your note cards according to the topics, subtopics, details, and subdetails in your outline. Start by writing the working title at the top of the first page. Then write an introduction that tells the reader what the paper will be about. Use your outline and note cards to write the body of the paper. As you write, insert any side headings and visual aids that will help the reader understand your topic. When you have finished writing about your topic, write a conclusion. The conclusion tells the reader what you have learned about the topic. Number each page in the top right-hand corner as you write. Be sure to circle the page numbers to keep them separate from other numbers in your research paper.

When you have finished writing a rough draft, reread it carefully and make any changes that will improve the paper.

The Revising Checklist shown below should be used for this purpose.

Revising Checklist

1. Does the introduction clearly introduce the topic?
2. Are side headings used to help the reader understand the paper?
3. Does the body contain all the facts needed?
4. Is each paragraph written with a main idea?
5. Does every sentence and paragraph add something to the paper?
6. Did I choose the best words to explain the ideas?
7. Does the conclusion follow from the facts?
8. Have I corrected all the misspelled words?
9. Have I capitalized all the appropriate words?
10. Have I used quotation marks to identify all quotations?
11. Have I reread the paper at least three times looking for ways to make it better?
12. Did I number all the pages?

You may need to write a paper more than once to get it in the best form. All good writers write their papers a number of times. Use the Revising Checklist to check each draft of a research paper. When the paper is in final form, write or type the final paper.

Preparing Footnotes

Credit must be given to sources from which you take quotations or major ideas. In a research paper, credit is given by using footnotes. On the page, a footnote reference number is written after the material for which credit is being given. The number is slightly raised above the line. Most often the footnotes are placed at the bottom of the page on which the quotation or main idea appears. A line is drawn to separate the text from the footnotes. Here is an example of a footnoted page. Notice how numbers are used in the text and in the footnotes to show how the references go together.

> The most common shoe size for men is size nine and for women it is size seven.[1] According to Donald Blake in the *Shoe Manufacturer's Journal,* "men and women are growing bigger feet."[2]
>
> ---
>
> 1. Phil Harris, *Shoe Sales,* p. 34.
> 2. Donald Blake, "Feet Are Getting Bigger," *Shoe Manufacturers' Journal,* Vol. 11, September 1990, p. 56.

Sometimes teachers prefer to have all the footnotes on one page at the end of the paper. When footnotes are listed at the end of a paper, the same format is used for writing the footnotes. The footnotes are numbered in the order the information is presented in the paper. Ask your teacher which way footnotes should be shown in your research paper.

1. When should you use footnotes?

2. In what two places can footnotes appear?

3. Who decides where the footnotes should appear in a research paper?

4. Is the same format used to write footnotes no matter where they appear?

5. What separates your writing from the footnotes when they are at the bottom of a page?

Preparing the Bibliography ━━━━━━━━━━━━━━━━━

At the end of a research paper you must provide a list of all the sources you used to gather information for the paper. This list of sources is called a **bibliography.** Here is a sample bibliography.

BIBLIOGRAPHY

Abbott, James. Director of the Regional Pollution Center, Zephyrhills, Florida 33541. Personal letter, November 12, 1992.

"Covering Up the Pollution Story." Atlanta Constitution, December 9, 1992, p. 4.

Frank, Steven. "What Are They Doing to Our Water?" Today's Health, January 1993, pp. 62–67.

"Pollution." World Book Encyclopedia, Volume 13, pp. 419–426.

Ruining Our World through Neglect. Videotape, 1993. 30 minutes. Distributed by Save Our Planet, San Diego, California.

Thompson, Robert. Our Polluted World: What Will We Leave for Our Children? Chicago: Delta Press, 1992.

To prepare a bibliography, you need a blank piece of paper and your bibliography cards. Write or type the word "Bibliography" in the center of a line 2 inches below the top of the sheet of paper. Then check to be sure all your bibliography cards are in alphabetical order by the first word on each card. Now write each reference as it appears on the bibliography card. The information on the cards is already in the correct format. Indent the second and following lines of each reference.

Now go ahead and prepare a bibliography using the following bibliography cards. Prepare your bibliography on a blank piece of paper.

```
Zayre, Albert. The Russian State.

Williams House Publishers,

New York, 1990.
```

Mann, Mark. "The Mongols Take Over Russia."

Historical Review. April 1990, pp. 10–12.

Bos, Candy. Director of the Miami Historical Center,

Miami, Florida 33122. Personal letter, May 25, 1990.

"Russian Tsars," Encyclopedia Britannica,

Volume 23, pp. 367–382.

"Government in the Early Years of the USSR,"

San Francisco Daily News, June 15, 1990, p. 20.

Touring the Kremlin. Videotape, 1988. 60 minutes.

Distributed by International Video Productions,

Dallas, Texas.

Thompson, Mary Ellen. Russian Language Teacher,

Willow School, Minneapolis, Minnesota 48767.

Personal conversation, June 4, 1990.

Striker, Sally. "Beautiful Icons."

Modern Art. July 1990, pp. 23–27.

Preparing the Title Page and Table of Contents

The title page is the first page of the research paper. It includes the title of the research paper, the name of the writer, and the date on which the paper is due. Look at the sample title page as you read the information in the box about it.

> To prepare the title page, you need a blank piece of paper. Three inches from the top of the sheet of paper, write or type the title using all capital letters. Be sure to center the title. About six inches from the top and bottom of the sheet of paper and centered, type the word "by." Two lines below the word "by," and centered, write your name. Two lines below your name, and centered, write the date the paper is due.

SOYBEAN PRODUCTION IN THE UNITED STATES

by

Mary Hardy

January 17, 1991

The table of contents is the second page of the research paper. Look at the sample table of contents as you read the information in the box about it.

> To prepare the table of contents, you need a blank piece of paper. Three inches from the top of the sheet of paper and centered, write or type the words "Table of Contents." Capitalize only the first letter of the word "Table" and the first letter of "Contents." Leave a one-inch margin on both the left and right sides of the piece of paper. The table of contents lists the main topics and important subtopics, and the pages on which each is introduced in a research paper. Capitalize each major word in each entry in the table of contents.

TABLE OF CONTENTS

	Page
Introduction	1
Northeastern states	2
Midwestern states	3
Southern states	5
Western states	9
Conclusion	10
Bibliography	12

Use the following information to prepare a Title Page and Table of Contents.

Lumbering in the forests of California. By Jane Diane Ross. Paper due November 21, 1991.

Introduction, page 1
A land of many trees, page 2
Glorious hardwoods, page 3
Beautiful firs, page 4
Graceful maple trees, page 5
Rapid growth in population, page 6

More housing needed, page 8
Other needs for wood, page 10
Saving the forest, page 12
Conclusion, page 15
Bibliography, page 17

Final Proofing

Read through your research paper one last time before submitting it to your teacher. Use the questions in the Final Checklist to look for the common errors found by teachers in research papers. Place a checkmark (√) in the "Yes" or "No" column for each question

FINAL CHECKLIST

	Yes	No
1. Do I have a title page?	_____	_____
2. Do I have a table of contents?	_____	_____
3. Are the pages numbered correctly?	_____	_____
4. Have I included all the footnotes?	_____	_____
5. Do I have a bibliography?	_____	_____

When you can answer "yes" to each of these questions, you are ready to submit your research paper to your teacher. Before you do, make a second copy for your own files in case your original copy gets lost. Then place the original copy of the research paper in a folder to protect it and submit it on the date due.

What I Have Learned

Directions: Show what you have learned about writing a research paper by writing an answer for each of the following:

1. What kind of information is found in a research paper?

2. What problem will you have if you choose a topic that is too broad? Too narrow?

3. Where should you begin looking for information?

4. In what type of printed reference will you find the most current information about a topic?

5. Must you prepare a bibliography card for every reference you use?

6. On a note card, what does 6-2 mean?

7. Label each part of the following outline:

    I. _____

      A. _____

        1. _____

          a. _____

8. What is each rewriting of the research paper called?

9. What is the purpose of the Revising Checklist?

10. Why must you use footnotes?

11. What is the title for the list of sources at the end of the research paper?

12. What is the first page of the research paper called?

13. What is the second page called?

14. What is the purpose of the Final Checklist?

Answers for Chapter 8 Reproducibles

8-1 Notes will vary.

8-2 1. Too broad. There are many forms of agriculture in America. 2. Too narrow. Too small a geographical area to focus on. 3. Suitable. Refers to a specific crop in a large enough geographical area. 4. Too broad. There are many uses for computers. 5. Too narrow. Focuses on a very minor use of computers. 6. Suitable. Refers to one important skill that can be developed through the use of computers.

8-3 Answers will vary.

8-4 Answers will vary.

8-5 Answers will vary.

8-6 No writing required.

8-7 1. Brown, Jake. Water All Around Us.
University of Michigan Press,
Lansing, Michigan, 1989.

2. Duda, Frances. "Stop Polluting My Drinking Water."
Great Lakes Monthly Magazine.
September 25, 1990, p. 44.

3. "Polluting America's Great Lakes,"
World Book Encyclopedia,
Volume 18, pp. 45–46.

8-8 1. Clark, Kathy. Director of Public Works,
Chicago, Illinois
Personal conversation, 16 September 1991

2. Boating the Great Lakes.
Audiocassette, 1990. 30 minutes.
Distributed by LTM Audiotapes,
Milwaukee, Wisconsin.

3. "What I Saw on the Beach Made Me Sick,"
Minneapolis Times,
1 October, 1991, p. 24.

8-9 NOTE CARD   (7-1)

Great Lakes—in U.S. and Canada. Largest fresh water source in world. Water better since industries stopped polluting it. Now can drink water and eat fish. Gov't and industry solved problem. Used for water, food, and fun by Americans and Canadians.

8-10 1. The effects of pollution on people who get their water from the Great Lakes.

2. I. Water for drinking.
II. Fish for eating.
III. Recreation.

3. 3.

4. 1. Getting the wood to the paper mills.
    2. Chemicals used to make paper.

5. a. truck.
    b. railroad.
    c. floating logs down rivers.
    6. An outline provides a plan for writing a paper.

8-11 No writing required.

8-12 1. When credit must be given to sources from which you take quotations or major ideas. 2. At the bottom of a page or at the end of the paper. 3. The teacher. 4. Yes. 5. A line that is drawn to separate the footnotes from the text of the paper.

8-13 Use the bibliography shown in Figure 8.4 as the answer key.

8-14 Use the title page as shown in Figure 8.5 and the table of contents as shown in Figure 8.6 as the answer keys.

8-15 No writing required.

8-16 Factual information obtained by doing research on a topic. 2. If too broad, you will not be able to complete the paper in the assigned number of pages. If too narrow, you will not find enough information to write the paper. 3. The school or community library. 4. Newspapers. 5. Yes. 6. Bibliography card 6, note card 2. 7. I. Main topic. A. Subtopic. 1. Detail. a. Subdetail. 8. Draft. 9. To help you identify things you can change to improve your paper. 10. To give credit to sources from which you take quotations or major ideas. 11. Bibliography. 12. Title page. 13. Table of contents. 14. To locate common errors so you can correct them before handing in the paper.

CHAPTER 9

Taking Tests

■ Purposes

The purposes of this chapter are to:
1. teach students with learning disabilities a strategy for preparing to take a test.
2. teach students with learning disabilities strategies for taking five types of tests.
3. provide reproducibles that can be used to help students learn to how prepare for and take tests.

■ Titles of Reproducibles

■ RATIONALE

Teachers give tests for a very important reason—to determine if students have learned new concepts and their application (Bos & Vaughn, 1988). As Vogel (1987) observed, tests also provide feedback to students. If students do poorly on a test, this is a warning signal they should seek assistance from the teacher. On the other hand, a high score on a test provides assurance to students that they are successfully meeting instructional objectives. And, of course, teachers use test results to assign grades to students.

It is important that tests measure students' knowledge of information and concepts, rather than reflect their lack of test taking skills (Hoover, 1988a). Students with learning disabilities often have poor test preparation and test-taking skills (Lee & Alley, 1984; Scruggs & Mastropieri, 1988). They must be taught these skills for several reasons:

1. Students with learning disabilities are often allowed to meet course requirements by completing projects, preparing written reports, or giving oral presentations rather than demonstrating what they have learned by taking traditional tests. Consequently, when they are required to take traditional tests, they are at a disadvantage. As Scruggs and Mastropieri (1988) noted, when taking tests, students who lack appropriate test-taking skills are at a disadvantage relative to students who have equal knowledge and effective test-taking skills.

2. As students with learning disabilities proceed through the school years and are mainstreamed into different subject area classes, they will increasingly be required to demonstrate what they have learned by taking a variety of tests. Some of the traditional forms of tests they will be required to take are: multiple-choice, true/false, matching, completion, and essay. Students with learning disabilities must be taught how to prepare for and take these tests so they can demonstrate what they have learned.

3. When students with learning disabilities do poorly on a test because of poor test-taking skills rather than lack of mastery of what has been taught, a teacher may reach two erroneous conclusions. The first is the students have not achieved mastery of what has been taught. The second is that the instruction has not been appropriate.

■ BACKGROUND INFORMATION

Students with learning disabilities need a strategy for preparing to take tests. They also need strategies for taking the different types of tests commonly given by teachers. These include multiple choice, true/false, matching, completion, and essay tests.

■ TEST PREPARATION STRATEGY

Students with learning disabilities frequently wait until the last day or two before beginning to prepare for a test. Then, when they do begin preparing, they often find they do not have all the information they need. It is not uncommon for students with learning disabilities to spend more of their time trying to obtain the information than attempting to master it. These students need a test preparation strategy that enables

300

them to begin preparing a sufficient time before the test is given. An appropriate strategy provides students with all the time they need to locate the information covered by the test while still giving them all the time they need to master the information.

Because they wait until the last day or two to begin preparing, students with learning disabilities must attempt to cram information into their memory. This overtaxes their memory span and builds up excessive anxiety. To counter this, we propose teaching these students a five-day test preparation plan that allows them sufficient time to prepare for a test.

Five-Day Test Preparation Plan

The five-day test preparation plan will help students with learning disabilities to better prepare for tests and consequently receive higher grades. The plan is divided into two parts:

Part I. *Getting Ready.* There are a number of things students with learning disabilities can do to get ready to prepare to take a test. These students should be taught to:

1. Ask the teacher what information will be covered on the test.

2. Ask the teacher what type of test will be given.

3. Use the SQ3R textbook reading strategy described in Chapter 2 to read all textbook assignments and take appropriate notes.

4. Use the notetaking strategy described in Chapter 4 to record all important information provided by the teacher.

5. Schedule their time to begin studying five days before a test is given.

Part II. *Preparing for the Test.* Students should be encouraged to begin preparing for a test five days before the test is given. This requires teachers to give students sufficient advance notice of tests. Here is the five-day test preparation plan students with learning disabilities should be taught to follow.

Day 5. On this day students should review their textbook notes for all assigned chapters in their textbooks. Textbook notes were introduced in Chapter 2 as part of the SQ3R textbook reading stratgegy. Students should also review their written class notes. The notetaking strategy was introduced in Chapter 4. Any information that is not understood should be brought to the teacher for clarification.

Day 4. On this day, students should use the techniques for remembering presented in Chapter 1 as they study the information in their textbook notes and class notes. Students should begin to commit this information to memory by reviewing it as least three times on this day.

Day 3. On this day, students should rewrite both their textbook notes and their class notes in a briefer form. Encourage the students to use terse language and abbreviations when rewriting their notes. The rewriting gives students a multimodal review of the information.

Day 2. On this day, students should write questions they think will be on the test. They should then write answers to these questions using their rewritten textbook and class notes as necessary.

Day 1. This is the day the students take the test. On this day students should review their rewritten textbook and class notes before the school day begins. A good time to do this is at breakfast or while riding to school. Just before the test, students should do a final review of these notes, particularly any parts they are having difficulty remembering.

■ STRATEGIES FOR TAKING TESTS

We present a different strategy for taking each of five types of tests. The strategies are based upon recommendations from a number of sources (Alley & Deshler, 1979; Austin Community College, 1989; Bos & Vaughn, 1988; Mastropieri & Scruggs, 1987; Sedita, 1989; Shepherd, 1982; Wallace & Kaufman, 1986). When using any of the strategies, students are taught to:

1. Read test directions carefully and ask for clarification of any directions not clearly understood.

2. Look over the entire test to get a feel for how much has to be done.

3. Determine how much time should be used to answer each item on the test.

4. Answer easy or known items first and then go back to answer more difficult items.

5. Check to make certain that all required items have been completed as well as possible.

■ TYPES OF TESTS

In this section we present the five most common types of tests that students with learning disabilities will be required to take in school. Multiple-choice, true/false, and matching tests are frequently used by teachers to test for factual recall. Completion and essay tests are typically used to test for conceptual understanding. Descriptions of each of these types of tests and the strategies that students with learning disabilities should use to take them follow.

Multiple-Choice Tests. Shepherd (1982) identified two types of multiple-choice items. One consists of an incomplete statement (stem) followed by possible ways the statement may be completed (answer choices). The second consists of a question (stem) followed by possible answers (answer choices). Typically there are four answer choices for each question, and students are instructed to choose the correct one and mark it in some manner. Here are examples of the two types of multiple-choice items.

Type 1: There are _____ months in a year.

a. 9

b. 12

c. 52

d. 7

Type 2: How many months are there in a year?

a. 9

b. 12

c. 52

d. 7

Students with learning disabilities should be taught to do the following when taking multiple-choice tests:

1. Read the question stem and underline any key words such as *not, except, incorrect,* and *false.*

2. Read the stem of the question with each possible answer choice to decide which is correct.

3. Cross out each incorrect answer choice. If one choice is left, select that choice as the answer. If more than one choice remains, reread each choice with the stem and choose the best answer.

4. Do not change an answer unless you are certain it is incorrect.

5. Answer all items unless there is a penalty for guessing.

In addition, students should be encouraged to look for clues to the correct answer. The following list, though not foolproof, gives some clues that students with learning disabilities might find useful.

1. When one of the answer choices is "All of the above" it is usually the correct answer.

2. Answer choices with qualifiers such as "Most people . . ." are usually correct.

3. Answer choices with absolute statements such as "All . . ." or "There is no . . ." are usually incorrect.

4. If two answer choices are opposites, one of them is likely to be correct.

5. If two answer choices are similar, neither one is likely to be correct.

6. The most general answer choice is likely to be the correct one.

7. The longest or most complete answer choice is likely to be the correct one.

8. An answer choice containing familiar language is likely to be the correct one.

9. An answer choice containing technical language is likely to be the correct one.

True/False Tests. For a true/false item, students must read a statement and decide if it is true or false. The item is usually answered by circling TRUE (T) or FALSE (F). An example of a true/false item is:

T   F   The sun rotates around the earth.

Students with learning disabilities should be taught to do the following when taking true/false tests:

1. Assume an answer is true unless the statement can be proved false.

2. Be certain that *all* parts of a statement are correct before marking it true.

3. Watch for negatives such as *not* or prefixes such as *in,* as in the word *infrequently.* Students should be shown that negatives can completely change the meaning of a statement. For example, the statement "I frequently eat a sandwich for lunch" is completely changed by saying "I infrequently eat a sandwich for lunch."

4. Simplify statements that contain a double negative by eliminating both negatives. Doing this makes such statements much easier to understand. For example, the statement, "You cannot ride a bicycle if you don't keep your balance," can be simplified to, "You can ride a bicycle if you keep your balance."

5. Assume that absolute statements are FALSE whereas qualified statements are TRUE.

6. Answer all items unless there is a penalty for guessing.

Matching Tests. Shepherd (1982) described matching tests as the presentation of two lists of items with the requirement that test takers associate items in one list with items in the other. The items within a list are of a similar type. An example of a matching test is as follows:

Directions: Match the symbols for holidays in the first column with the holidays in the second column. Write the number of the symbol that goes with a holiday on the line next to the holiday.

1. turkey	_____	Fourth of July
2. Santa Claus	_____	Thanksgiving
3. U.S. flag	_____	Christmas
4. firecracker	_____	Memorial Day

Students with learning disabilities should be taught to do the following when taking matching tests:

1. Read all the items in both columns before answering.

2. Start by making the easiest matches.

3. Make all the correct matches possible before guessing at any of the other matches.

4. Cross out items in both columns as they use them.

5. Make their best guess for the remaining items unless there is a penalty for guessing.

Completion Tests. In a completion test, statements are presented with a deleted portion (blank line) that must be filled in by the test taker. The correct response to a completion item may be one or more words in length. An example of a completion item is:

The capital of the United States is _____.

Students with learning disabilities should be taught to do the following when taking completion tests:

1. Read the statement and think about what is missing.

2. Write an answer that logically fits the blank line.

3. Write an answer that fits the blank line grammatically. For example, the word *an* just before the blank line means that the answer must begin with a vowel sound.

4. Use the length of the blank line as a clue to the length of their answer unless the length of the blank line is the same for every item on the test.

5. Reread the statement with their answer in it to be sure it makes sense.

Essay Tests. This test form consists of questions or statements to which test takers must write an answer. Essay questions can vary in what they require. Shepherd (1982) pointed out that essay questions include **direction words** such as *discuss, compare,* and *contrast.* Direction words tell what the test taker has to do to answer the question.

It is important to teach students with learning disabilities to recognize and interpret direction words. Shepherd (1982) noted that different direction words often mean essentially the same thing. It is a good idea, therefore, to teach direction words as sets of similar words. Students should be taught the following sets of direction words and their meanings:

discuss, describe, explain. These three direction words tell students to write as much as they can about a question or statement.

diagram, illustrate. These two direction words tell students to make a drawing with each part labeled.

compare, contrast. *Compare* directs students to tell how two or more things are alike as well as how they are different. *Contrast* directs students to tell only how they are different.

relate, trace. *Relate* tells students to show how two or more things are connected. *Trace* directs them to state a series of things in some logical order.

criticize, evaluate, justify. These three direction words require students to reach a conclusion about the value of something. *Criticize* and *evaluate* each require them to think about the positive and negative aspects of something before coming to a conclusion about it. *Justify* requires students to provide reasons that explain an action or decision.

list, outline. *List* tells students to present information in an item-by-item series, usually with each item numbered. *Outline* tells them to provide the main points in some detail, usually using both numbers and letters.

summarize. *Summarize* directs students to write a brief statement that tells something about all the important ideas.

In addition to learning about direction words, students with learning disabilities should also be taught to do the following when taking essay tests:

1. Read and restate a question or statement in their own words before attempting to answer it. If they are unable to do this, they probably do not understand the question and should ask the teacher for clarification.

2. Make a brief outline before writing their answer. This helps students organize what they will write.

3. Answer all parts of a question.

4. Write directly to the point of the question, rather than write about something they are interested in or something else they happen to know.

5. Use pictures and diagrams where appropriate to help explain ideas.

6. Write neatly. Students should be reminded that teachers will not give credit for something that cannot be read.

7. Proofread their answers for clarity, spelling, and grammar.

8. When running out of time, list all the information they know about the question or statement.

■ TEACHING PLAN

Here is a plan for teaching students with learning disabilities how to prepare for and take tests.

1. Tell students they will be learning how to prepare for and take tests. Emphasize that this will help them get better grades in school. Distribute copies of Reproducible 9-1, "Preparing for Tests." Discuss the four suggestions presented. Then have students write a sentence telling about each.

2. Bring out the fact that to prepare effectively, students need a plan. Use Reproducible 9-2, "Five-Day Test Preparation Plan," to demonstrate a way students can systematically prepare for tests. Highlight what students should do each day as they get closer to taking a test. Have the students complete the page activity.

3. Reproducible 9-3, "Things to Do When Taking Tests," should be used to teach students five things they should do when taking any type of test. Discuss the five suggestions and have the students complete the written activity.

4. Distribute Reproducible 9-4, "Learning about Multiple-Choice Tests." Use 9-4 to teach students about two types of multiple-choice test items. Make certain students recognize that multiple-choice items consist of a stem and a set of answer choices. Have the students prepare an example of each of the two types of multiple-choice items using the information provided.

5. Have the students take notes using Reproducible 9-5, "Guidelines for Taking Multiple-Choice Tests," as you elaborate on the guidelines for taking multiple-choice tests.

6. Have students take the practice test on Reproducible 9-6, "Practice Taking a Multiple-Choice Test." Remind the students to apply the guidelines they learned for taking multiple choice tests. There is a five-minute time limit for this test. When the test is completed, go over the answers and have the students score and grade their test.

7. Have the students take notes using Reproducible 9-7, "More Guidelines for Taking Multiple-Choice Tests," as you elaborate on these additional suggestions.

8. Have the students take notes using Reproducible 9-8, "Guidelines for Taking True/False Tests," as you elaborate on the guidelines for taking true/false tests.

9. Have students take the practice test on Reproducible 9-9, "Practice Taking a True/False Test." Remind the students to apply the guidelines they learned for taking true/false tests. There is a five-minute time limit for this test. When the test is completed, go over the answers and have the students score and grade their test.

10. Have the students take notes using Reproducible 9-10, "Guidelines for Taking Matching Tests," as you elaborate on the guidelines for taking matching tests.

11. Have students take the practice tests on Reproducible 9-11, "Practice Taking Matching Tests." Remind the students to apply the guidelines they learned for matching tests. There is a seven-minute time limit for the three tests on this reproducible. When the tests are completed, go over the answers and have the students score and grade them.

12. Have the students take notes using Reproducible 9-12, "Guidelines for Taking Completion Tests," as you elaborate on the guidelines for taking completion tests.

13. Have the students take the practice test on Reproducible 9-13, "Practice Taking a Completion Test." Remind the students to apply the guidelines they learned for completion tests. There is a five-minute time limit for this test. When the test is completed, go over the answers and have the students score and grade their test.

14. Distribute Reproducible 9-14, "Learning about Direction Words in Essay Tests." Use 9-14 to teach students about the meaning and use of direction words. Emphasize that many direction words mean the same thing. After the discussion, have students write statements that tell what the direction words mean.

15. Have the students take notes using Reproducible 9-15, "Guidelines for Taking Essay Tests," as you elaborate on the guidelines for taking essay tests.

16. Review the material learned in this chapter with the students. Then have the students take the practice test on Reproducible 9-16, "Practice Taking an Essay Test." Remind the students to apply the guidelines they learned for essay tests. There is a thirty-minute time limit for this test. When the test is completed, collect, score, and return it.

17. Distribute Reproducible 9-17, "What I Have Learned." Use this reproducible to evaluate how well your students have learned the information taught in this chapter. As needed, use any of the reproducibles to review what was presented in this chapter.

Preparing for Tests

Do you want to get better grades on your tests? Most students do. You can too if you follow these suggestions:

1. Ask your teacher to explain what will be on the test. Also ask what will not be on the test. This way you know exactly what you need to study for the test.

2. Review your textbook notes to be sure they are complete. Compare your notes with those taken by other students. Ask your teacher to clarify anything you do not understand.

3. Review your class notes to be sure they are complete. Compare your class notes with notes taken by other students. Ask your teacher to clarify anything you do not understand.

4. To learn all you need to know to do well on a test and get a good grade, you need to begin to prepare early. Schedule your time so you will be able to start preparing five days before the test is given.

Think about the four things you need to do to get ready for your next test. In your own words, write a sentence telling about each.

1.

2.

3.

4.

Five-Day Test Preparation Plan

Here is a five-day plan you can use to prepare for a test. The five-day plan shows what you should do each day to get ready for the test. If you follow the five-day plan, each day you will find yourself more ready to take the test. You will be so ready for the test that you will look forward to taking it.

Here is what you need to do each day:

Day Five Read the notes you took in class. Read the notes you took from your textbook. Read over all the handouts provided by your teacher. On this day you should identify all the important information you must know and remember for the test. Highlight or underline the important information in your notes.

Day Four Use the techniques you have learned, such as visualization, association, application, repetition, and mnemonics, to help you remember the important information you identified on Day Five. Review your notes until you can remember all the important information. The more information there is to remember and the more difficult the information is, the more times you will need to review it.

Day Three Rewrite the important information in a brief form using the fewest words you can. Use abbreviations wherever possible. Review your rewritten notes at least twice on this day.

Day Two Make a list of questions you think your teacher will ask on the test. Write answers for these questions.

Day One This is the day you take the test. Review your rewritten notes from Day Three. Also review the questions and answers you prepared on Day Two. A good time to do this is while eating breakfast or while riding to school. Just before the test, review anything you are having difficulty remembering.

Think about what you must do each day to prepare for a test. In your own words, write a sentence telling what you will do each day.

Day Five.

Day Four.

Day Three.

Day Two.

Day One.

Things to Do When Taking Tests

While you are taking a test, there are some important things you can do to improve your score. Here are five things you should do to improve your test score on any test.

1. Read the test directions carefully. Ask the teacher to explain any directions or words you do not understand.

2. Look over the entire test to see how much there is to do.

3. Decide how much time you can spend answering each question on the test. You should be guided by the number of questions as well as how many points each question counts. Plan to spend more time on those questions that count for the most points.

4. Answer the easiest questions first. Then go back and answer as many of the more difficult questions as you can.

5. Review your answers to be sure they are correct. Do not hand in your test until you have reviewed your answers.

What five things should you do while taking a test?

1.

2.

3.

4.

5.

Learning about Multiple-Choice Tests

There are two types of multiple-choice test items. Both have a stem and a number of answer choices.

The first type has an incomplete statement followed by possible answers to complete the statement. Your job is to identify the answer that correctly completes the statement. Here is an example of this type of item.

There are _____ months in a year. (Stem)

(Answer choices)

a. 9

b. 12

c. 52

d. 7

The second type has a question followed by possible answers. Your job is to identify the choice that correctly answers the question. Here is an example of this type of item.

How many months are there in a year? (Stem)

(Answer choices)

a. 9

b. 12

c. 52

d. 7

Use the information in the box to write multiple-choice test items. Write one item for each type.

> *Year:* 1492.
>
> *Event:* Columbus discovered America.

1.

a.

b.

c.

d.

2.

a.

b.

c.

d.

Guidelines for Taking Multiple-Choice Tests ━━━

There are a number of things you can do to choose the correct answer in a multiple-choice test item. Here are some guidelines for answering multiple-choice test items. Add information to each guideline as your teacher tells you more about it.

- Read the stem and underline key words such as *not, except, incorrect, false.* These words give you clues to the correct answer.

- Read the stem with each possible answer choice to decide which answer choice is correct.

- As you decide an answer choice is incorrect, draw a line through it.

- If there is one answer choice left, it is the answer you should select.

- If there is more than one answer choice left, reread each with the stem and choose the best answer.

- Do not change your answer unless you are sure it is wrong.

- Answer all items unless there is a penalty for guessing.

Practice Taking a Multiple-Choice Test

Take the following multiple-choice test. Apply the guidelines you learned for answering multiple-choice test items. There is no penalty for guessing. Each correct choice is worth one point. You will have five minutes to complete the test.

Directions: Circle the best answer for each of the following:

1. Do not answer questions for which you are unsure of the answer when:

    a. you are running out of time.

    b. a question is difficult

    c. there is a guessing penalty.

    d. you don't like the question.

2. You should _____ an answer choice when you decide it is incorrect.

    a. choose

    b. reread

    c. rewrite

    d. draw a line through

3. You should _____ key words in a stem.

    a. underline

    b. ignore

    c. cross out

    d. look up

4. Change your answer when it is:

    a. too long.

    b. correct.

    c. wrong.

    d. too short.

5. Read the _____ with each answer choice to decide which answer is correct.

    a. first word of a question

    b. last word of a question

    c. stem

    d. key word

Number Correct _____

    5 = Excellent

    4 = Good

    0–3 = Reread the information on Reproducibles 9-4 and 9-5

More Guidelines for Taking Multiple-Choice Tests

Here are some more guidelines that will help you select correct answers on multiple-choice tests. Add information to each guideline as your teacher discusses it with you.

- When one of the answer choices is "all of the above," it is usually the correct answer. Before choosing "all of the above," check to be sure all the answer choices are correct.

- If two of the answer choices are opposites, one of them is likely to be the correct answer.

- If two of the answer choices are almost the same, neither one is likely to be the correct answer.

- The most general answer choice is often the correct answer.

- The most complete answer choice is often the correct answer.

- An answer choice containing language that your teacher or textbook used is likely to be the correct answer.

- An answer choice containing technical language is often the correct answer.

Guidelines for Taking True/False Tests ━━━━━━━━━

Here are some things you can do to improve your score on a true/false test. By following these guidelines you will have a better chance of selecting correct answers. Add information to each guideline as your teacher tells you more about it.

- Choose TRUE unless you can prove that a statement is FALSE.

- For a statement to be TRUE, all parts of the statement must be true. For example, the statement below is FALSE because not all parts of it are true.

  All mammals have hair, are warm blooded, and can talk.   True *False*

  This answer is FALSE because, although all mammals have hair and are warm blooded, not all mammals can talk.

- Be careful when reading statements that contain negatives such as *not, don't,* or *in (infrequent)* and *un (unfriendly)*. A negative can completely change the meaning of a statement. For example:

  1. Jane is going to the party.
  2. Jane is not going to the party.

  1. He comes to school frequently.
  2. He comes to school infrequently.

- If a statement has two negatives in it, get rid of both negatives. This makes the statement much easier to understand. For example, look at the two statements that follow. The second one is easier to understand because the two negatives have been taken out.

  1. You can not get good grades if you do not study.
  2. You can get good grades if you study.

- Absolute statements are usually FALSE. Qualified statements are usually TRUE. For example, statement 1 is FALSE and statement 2 is TRUE.

    1. *All* people like to go to the movies on Friday.

    2. *Some* people like to go to the movies on Friday.

- If you are uncertain about an item, take a guess at the answer unless there is a penalty for guessing.

Practice Taking a True/False Test ━━━━━━━━

Answer the following about taking true/false tests. Use what you learned about answering true/false test items. There is no penalty for guessing. Each item is worth one point. You will have five minutes to complete the test.

Directions: Circle TRUE or FALSE for each of the following.

TRUE   FALSE   1. If a statement has two negatives, you should get rid of one of the negatives to make the statement easier to understand.

TRUE   FALSE   2. Absolute statements are usually false.

TRUE   FALSE   3. If any part of a statement is true, then the statement is true.

TRUE   FALSE   4. If you cannot prove a statement is false, you should consider it to be true.

TRUE   FALSE   5. A negative can completely change the meaning of a statement.

TRUE   FALSE   6. If you are uncertain about an answer, guess even if there is a guessing penalty.

TRUE   FALSE   7. A choice containing familiar language is usually not true.

TRUE   FALSE   8. Qualified statements are usually false.

Number Correct _____

Grading Scale

   8 = Excellent

   7 = Good

0–6 = Reread the information on Reproducible 9-8

Guidelines for Taking Matching Tests

Read the directions for the following matching test. Notice that the directions tell you how to match items in the first column with items in the second column. The matching test has been completed to show you how the matches are made.

Directions: Match the words in the first column with the holidays in the second column. Write the number of the word that goes with the holiday on the line next to the holiday.

1. turkey   ___4___ 4th of July

2. Santa Claus   ___1___ Thanksgiving

3. U.S. flag   ___2___ Christmas

4. firecracker   ___3___ Memorial Day

Here are some things you can do to improve your score on matching tests. If you follow these guidelines, you will have a better chance of making correct matches. Add information to each of the following guidelines as your teacher discusses them with you.

- Read all the items in both columns before making any matches. In the example, you might have matched *U.S. flag* with *4th of July* if you had not read all the way down to *firecracker*.

- Start by making the easiest matches.

- Make all correct matches before guessing at any matches.

- Cross out items in both columns as you make matches.

- Make your best guess for any remaining matches unless there is a penalty for guessing.

Practice Taking Matching Tests ━━━━━━━━━━━━━━━

Here are three matching tests. Follow the guidelines you learned for taking matching tests to complete them. You have seven minutes to complete the three tests. Each correct match is worth one point. Tthere is no penalty for guessing.

Directions for Test One: Match the sport terms in the first column with the sports in the second column. Write the number of the item in the first column on the line next to the item it goes with in the second column.

1. home run   _____ football

2. foul shot   _____ baseball

3. touchdown   _____ basketball

4. birdie   _____ tennis

5. serve   _____ golf

Directions for Test Two: Match the presidents with the statement that best describes them. Write the number of the item in the first column on the line next to the item it goes with in the second column.

1. Abraham Lincoln   _____ was once an actor

2. George Washington   _____ famous Civil War general

3. U. S. Grant   _____ first president

4. Franklin D. Roosevelt _____ ended slavery

5. Ronald Reagan   _____ elected four times

Sometimes you will be asked to match items in the second column with items in the first column as in the following.

Directions for Test Three: Write the number of the item in the second column on the line next to the item it goes with in the first column.

_____ physician   1. product

_____ broadcaster   2. airplane

_____ pilot   3. prescription

_____ salesperson   4. lesson

_____ teacher   5. news

Total Number Correct _____

Grading Scale

13–15 = Excellent

10–12 = Good

0–9 = Review the information on Reproducible 9-10.

Guidelines for Taking Completion Tests ▬▬▬▬▬▬

A completion test item consists of a statement with part of the statement missing. The missing part is shown by a blank line. The missing part can be anywhere in the statement, and it can be one word or more than one word. Your job is to write in the missing part. Here are examples of completion items with the missing part in different places.

1. The Bill of Rights states your _____ as a citizen of the United States.

2. The capital of the state of California is _____.

3. _____ is the current president of the United States.

Here are some things you can do to improve your score on a completion test. By following these guidelines you will have a better chance of completing items correctly. Add information to each guideline as your teacher discusses it.

• Read the statement and think about what is missing.

• Write an answer that logically completes the statement.

• Be sure the answer fits the statement grammatically.

• Use the length of the blank line as a clue to the length of the answer unless the length of the blank line is the same for every item in the test.

• Reread the statement with your answer in it to be sure it makes sense.

Practice Taking a Completion Test ━━━━━━━━

Here is an example of a completion test. Follow the guidelines you just learned as you take this test. You will have five minutes to take the test. Each correct completion is worth one point. There is no penalty for guessing.

Directions: Complete each statement by writing the missing part on the line.

1. Too much sun can cause _____.

2. The president of the United States is _____.

3. _____ live in igloos at the north pole.

4. Jim Fixx was the _____ of the best selling book on running titled *The Complete Book of Running.*

5. Milk is _____ in color.

6. Your _____ supply oxygen to your heart and brain.

7. The United States exploded an _____ at Hiroshima to end World War II.

8. The more you study, the _____ your grades will be.

9. _____ has the largest population of any country in the world.

10. The four seasons of the year are _____.

Number Correct _____

Grading Scale

9–10 = Excellent

7–8 = Good

0–6 = Review the information on Reproducible 9-12.

Learning about Direction Words in Essay Tests

In an essay test you must write an answer to a question or statement. Sometimes the answer will be very long and sometimes just a few words.

The key to writing a good answer is understanding the *direction word* in the question or statement. A **direction word** tells you what you have to do when writing an answer.

Many of the direction words you find in essay test items mean the same thing. Here are the common direction words used by teachers when they write essay test items.

discuss, describe, explain. These three direction words have the same meaning. When you see them in an essay test item, they are telling you to write as much as you can about a statement or question. For example,

Discuss
Describe the characteristics of good study habits.
Explain

These three direction words mean the same thing. They tell you to write as much as you know about what good study habits are like.

diagram, illustrate. These two direction words tell you to make a drawing and to label each part.

Diagram

how electricity flows through a light bulb.

Illustrate

compare, contrast. To *compare* means to tell how two or more things are alike as well as how they are different. To *contrast* means to tell only how they are different.

Compare the governing systems in the United States and the USSR.

To answer this item, you must tell how these two systems are alike and how they are different.

Contrast the governing systems in the USA and the USSR.

To answer this item, you must tell only how the two systems are different.

relate, trace. To *relate* means to show how two or more things are connected. To *trace* means to state a series of things in some logical order.

Relate good study habits to good grades.

To answer this item, you must tell how good study habits help you get good grades.

Trace the events leading to the American civil war.

To answer this item, you must state in chronological order the events that led to the war between the North and the South.

criticize, evaluate, justify. These three direction words tell you to write a conclusion about the value of something. *Criticize* and *evaluate* tell you to think about both the positive and negative aspects of something before you come to a conclusion about it. *Justify* tells you to provide reasons that explain an action or decision.

Criticize

the Supreme Court's decision on flag burning.

Evaluate

This tells you to consider the positive and negative parts of the decision made by the Supreme Court before you come to your own conclusion on flag burning.

Justify the Supreme Court's decision on flag burning.

This tells to you provide arguments as to why the decision made by the Supreme Court was correct.

list, outline. To *list* means to present information in some order. Each item is usually numbered. To *outline* means to give the main points. An outline usually contains numbers and letters. An outline is usually more detailed than a list.

List the four seasons of the year.

Here you present the seasons item by item.

1. winter

2. spring

3. summer

4. fall

Provide an **outline** for different forms of transportation.

Here you use numbers and letters to show the main points.

Different Forms of Transportation

1. land

    a. cars

    b. buses

325

       c. trains

       d. motorcycles

2. sea

       a. sailboats

       b. ocean lines

       c. motor boats

3. air

       a. jet airplanes

       b. helicopters

       c. hot air balloons

summarize. *A summary* is a short statement that tells something about all the important ideas.

Summarize what you learned about direction words.

To respond to this item, you have to tell what direction words are, identify the different direction words, and briefly tell what they mean.

Write a statement that tells what each of the following mean:

1. discuss, describe, explain

_____

2. diagram, illustrate

_____

3. compare, contrast

_____

4. relate, trace

_____

5. criticize, evaluate, justify

_____

6. list, outline

_____

7. summarize

_____

326

Guidelines for Taking Essay Tests

There are a number of things you can do to write a good answer to an essay test item. Here are some guidelines for answering essay test items. Add information to each guideline as your teacher tells you more about it.

- Read and restate each item in your own words before attempting to answer it. In this way, you check to see if you understand it.

- Decide if your answer needs to be long or just a few words. If your answer is going to be long, make a brief outline before writing your answer. This helps you organize your information.

- Answer all parts of the item.

- Write directly to the point of the item. This means that you must answer the question or statement and not write about something else you find interesting or happen to know about.

- Use pictures and diagrams to explain your ideas whenever it may be appropriate.

- Write neatly because teachers will not give you credit for something they cannot read.

- Proofread your answers for clarity, spelling, and grammar.

- When you are running out of time, quickly list the information you know about any remaining items so your teacher will see what you know. This may earn you partial credit.

Practice Taking an Essay Test

Here is an example of an essay test. Use the guidelines you learned to complete the test. You will have thirty minutes to complete the entire test. Your teacher will grade your answer for content, clarity, spelling, and grammar. Each item is worth 10 points.

Directions: Answer each of the following. You have 30 minutes to complete the test. Use the back if necessary.

1. **Describe** what you should do to get ready to study for tests.

2. **Outline** the five-day study plan.

3. **Summarize** the five things you should do when taking any test.

4. **Contrast** the two types of multiple-choice test items you learned about.

What I Have Learned ━━━━━━━━━━━━━━━━━━━

Directions: Show what you have learned about preparing for and taking different types of tests by writing an answer for each of the following:

1. Describe the four things you should do to get ready to study for a test.

2. List the steps in the five-day study plan.

3. Explain the five things you should do when taking any test.

4. Summarize what you should do when taking each of the following types of tests:

   Multiple choice

   True/false

   Matching

   Completion

   Essay

Answers for Chapter 9 Reproducibles

9-1   1. Find out what will be on the test. 2. Make sure your textbook notes are complete. 3. Make sure your class notes are complete. 4. Begin preparing five days before the test.

9-2   Day 5. Read all notes and handouts and highlight important information.

       Day 4. Use memory techniques to remember this information.

       Day 3. Rewrite important information in brief form; review at least twice.

       Day 2. Write answers for questions you believe your teacher will ask.

       Day 1. Review your rewritten notes and questions and answers before taking the test.

9-3   1. Read directions carefully. Ask your teacher to explain anything you do not understand. 2. Look at the entire test to decide what you have to do. 3. Decide how much time to use to answer each question. 4. Answer easier questions first. 5. Check your answers for correctness.

9-4   Answers will vary, but the format must match those shown on Reproducible 9-4.

9-5   Notes will vary.

9-6   1. c.   2. d.   3. a.   4. c.   5. c.

9-7   Notes will vary.

9-8   Notes will vary.

9-9   1. False.   2. True.   3. False.   4. True.   5. True.   6. False.   7. False.   8. False

9-10 Notes will vary.

9-11 Test One
       3 = football
       1 = baseball
       2 = basketball
       5 = tennis
       4 = golf

      Test Two
       5 = was once an actor
       3 = famous Civil War general
       2 = first president
       1 = ended slavery
       4 = elected four times

      Test Three
       3 = physician
       5 = broadcaster
       2 = pilot
       1 = salesperson
       4 = teacher

9-12 Notes will vary.

9-13 1. sun burn. 2. name of current president. 3. Eskimos. 4. author. 5. white. 6. lungs. 7. atomic bomb. 8. better. 9. China. 10. summer, fall, winter, spring (seasons can be in any order).

9-14 1. Write as much as you can about something. 2. Make a drawing and label the parts. 3. *Compare* means alike and different. *Contrast* means different. 4. *Relate* means how things are connected. *Trace* means to put things in a logical order. 5. Come to a conclusion about the value of something. 6. Both present information in an ordered way. 7. Brief statement of the important ideas.

9-15 Notes will vary.

9-16 Answers will vary but should contain the essential information found in the reproducibles as follows:
>   1—Reproducible 9-1
>   2—Reproducible 9-2
>   3—Reproducible 9-3
>   4—Reproducible 9-4

9-17 1. Same as for Reproducible 9-1. 2. Same as for Reproducible 9-2. 3. Same as for Reproducible 9-3. 4. Multiple choice: Strategies shown on Reproducibles 9-5 and 9-7. True/false: Strategies shown on Reproducible 9-8. Matching: Strategies shown on Reproducible 9-10. Completion: Strategies shown on Reproducible 9-12. Essay: Strategies shown on Reproducible 9-15.

CHAPTER 10

Using Time

■ Purposes

The purposes of this chapter are to:
1. teach students with learning disabilities a strategy for using time effectively
2. provide reproducibles that can be used to teach students to use time effectively.

■ Titles of Reproducibles

■ RATIONALE

Students with learning disabilities generally require more time than their non-learning-disabled peers to complete assignments and master instructional objectives. Although wasted time is a problem for all students, it is an especially acute problem for students with learning disabilities, who must take full advantage of available time to keep pace with their peers. Unfortunately, as their teachers realize, students with learning disabilities possess few or no effective strategies for scheduling and managing their time.

Heron and Harris (1987) pointed out that students with learning disabilities typically have not mastered a strategy for allocating time among tasks or designating sufficient time to complete tasks. Alley and Deshler (1979) described two time management patterns that characterize these students. In one pattern, the student has no schedule under the assumption that this provides maximum flexibility. As today's kids might put it, they "go with the flow." Alley and Deshler termed the result "confusion squared." The second pattern involves a rigid, minute-by-minute scheduling of time. Students who follow this pattern spend so much time planning a schedule that they have little time or energy left to do the work that needs to be done. Both patterns are nonproductive.

Given the need for students with learning disabilities to make the most of their time, and their lack of a strategy for doing so, it is important that they be taught how to use time effectively. In this chapter we offer a strategy that students with learning disabilities can use to organize their time to meet their school assignments and responsibilities. The goal is to have these students become effective self-managers, capable of deciding what is most important for them to do, how long it will take, and where and when to do it.

■ BACKGROUND INFORMATION

A Strategy for Using Time Effectively

Bos and Vaughn (1988) defined time management as "organizing and monitoring time so that tasks can be scheduled and completed in an efficient and timely manner" (p. 197). There are a number of techniques that can be used to help students with learning disabilities use their time effectively. We recommend a strategy that includes five components:

1. Semester Calendar

2. Weekly Planner

3. Daily Organizer

4. Study Habits Checklist

5. Study Place Checklist

Semester Calendar. The **semester calendar** gives students a place to record the important due dates for projects, reports, papers, and tests. It also provides a place for students to indicate the dates for initiating activities and evaluating progress. The semester calendar should include all the school dates, holidays, and special school events during one semester of school. It should also include the out-of-school special events in which students plan to be involved—for example, attending sporting events, going to club meetings, and going on family trips. Each month of the semester should be on a separate page, and should cover Mondays through Fridays. Space should be provided at the bottom for special notes. Students should use an asterisk (*) to indicate special notes they record at the bottom of the page. The first note should be highlighted as *, the second as **, and so on. The students' primary teacher should assist students to prepare the semester calendar at the beginning of each semester. Students should update the calendar as the semester progresses.

We recommend that the semester calendar be printed on heavy paper. Holes can be punched if necessary to allow students to keep the calendar in a three-ring notebook. A copy of the calendar should be given to the student's teacher and parents to allow them to monitor progress. All entries should be done in pencil to allow changes as they become necessary. As changes are made, students should be responsible for making these known so that teachers and parents can make the changes on their copies of the calendar. Figure 10.1 shows an example of a semester calendar for Marie, a ninth-grade student.

Using the semester calendar allows students to plan their work, determine when they must begin various activities, and monitor their progress over a semester. Use of the calendar also ensures that students do not "lose the forest for the trees." Since the teacher and the parents have a copy of the calendar, they can monitor student progress.

Weekly Planner. The semester calendar gives students an important long-range overview of what they have to do during the course of a semester to succeed in school. The **weekly planner** provides a more detailed view of what students have to do for a specified segment of the semester. During each weekend of the semester students should review their semester calendar and prepare a weekly planner. The weekly planner is considerably more detailed than the semester calendar. The boxes are larger to allow students to include more detail for each day. Information to be recorded includes dates and times of tests, meetings, and special events, and due dates for projects and papers. Out-of-school responsibilities such as household chores and employment should be included. Additional entries should be made during the week as necessary. Once again, entries should be written in pencil to allow changes. Because the weekly planner is *not* a schedule, things that occur each day at the same time are not recorded. For example, classes are not entered because students quickly memorize when and where these occur. Again, students should use an * to indicate special notes they record at the bottom of the page. Figure 10-2 shows an example of a weekly planner for Marie.

Students should be taught to do the following when developing their weekly planner:

1. Review their semester calendar to see what they already had planned to do during the week. Entries from the semester calendar should be copied over onto the weekly planner with more details added.

2. Review their notes from various classes to determine what else needs to be entered.

3. Add out-of school responsibilities.

Daily Organizer. The **daily organizer** is the most detailed level of planning. Yet it is really quite simple to prepare. Each evening before a school day students review their weekly planner and their notes for that day from their various classes. In addition, they determine those things they did not accomplish that day. They then

FIGURE 10.1 Marie's Semester Calendar

NAME _____Marie_____

SEMESTER _____Fall_____

YEAR _____1990_____

MONTH _____November_____

MONDAY	TUESDAY	WEDNESDAY	THURSDAY	FRIDAY
			1	2
English 5 Book Report Due	6	Trip to Art 7 Museum*	8	9
Math 12 Midterm History Midterm	Tryout for 13 Xmas Play	Science 14 Midterm	Awards 15 Assembly 9-12	16
School 19 Pictures**	20	Science 21 Project Due	22 THANKSGIVING HOLIDAY	23
26	27	Career 28 Day	29	30

NOTES: * Remember Permission Slip
       ** Buy New Blouse

FIGURE 10.2 Marie's Weekly Planner

NAME _____Marie_____

WEEK OF ____11/12–11/18____

	MONDAY	TUESDAY	WEDNESDAY	THURSDAY	FRIDAY	SATURDAY	SUNDAY
9:00	Math Midterm				Awards Assembly***	Clean Room	Family Visit to Aunt Martha
10:00			Science Midterm			Laundry	
11:00							
12:00							
1:00	History Midterm						
2:00						Science Project with Paul	
3:00						& Sally at my house****	
4:00		Tryout for Xmas Play	Photog. Club*	Interview for job at Jones' Store**			
5:00							
6:00	Homework		Homework				

FIGURE 10.2 Continued

7:00	Study for Science Test with Jane	Homework	Work on Science Project with Paul	Homework			Homework
8:00	at her house	Study for Science Test	& Sally at Sally's House		Community Center Dance	Date with Bob	Complete Weekly Planning for 11/19–11/25
9:00							
10:00							

Notes: *Have camera checked for spot on lens.
**Fill out application and drop off before Thursday.
***Get congratulations card for Roberta.
****Get snacks and soda.

record everything they have to do the next day and precisely when they will do it. Space is provided at the bottom of the page for special notes. The daily organizer is in effect a "To Do" list that students can use to move effectively and efficiently through their day.

As with the semester calendar and the weekly planner, entries in the daily organizer should be written in pencil. Students should cross off assignments or activities as they are completed. This accomplishes three things. First, students gain a sense of fulfillment when they record successful completion of an assignment or activity. Second, at any given time during the day, students can see what they still need to do. Third, at the end of the day, students can determine what they did not accomplish and, consequently, will need to do the next day or at some later time.

Figure 10.3 shows an example of a daily organizer for Marie. A daily organizer gives students with learning disabilities a concrete tool they can use to ensure they do what is necessary. The practical nature of the daily organizer makes it well suited to students with learning disabilities, who characteristically require considerable structure to succeed. The thorough organization implicit in the daily organizer provides order in place of chaos, a system in place of random effort, thereby reducing "confusion squared." Its simplicity ensures that students spend most of their time doing things, rather than spending a great deal of time in inefficient efforts to "plan" what they have to do.

Study Habits Checklist. Regardless of how well students with learning disabilities schedule their time, without effective study habits they will not be able to complete their assignments successfully. Students must develop appropriate study habits to carry out their plans. We propose the following study habits as the most important to teach students with learning disabilities to use consistently:

338

1. Start working on time.

2. Don't daydream.

3. Tell your friends not to call you during your study time.

4. Take short breaks when you feel fatigued.

5. Begin with the hardest assignment.

6. Review your notes before beginning an assignment.

7. Review your notes for courses for which you do not have an assignment.

8. Finish one assignment before going on to another.

9. Have a "study buddy" you can contact when you get stuck.

10. Begin studying for a test five days before it will be given.

FIGURE 10.3 Marie's Daily Organizer

NAME _____Marie_____

DAY/DATE ___Wed. 11/14___

9:00	Ask Mr. Renaldo to explain rate problem.
10:00	Ask Mrs. Wallace for good book about Shakespeare.
11:00	Science midterm
12:00	Lunch—Talk with Paul & Sally about science project.—Pay Miss Smith 80 cents I owe from yesterday.
1:00	
2:00	
3:00	
4:00	Photography Club—Bring in 3 best photos I've taken.
5:00	
6:00	Homework
7:00	Science project at Sallay's. Bring encyclopedia volume about snakes.
8:00	
9:00	
10:00	

NOTES: Check drama bulletin board for tryout results.
Clean out PE locker and bring uniform home to wash.

11. Keep working on long-term assignments.

12. Write down questions you will need to ask your teacher.

FIGURE 10.4 Marie's Study Habits Checklist

NAME _____ Marie _____

DATE _____ 9/12/90 _____

Study Habits Checklist

You need good study habits to get good grades. Good grades just don't happen, they come as a result of study. Evaluate your study habits using the following checklist. Read each statement and for each place a (√) under "Rarely," "Generally," or "Always." Use this guide to help you make your decisions.

Rarely means almost never.

Generally means about half the time.

Always means all of the time.

Statements	Rarely	Generally	Always
I start working on time.			√
I avoid daydreaming.		√	
I tell my friends not to call me during my study time.		√	
I take short breaks when I feel tired.			√
I begin with the hardest assignment.	√		
I review my notes before beginning an assignment		√	
I review my notes for courses for which I do not have an assignment.	√		
I finish one assignment before going on to another.		√	
I have a "study buddy: I can contact when I get stuck.	√		
I begin studying for a test at least five days before it will be given.	√		
I keep working on long-term assignments.			
I write down questions I will need to ask my teacher.		√	

The **study habits checklist** shown in Figure 10.4 can be used to introduce students to these important study habits. Students should complete the study habits checklist at the beginning of the school year. Figure 10.4 records Marie's responses to the statements. It is clear from her responses that she needs to improve some of her study skills.

By completing the study habits checklist, students will be able to see the things they have to do to develop good study habits. Students should periodically complete the study habits checklist to evaluate the extent to which they have developed good study habits.

Study Place Checklist. Students with learning disabilities need more than just good study habits. They also need a good place in which to study. Most study time occurs either in the library or at home. School libraries are designed to facilitate intensive study and provide a good study environment. The home environment, however, is typically not a good study place because it is not designed as a place to study.

Most home environments are busy places full of distractions. It is difficult to concentrate when surrounded by the sounds of conversation, cooking, cleaning, and loud television sets and stereos. It is difficult to concentrate when temptations abound such as food to eat, people to talk to on the telephone, television programs to watch, or a favorite magazine to read.

Students must make an effort to develop a good study place in their home. Parents and siblings must cooperate in this effort. A good study place at home has the following characteristics:

1. It is quiet.

2. There are no visual distractions.

3. There is good light.

4. The temperature is comfortable.

5. There is a comfortable chair.

6. All necessary work and reference materials are available.

7. There is a desk or table large enough to hold all materials.

8. It is available for designated periods of time.

Students can be introduced to the need to develop a good study place by completing at the beginning of the school year the study place checklist shown in Figure 10.5. In this way students will see the things they have to do to create a good study place at home. Figure 10.5 shows Marie's responses to the items of the study place checklist. Marie appears to have a fairly good study place for her use, but some aspects can be improved.

■ TEACHING PLAN

Here is a plan for teaching students with learning disabilities the five components of the strategy for using time effectively. The plan should be introduced as early in the school year as possible.

1. Lead the students in a discussion of the importance of using time efficiently. Bring out the fact that successful students schedule and manage their time in a manner that allows them to complete all their work and responsibilities, yet have time remaining

FIGURE 10.5 Marie's Study Place Checklist

NAME _____ Marie _____

DATE _____ 9/12/90 _____

Study Habits Checklist

In addition to using good study habits, you need a good study place at home in which to do your school work. Your study place needs to be arranged for studying with all temptations to do anything else removed.

How you arrange your study place has a lot to do with how well you will study and learn. If your study place is a noisy, busy place that is full of distractions you won't learn much. If there is a telephone, radio, stereo, or television nearby, the temptations to use them may be too much for you. Thinking about people to call, songs to listen to, or programs to watch takes time away from study. Time away from studying lowers your grades.

Evalute your study place using the following checklist. Read each statement and for each place a (√) under "Rarely," "Generally," or "Always." Use this guide to help you make your decisions.

Rarely means almost never.

Generally means about half the time.

Always means all of the time.

Statements	Rarely	Generally	Always
I Have a quiet study place.		√	
There are no visual distractions.	√		
There is good light.			√
The temperature is comfortable.		√	
There is a comfortable chair.			√
All necessary work and reference materials are there.		√	
There is a desk or table large enough to hold all my materials.			√
I can use this study place whenever I need it.		√	

for recreational activities. Then distribute Reproducible 10-1, "A Strategy for Using Time Effectively," to the students. Discuss each of the five components of the strategy. Then have the students write on the reproducible the five steps in the strategy.

2. Distribute Reproducible 10-2, "Using a Semester Calendar." Discuss the purposes of a semester calendar. Review the four steps students need to follow to make a semester calendar. Then have the students list their school assignments, school activities, and out-of-school activities they know they will be involved with during the semester. Make sure they include dates. Tell the students they can record special notes about the things they have to do in the section headed "NOTES" at the bottom

. of the semester calendar. Show students how to use the asterisk. Explain that the first note should be shown with an *, the second note with **, and so on.

3. Add the dates to Reproducible 10-3, "Semester Calendar," for each month of the semester. Distribute one copy of 10-3 for each month of the semester to each student. Have the students record the information they wrote on Reproducible 10-2 on the appropriate page (month) of Reproducible 10-3. Explain that they should keep their semester calendar in a notebook or looseleaf binder they bring to school each day. Tell students they should make entries on their calendars in pencil so that they can make changes in it throughout the semester.

4. Distribute Reproducible 10-4, "Using a Weekly Planner." Discuss the purposes of a weekly planner. Review the three steps students need to complete to make a weekly planner. Then for the coming week have students use their semester calendar and class notes to list things they need to do that week. Have the students also list out-of-school things they need to do. Tell students they should not list things that they do each day at the same time.

5. Have the students record the information they listed on Reproducible 10-4 on Reproducible 10-5, "Weekly Planner," fitting the information into appropriate blocks of time. Tell the students they can record special notes about the things they have to do in the section headed "NOTES" at the bottom of the weekly planner. Show students how to use the asterisk. Explain that the first note should be shown with an *, the second note with **, and so on. Tell students they should keep the current weekly planner in a notebook they bring to school each day. They also need to know that they will need a blank copy of the weekly planner for each week of the semester.

6. Distribute Reproducible 10-6, "Using a Daily Organizer." Discuss the purposes of a daily organizer. Review the five steps students need to follow to make a daily planner. Then have the students list things from their weekly planner they will need to do the next day. Have them also list things from their class notes they know they will have to do, as well as anything they are aware of not having completed the previous day.

7. Have the students record the information they listed on Reproducible 10-6 onto Reproducible 10-7, "Daily Organizer," fitting the information into appropriate blocks of time. Explain how to cross off entries as they are accomplished. Point out that there is space at the bottom to write special notes. Tell the students they need one blank copy of the daily organizer for each day of the semester. Tell them to bring their current daily organizer to school each day.

8. Lead the students in a discussion of the importance of good study habits. Then, on the chalkboard, write the twelve good study habits listed in the background information section. Briefly discuss each one of these study habits. Then have the students complete Reproducible 10-8, "Study Habits Checklist."

9. After the students have completed the study habits checklist, distribute Reproducible 10-9, "Improving Your Study Habits." Have the students list any study habit for which they checked "Rarely." For each study habit listed, have them write a suggestion for improving it. Have the students share their suggestions with the entire class.

10. Lead the students in a discussion of the importance of having a good place to study. Then, on the chalkboard, write the eight characteristics of a good study place listed

in the background information section. Briefly discuss each one of these characteristics. Then have the students complete Reproducible 10-10, "Study Place Checklist."

11. After the students have completed the study place checklist, distribute Reproducible 10-11, "Improving Your Study Place." Have the students list any characteristic for which they checked "Rarely." For each characteristic listed, have then write a suggestion for improving it. Have the students share their suggestions with the entire class.

12. Distribute Reproducible 10-12, "What I Have Learned." Use this reproducible to evaluate how well your students have learned to use the information taught in this chapter. As needed, use any of the reproducibles to review what was presented in this chapter.

A Strategy for Using Time Effectively ▬▬▬▬▬

Do you ever wonder how some students seem to get their work done and still have lots of time to do other things? Well, these students schedule their time so they can get everything done they want to do. They also manage their time so there is time for school as well as lots of time for other activities. These students have an effective strategy for using time. You must also have an effective strategy for managing your time. This means you must do the following:

1. Prepare a **Semester Calendar** that shows all your major school and out-of-school activities and assignments for a semester. This is your long-term plan and should be prepared at the beginning of each semester or term. As the semester goes on, you will continually add new items to the calendar.

2. Prepare a **Weekly Planner** that shows your school and out-of-school activities and assignments due for the upcoming week. This is your short-term plan and should be prepared over the weekend before each week begins.

3. Prepare a **Daily Organizer** to show what you must do each day and when you plan to do it. This is your daily plan and should be prepared each night for the next day.

4. Evaluate your **Study Habits** to find ways you can improve them. Study habits are the routines you follow to finish assignments on time and to prepare for tests.

5. Evaluate your **Study Place** to find ways you can improve it. A study place is an area in your home where it is easy and comfortable to study.

List the five steps in the strategy for effectively using time.

1.

2.

3.

4.

5.

Using a Semester Calendar

To do all the things you want to do each semester, you need to schedule your time. A semester calendar will remind you when you need to start and finish important school and out-of-school activities. It will help you plan your time so you do not schedule more things than you can possibly do.

A **Semester Calendar** helps you to organize your school and out-of-school activities. Here is how you use it:

1. Ask each of your teachers for a list of assignments and dates and place them on your semester calendar. Be sure to enter all the regular, midterm, and final examination dates as well as the dates that papers and projects are due.

2. Get a list of the school activities for the current semester. Enter the activities you plan to be part of on your semester calendar.

3. Make a list of the out-of-school special events in which you plan to be involved. These include such things as attending sporting events, going to club meetings, and going on family trips. Enter each on your semester calendar.

4. Record any special notes about the things you have to do in the section headed "NOTES" at the bottom of the semester calendar. Use an * for the first note, ** for the second note, and so on.

Now list the school assignments you know you will have this semester. Also provide their dates.

Then list the school activities you know you will be involved with this semester. Also provide their dates.

Next list the out-of-school activities you know you will be involved with this semester. Also provide their dates.

Finally, list any special notes.

Use these lists to complete the semester calendar provided to you by the teacher.

Semester Calendar

NAME _____

SEMESTER _____

YEAR _____

MONTH _____

MONDAY	TUESDAY	WEDNESDAY	THURSDAY	FRIDAY

NOTES:

Using a Weekly Planner

During each weekend you need to spend some time preparing your plan for the upcoming week. A weekly planner will help you do this. The weekly planner is used to show in detail what you are planning to do during any week. Here is how to prepare your weekly planner:

1. Review your semester calendar to see what you planned to do during the week. Enter this information into your weekly planner.

2. Review notes from your classes to see what else needs to be added to your weekly planner.

3. Think about the out-of-school things you need to do during the upcoming week. Add them to your weekly planner.

Now list items from your semester calendar that you need to record in your weekly planner.

Next list items from your notes that need to be recorded in your weekly planner.

Then list out-of-school things you need to do.

Finally, list any special notes.

Use these lists to complete the weekly planner provided to you by your teacher.

Weekly Planner

NAME _____

WEEK OF _____

	MONDAY	TUESDAY	WEDNESDAY	THURSDAY	FRIDAY	SATURDAY	SUNDAY
9:00							
10:00							
11:00							
12:00							
1:00							
2:00							
3:00							
4:00							
5:00							
6:00							

7:00						
8:00						
9:00						
10:00						

NOTES:

Using a Daily Organizer

Each evening before a school day, you need to prepare a daily organizer. The daily organizer shows how you will use every hour of your day. It helps you arrange your time so you get everything done you want to do. It keeps you from wasting time. Here is how to prepare your daily organizer.

1. Review your weekly planner to see what you need to do tomorrow.

2. Review your class notes to see what else you need to add.

3. Review your daily organizer for today to determine what you did not get done. Add these things to your daily organizer for tomorrow.

4. For each thing you need to do tomorrow, decide how much time you need to do it.

5. Decide when you will do each thing. Write the thing you need to do in the appropriate time period in your daily organizer.

Now list the things from your weekly planner that you need to do tomorrow. Next to each, tell how much time you need to do it.

Then list things from your class notes you know you need to do tomorrow. Tell how much time you will need to do each thing.

Next list things you did not finish today and that you will need to do tomorrow. Tell how much time you will need to do each thing.

Finally, list any special notes.

Use your list to complete the daily organizer provided by your teacher.

Daily Organizer

NAME _____

DAY/DATE _____

9:00	_____
10:00	_____
11:00	_____
12:00	_____
1:00	_____
2:00	_____
3:00	_____
4:00	_____
5:00	_____
6:00	_____
7:00	_____
8:00	_____
9:00	_____
10:00	_____

NOTES:

Study Habits Checklist ━━━━━━━━━━━━━━━━━━━━━━

NAME _____ DATE _____

You need good study habits to get good grades. Good grades just don't happen—they come as a result of studying. Use the following checklist to see how good your study habits are. Read each statement and place a (√) under "Rarely," "Generally," or "Always." Use this guide to help you make your decisions.

Rarely means almost never.

Generally means about half the time.

Always means all the time.

Statements	Rarely	Generally	Always
I start working on time.			
I avoid daydreaming.			
I tell my friends not to call me during my study time.			
I take short breaks when I feel tired.			
I begin with the hardest assignment.			
I review my notes before beginning an assignment			
I finish one assignment before going on to another.			
I have a "study buddy" I can contact when I get stuck.			
I begin studying for a test at least five days before it will be given.			
I keep working on long-term assignments.			
I write down questions I will need to ask my teacher.			

Improving Your Study Habits

List the study habits you need to improve in order to get better grades. Include anything for which you checked "Rarely" when completing the Study Skills Checklist on Reproducible 10-8. For each one listed, write something you can do to improve it.

Study habit to be improved: _____

_____

Suggestion for improving it: _____

_____

_____

_____

Study habit to be improved: _____

_____

Suggestion for improving it: _____

_____

_____

_____

Study habit to be improved: _____

_____

Suggestion for improving it: _____

_____

_____

_____

Study habit to be improved _____

_____

Suggestion for improving it: _____

_____

_____

_____

Study habit to be improved: _____

_____

Suggestion for improving it: _____

_____

_____

_____

Study habit to be improved: _____

_____

Suggestion for improving it: _____

_____

_____

_____

Study Place Checklist

You need a good study place at home. How you arrange your study place has a lot to do with how well you will study and learn. If your study place is a noisy, busy place that is full of distractions, you won't learn much. If there is a telephone, radio, stereo, or television nearby, the temptation to use them may be too much for you. Thinking about people to call, songs to listen to, or programs to watch takes time away from studying. Time away from studying lowers your grades.

Evaluate your study place using the following checklist. Read each statement and for each place a (√) under "Rarely," "Generally," or "Always." Use this guide to help you make your decisions.

Rarely means almost never.

Generally means about half the time.

Always means all of the time.

Statements	Rarely	Generally	Always
I have a quiet study place.			
There are no visual distractions.			
There is good light.			
The temperature is comfortable.			
There is a comfortable chair.			
All necessary work and reference materials are there.			
There is a desk or table large enough to hold all my materials.			
I can use this study place whenever I need it.			

Improving Your Study Place ▬▬▬▬▬

List the things about your study place that need to be improved. Include anything for which you checked "Rarely" when completing the Study Place Checklist on Reproducible 10-9. For each thing listed, write something you can do to improve it.

Thing that needs to be improved: _____

_____

Suggestion for improving it: _____

_____

_____

_____

Thing that needs to be improved: _____

_____

Suggestion for improving it: _____

_____

_____

_____

Thing that needs to be improved: _____

_____

Suggestion for improving it: _____

_____

_____

_____

Thing that needs to be improved _____

_____

Suggestion for improving it: _____

_____

_____

_____

Thing that needs to be improved: _____

_____

Suggestion for improving it: _____

_____

_____

_____

Thing that needs to be improved: _____

_____

Suggestion for improving it: _____

_____

_____

_____

What I Have Learned

Directions: Show what you have learned about managing your time by writing an answer for each of the following:

1. Why do you need to prepare a semester calendar?

2. What will a weekly planner help you do?

3. What do you use the daily organizer for?

4. List five good study habits you should have.

5. Write five things that should be true about your study place.

Answers for Chapter 10 Reproducibles

10-1   1. Prepare a semester calendar showing major things to do both in and out of school for the semester. 2. Prepare a weekly calendar showing in- and out-of-school activities for the upcoming week. 3. Prepare a daily organizer to show what must be done tomorrow. 4. Improve study habits. 5. Improve study place.

10-2   Answers will vary.

10-3   Entries will vary according to the information recorded on Reproducible 10-2.

10-4   Answer will vary.

10-5   Entries will vary according to the information recorded on Reproducible 10-4.

10-6   Answers will vary.

10-7   Entries will vary according to the information recorded on Reproducible 10-6.

10-8   Answers will vary.

10-9   Entries will vary according to the information recorded on Reproducible 10-8.

10-10   Answers will vary.

10-11   Entries will vary according to the information recorded on Reproducible 10-10.

10-12   1. To have a long-range plan for organizing your in-school and out-of-school activities for the semester. 2. Prepare for the requirements of the upcoming week. 3. Shows what you must do each day and when you expect to do it. 4. Any of the eleven statements of the Study Habits Checklist shown on Reproducible 10-8. 5. Any of the eight statements from the Study Place Checklist shown on Reproducible 10-10.

References and Bibliography

Adler, B. (1988). *The student's memory book*. New York: Doubleday.

Alley, G., & Deshler, D. (1979). *Teaching the learning disabled adolescent: Strategies and methods*. Denver, CO: Love.

Anderman, R. C., & Williams, J. M. (1986). *Teaching test-taking and note-taking skills to learning disabled high school students*. Paper presented at the 68th Annual Convention of the Council for Exceptional Children, New Orleans, Louisiana, April 1.

Austin Community College Study Guide Series. (1989). *Academic Therapy*, 24:329–363.

Beirne-Smith, M. (1989). A systematic approach for teaching notetaking skills to students with mild learning handicaps. *Academic Therapy*, 24:425–437.

Bos, C. S., & Vaughn, S. (1988). *Strategies for teaching students with learning and behavior problems*. Needham Heights, MA: Allyn and Bacon.

Choate, J. S., Bennett, T. Z., Enright, B. E., Miller, L. J., Poteet, J. A., & Rakes, T. A. (1987). *Assessing and programming basic curriculum skills*. Newton, MA: Allyn and Bacon.

Clark, E. L., Deshler, D. D., Schumaker, J. B., Alley, G. R., & Warner, M. M. (1984). Visual imagery and self-questioning: Strategies to improve comprehension of written material. *Journal of Learning Disabilities*, 17:145–149.

Colligan, L. (1982). *Taking tests*. New York: Scholastic Book Services.

Cronin, M. E., & Currie, P. S. (1984). Study skills: A resource guide for practitioners. *Remedial and Special Education*, 5:61–69.

Derr, A. M., & Peters, C. L. (1986). The geometric organizer: A study technique. *Academic Therapy*, 21:357–366.

Deshler, D. D., & Schumaker, J. D. (1986). Learning strategies: An instructional alternatives for low-achieving adolescents. *Exceptional Children*, 52:583–590.

Devine, T. G. (1981). *Teaching study skills*. Boston: Allyn and Bacon.

Ellis, E. S., Sabournie, E. J., & Marshall, K. J. (1989). Teaching learning strategies to learning disabled students in postsecondary settings. *Academic Therapy*, 24:491–501.

Forgan, H. W., & Mangrum, C. T. (1989). *Teaching content area reading skills*, 4th ed. Columbus, OH: Merrill.

Fraenkel, J. R., Kane, F. T., & Wolf, A. (1990). *Civics, government, and citizenship*. Englewood Cliffs, NJ: Prentice Hall.

Gearheart, R. B., & Gearheart, C. J. (1989). *Learning disabilities*, 5th ed. Columbus, OH: Merrill.

Giordano, G. (1982). Outlining techniques that help disabled readers. *Academic Therapy*, 17:517–522.

Gleason, M. M. (1988). Teaching study strategies. *Teaching Exceptional Children*, Spring: 52–57.

Hallahan, D. P., Kauffman, J. M., & Lloyd, J. W. (1985). *Introduction to learning disabilities*, 2nd ed. Englewood Cliffs, NJ: Prentice-Hall.

Hauer, M. G., Murray, R. C., Dantin, D. B., & Bolner, M. S. (1987). *Books, libraries, and research*, 3rd ed. Dubuque, IA: Kendall/Hunt.

Hoover, J. J. (1988). *Teaching handicapped students study skills*, 2nd ed. Lindale, TX: Hamilton Publications.

Hoover, J. J. (1989a). Implementing a study skills program in the classroom. *Academic Therapy,* 24:471–476.

Hoover, J. J. (1989b). Study skills and the education of students with learning disabilities. *Journal of Learning Disabilities,* 22:452–455.

Horton, S. V., Lovitt, T. C., Givens, A., & Nelson, R. (1989). Teaching social studies to high school students with academic handicaps in a mainstreamed setting: Effects of a computerized study guide. *Journal of Learning Disabilities,* 22:102–107.

Kirk, S. A., & Chalfant, J. C. (1984). *Academic and developmental learning disabilities.* Denver, CO: Love.

Leal, L., & Rafoth, M. A. (1991). Memory strategy development: What teachers do makes a difference. *Prevention,* 26:234–237.

Lee, P., & Alley, G. R. (1984). *Teaching junior high school LD students to use a test-taking strategy.* Research Report No. 38, Institute for Research in Learning Disabilities, University of Kansas.

Lenz, B. K., Alley, G. R., & Schumaker, J. B. (1987). Activating the inactive learner: Advance organizers in the secondary content classroom. *Learning Disability Quarterly,* 10:53–67.

Lovitt, T. C. (1989). *Introduction to learning disabilities.* Needham Heights, MA: Allyn and Bacon.

Lovitt, L. C., & Horton, S. V. (1987). How to develop study guides. *Reading, Writing, and Learning Disabilities,* 3:333–343.

Mandelbaum, L. H., & Wilson, R. (1989). Teaching listening skills in the special education classroom. *Academic Therapy,* 24:449–459.

Mann, P. H., Suiter, P. A., & McClung, R. M. (1987). *Handbook in diagnostic-prescriptive teaching,* 3rd ed. Newton, MA: Allyn and Bacon.

Mastropieri, M. A. (1988). Using the keyboard method. *Teaching Exceptional Children,* Winter: 4–8.

Mastropieri, M. A., & Scruggs, T. E. (1987). *Effective instruction for special education.* Boston: College-Hill Press.

McKenzie, R. G. (1991). Developing study skills through cooperative learning activities. *Prevention,* 16:227–229.

McLoughlin, J. A., & Lewis, R. B. (1986). *Assessing special students,* 2nd ed. Columbus, OH: Merrill.

Mercer, C. D. (1991). *Students with learning disabilities,* 4th ed. New York: Merrill.

Pavlak, S. A. (1985a). *Classroom activities for correcting specific reading problems.* West Nyack, NY: Parker.

Pavlak, S. A. (1985b). *Informal tests for diagnosing specific reading problems.* West Nyack, NY: Parker.

Pope, L. (1982). *Guidelines for teaching children with learning problems.* Brooklyn: BOOK-LAB.

Robinson, H. A. (1978). *Teaching reading and study skills: The content areas,* 2nd ed. Boston: Allyn and Bacon.

Rooney, K. J. (1989). Independent strategies for efficient study: A core approach. *Academic Therapy,* 24:383–390.

Rothman, R. W., & Cohen, J. (1988). Teaching test taking skills. *Academic Therapy,* 23:341–347.

Saski, J., Swicegood, P., & Carter, J. (1983). Notetaking formats for learning disabled adolescents. *Learning Disability Quarterly,* 6:265–272.

Scheid, K. (1989). *Cognitive and metacognitive learning strategies—Their role in the education of special education students.* Columbus, OH: LINC Resources.

Schewel, R. (1989). Semantic mapping: A study skills strategy. *Academic Therapy*, 24:439–447.

Schumaker, J. B., Deshler, D. D., Alley, G. R., Warner, M. M., & Denton, P. H. (1982). Multipass: A learning strategy for improving reading comprehension. *Learning Disabilitiy Quarterly*, 5:295–304.

Scruggs, T. E., & Mastropieri, M. A. (1984). Improving memory for facts: The "keyword" method. *Academic Therapy*, 20:159–165.

Scruggs, T. E., & Mastropieri, M. A. (1988). Are learning disabled students "test-wise"? A review of recent research. *Learning Disabilities Focus*, 3:87–97.

Sedita, J. (1989). *Landmark study skills guide*. Prides Crossing, MA: Landmark Foundation.

Shepherd, J. R. (1982). *The Houghton Mifflin study skills handbook*. Boston: Houghton Mifflin.

Shields, J. M., & Heron, T. E. (1989). Teaching organizational skills to students with learning disabilities. *Teaching Exceptional Children*, Winter: 8–13.

Slade, D. L. (1986). Developing foundations for organizational skills. *Academic Therapy*, 21:261–266.

Smith, C. R. (1983). *Learning disabilities*. Needham Heights, MA: Allyn and Bacon.

Smith, D. D. (1989). *Teaching students with learning and behavior problems*, 2nd ed. Englewood Cliffs, NJ: Prentice Hall.

Smith, T. E. C., & Dowdy, C. A. (1989). The role of study skills in the secondary curriculum. *Academic Therapy*, 24:479–490.

Vogel, S. A. (1987). Issues and concerns in LD college programmaing. In D. J. Johnson & J. W. Blalock (Eds.), *Adults with learning disabilities*. Orlando, FL: Grune and Stratton.

Wallace, G., & Kauffman, J. M. (1986). *Teaching students with learning and behavior problems*, 2nd ed. Columbus, OH: Merrill.

Wallace, G., & McLoughlin, J. A. (1988). *Learning disabilities: Concepts and characteristics*, 3rd ed. Columbus, OH: Merrill.

Wehrung-Schaffner, L., & Sapona, R. H. (1990). May the FORCE be with you: A test preparation strategy for learning disabled adolescents. *Academic Therapy*, 25:291–300.

Weinstein, C. E., Goetz, E. T., & Alexander, P. A. *Learning and study strategies*. San Diego, CA: Academic Press, 1988.

Wesson, C. L., & Keefe, M. (1989). Teaching library skills to students with mild and moderate handicaps. *Teaching Exceptional Children*, Spring: 29–31.

Wood, J. W., White, B. L., & Miederhoff, J. E. (1988). Notetaking for the mainstreamed student. *Academic Therapy*, 24:107–112.

Index